Daily Mail TAX GUIDE 2012/2013

JANE VASS

D0238199

P
PROFILE BOOKS

For my family, Ian, William and Jessica,
who have survived their constant exposure to tax with grace and humour.

In memoriam W.J.D.V.

This edition first published in 2012

First published in Great Britain in 2003 by
Profile Books Ltd
3A Exmouth House
Pine Street
Exmouth Market
London ECIR OJH
www.profilebooks.com

Typeset in Plantin by MacGuru Ltd
info@macguru.org.uk

Printed and bound in Great Britain by
Clays, Bungay, Suffolk

A CIP catalogue record for this book is available from the British Library.

ISBN 978 1 84668 629 0
eISBN 978 1 84765 838 8

Contents

Acknowledgements

This is the tenth edition of this book, and the same team has worked on each edition – Stephen Brough, Jonathan Harley and Penny Williams. Each year, they have dealt with my corrections with professionalism and patience and remained cheerful throughout. Lynette Davidson compiled the index – a vital part of the book. I am deeply grateful to them all, and to James Coney of *Money Mail* for his support for the book.

Special thanks are due to Jane Moore, who for the past ten years has reviewed the book on behalf of the Low Incomes Tax Reform Group (LITRG). The LITRG aims to help people on low incomes to cope with their tax and campaigns for a simpler and more accessible tax and benefits system. Jane has contributed far more than just her considerable technical expertise, and her practical experience of the problems people face when grappling with their tax has been invaluable.

However, all errors remain my own, and I welcome comments, via the publisher.

Jane Vass

NOTE

Everyone's personal circumstances are different and tax rules can change. This book has been carefully researched and checked. If by chance a mistake or omission has occurred I am sorry that neither I, the *Daily Mail*, nor the publisher can take responsibility for any loss or problem you suffer as a result. But if you have any suggestions about how the content of the guide could be improved, please write to me, care of the publisher, Profile Books, 3A Exmouth House, Pine Street, London ECIR OJH.

Introduction

With each Budget most family finances take another blow. Bankers, millionaires and tax evaders have been targeted, but we've all had to suffer tax rises and benefits cuts to help the UK economy recover.

The impact on squeezed families who have already seen huge increases in the cost of essential services such as energy and an increase in VAT to 20 per cent has been, arguably, greater. And pensioners, who are suffering from low pension payouts and three years of historically low interest rates, are not untouched.

Even before the Chancellor George Osborne got to his feet on Budget day in March 2012, taxpayers faced a host of changes that he and his predecessors had put in place. Some of these took effect on 6 April this year – such as changes to tax credits for many middle-income families. But others, including changes to the way pensioners are taxed and the removal of child benefit for wealthier families, are still in the pipeline.

One of the most controversial announcements of the recent Budget was the removal of allowances for those aged over 65, which has been nicknamed the 'granny tax'. Currently, pensioners get higher allowances than younger workers – those aged over 65 can have income of £10,500 a year before paying tax, and the over 75s need to have an income above £10,660.

Anyone turning 65 from 6 April 2013 will not qualify for the perk, and instead will get only the regular personal allowance. Those who can still claim the extra amount will have it frozen until the regular allowance is raised to the same level.

A further much-debated change happens from 7 January 2013, two-thirds of the way through this current tax year. From then any family where a person earns £50,000 or more a year will start to lose their child benefit, currently worth £20.30 a week for a first child and £13.40 for each additional child. Those earning more than £60,000 will get nothing. Anyone caught by this rule who continues to claim the benefit may be asked to fill out a self-assessment tax form, and will be made to repay some or all of what they have been given.

The Chancellor has delivered some good news. The personal allowance has increased rapidly, from £8,105 in 2012–13 to £9,205 in 2013–14, and the government's aim is to increase it to £10,000 in 2014–15. And there will be a cut in the top rate of income tax from 50 per cent to 45 per cent for those earning over £150,000 a year. But at the same time, the point at which 40 per cent tax starts being paid is falling.

Income tax and National Insurance contributions can be fiendishly complicated – and the recent changes can make it extremely difficult to keep on top of your affairs. Only the wealthiest have the resources to employ expensive accountants to help them pay less tax. And pensioners who have spent their working lives having their affairs dealt with by an employer are often expected to become tax experts overnight.

After two terrible years in which its customer service has come under heavy criticism, HMRC has taken great strides to prevent people from paying the wrong amount of tax. But those with many sources of income or whose circumstances change are often caught out. HMRC's phone lines can still be clogged with callers, making it exasperating to get a simple question answered.

That is where this book comes in. You can't avoid paying tax altogether, but you can keep it to a minimum.

This book will help make the most of the reliefs and allowances you are entitled to. It is written by Jane Vass in the same straightforward, concise style you have come to expect from *Money Mail*. It aims to give simple explanations to complex issues and show you how to fill out tax forms.

I hope you find it as helpful in planning your tax affairs as I always find it in planning mine.

James Coney
Money Mail editor
March 2012

How this book can help you

Over recent years, Her Majesty's Revenue & Customs (HMRC) has become bigger and more faceless, swallowing up other government departments but at the same time shedding front-line staff. Now, more than ever, you need to keep an eye on your tax affairs, and this book aims to explain how the tax system works, how to keep your tax bill low and how to make dealing with your tax as simple as possible.

It is organised in three parts:

- *Part 1 – The basics.* This gives you an introduction to the different types of tax covered in the book and how tax is collected, and advises you on trouble-shooting and where to get more help.
- *Part 2 – Planning to save tax.* Each chapter in Part 2 covers particular situations, e.g. work, retirement, property. Chapters 14 and 15 explain capital gains tax and inheritance tax.
- *Part 3 – Filling in the forms.* This section tells you what sorts of form you may get and how to fill in the full tax return, the short return and the form R40 that you may be sent if you want to reclaim tax.

Watch out for the tips throughout the text – our top tips appear at the start of each chapter. The 'record-keeping' section at the end of each chapter in Parts 1 and 2 will help you organise your papers.

The Fact file at the end of the book summarises some key facts and figures and has lists of useful publications, HMRC helplines and addresses for all the organisations mentioned in the book.

What's changing?

As the government struggles to reduce the deficit, the tax system has not been immune. Although there have been rises in the personal allowance for people under 65, taking more than 1 million people out of tax, and (from April 2013) a cut in the top rate of tax, the cost is being recovered largely through changes to tax allowances for pensioners.

More positively, there have been a number of initiatives to make tax simpler to understand and improve tax administration.

Mixed news for individuals

There has been no change to income tax rates in 2012–13, but in 2013–14 the top rate of tax (payable on income above £150,000) will fall from 50 per cent to 45 per cent. However, if you are under 65 there is a big rise in the amount you can have tax-free each year. From 6 April 2012, the basic personal allowance rose to £8,105 and it will rise again to £9,205 from April 2013. In 2012–13 higher-rate taxpayers will not benefit, because the threshold at which you start to pay higher-rate tax fell from £35,000 to £34,370 in April 2012. It will fall again to £32,245 from April 2013.

Most taxpayers will be affected by the decision to index-link allowances (except the blind person's allowance) in line with the Consumer Prices Index, rather than the generally faster-rising Retail Prices Index, from April 2012. However, pensioners will be hit by the government's proposal to freeze the higher age-related allowances at the 2012–13 rates. Higher allowances will not be available at all if you turn 65 after 5 April 2013.

Gloomy news for families

In April 2011, the tax credits means test got tougher and the childcare tax credit was cut. From April 2012, the means test got tougher still, many tax credits were frozen and most couples with children have to work at least 24 hours a week between them to qualify. And from October 2013, tax credits will start to be replaced with a new benefit, Universal Credit.

If your income is above £50,000, or your partner's is, you also face the loss of child benefit in 2013. See page 55.

Tax simplification

The independent Office of Tax Simplification (OTS) was set up in 2010 to advise the government. So far it has investigated:

- *Tax reliefs* – recommending the abolition of a number of outdated reliefs, such as tax-free luncheon vouchers (15p a day). These have been abolished from April 2013.
- *Small business taxation* – the OTS has recommended changes to make tax simpler for the smallest businesses and to allow more expenses to be claimed on a flat-rate basis. The government has said that it will adopt these recommendations from April 2013.
- *The taxation of pensioners* – looking at a wide range of issues, including the impact of the tax system on people who have a number of different sources of income.
- *Employee share schemes* – this investigation is still at an early stage.

'Real time' tax

Currently your employer deducts tax every time you are paid (or get your pension) but tells your tax office how much has been paid after the end of the tax year. This leads to a number of problems, particularly if you change your job or have more than one job or pension, and after the end of each tax year many people receive P800 *Tax Calculation* notices showing tax underpayments or overpayments. Between April 2013 and October 2013 HMRC plans to move to collecting the information during the year, online.

Jam tomorrow?

The government's most ambitious simplification plan is to merge the operation of income tax and National Insurance. The basis of the two taxes will not change, however, and the government has said it will not extend National Insurance to people above state pension age or to types of income that are not currently liable such as pensions. This major change is unlikely to come before 2017. In the meantime, checking your tax bill has never been so important.

Part 1
The basics

1

The taxes you might pay

Tax covers virtually every area of our lives, from our work to our spending. This book concentrates on the taxes you can do something about, either by planning ahead to save tax, or by filling out tax forms efficiently so that you pay the right amount of tax. This chapter introduces all the various forms of tax covered in the book and tells you which chapter to go to for further information.

Top tips

- If you've forgotten to claim a relief or allowance, you can usually still do so providing you act within four years of the end of the tax year to which it relates. So if you claim by 5 April 2013, you can get relief for tax years back to 2008–09 (see page 37). However, shorter deadlines apply for some business reliefs.
- Watch out for tax changes – you may need to reassess your tax plans.
- You have a legal obligation to keep records to back up your tax return or claim. Make a habit of keeping key documents.
- Check your National Insurance record (see page 13 for how to do this). If you have not paid enough National Insurance, your entitlement to a state retirement pension or other benefits may be affected. You can pay extra to boost your entitlement.

How tax is collected

The mammoth government department that administers our taxes is Her Majesty's Revenue & Customs, or 'HMRC' for short. Everyone, including children, is likely to come into contact with it at some point. It collects our taxes, National Insurance contributions and student loan repayments. It administers VAT and customs and excise duties and enforces the National Minimum Wage. And it is responsible for paying out tax credits and child benefit.

HMRC aims to collect as much tax as possible from your income before you get it. It requires:

- employers to deduct tax from your salary under the Pay As You Earn (PAYE) system
- building contractors to deduct tax from some subcontractors' pay
- pension schemes to deduct tax from your pension, usually under PAYE
- financial organisations and companies to deduct tax from savings interest and dividends.

Not all your tax may be collected this way – e.g. if you have profits from a business or letting out property. If so, or if your affairs are complex, you will probably get a tax return. Chapter 2 covers how tax is collected.

Tax years

You pay tax on income or gains made in a 'tax year'. The tax year runs from 6 April until 5 April in the next year. So the 12-month period starting on 6 April 2011 and ending on 5 April 2012 is called the '2011–12 tax year'.

Rates of tax for each tax year are usually set in the Budget (traditionally in March), but tax allowances for the coming year are usually announced before Christmas and tax changes may be made at any time. Budget proposals become law only when Parliament passes a Finance Act, and they may be rejected or amended, so do not count on a proposal going through.

This book covers two tax years – the tax year just ended (2011–12) and the current tax year (2012–13). If you are planning ahead to save tax you should use the 2012–13 tax rules, but you need to use the 2011–12 rules when checking your tax and filling in your tax return, if you get one.

Income tax

Your taxable income includes: pay from a job (after deducting contributions to your employer's pension scheme, 'payroll giving' to charity and some expenses); pensions; business profits and rental income (after expenses and investment allowances); and the before-tax amount of any savings interest or investment income and share dividends.

Some types of income are completely tax-free, such as maintenance from an ex-spouse and tax credits. There is a list of tax-free income in each of Chapters 4 to 11, but see Table 1.1 on page 10 for a quick checklist.

Calculating your tax

Your taxable income from all sources is added up, but you get the first slice tax-free – this is called your personal allowance. In 2012–13 the personal allowance is £8,105 (a rise of £630 on the 2011–12 allowance of £7,475), or £10,500 if you are at least 65 at any point in the tax year, £10,660 if you are at least 75 (up from £9,940 and £10,090 in 2011–12). However, as explained in Chapter 6, the extra age-related amount is reduced if your income is above £25,400 in 2012–13 (£24,000 in 2011–12). And, irrespective of age, your personal allowance is reduced by £1 for every £2 of income above £100,000. There is also an extra allowance for blind people of £2,100 in 2012–13 (£1,980 in 2011–12).

At this stage you can also deduct from your taxable income a few items which qualify for full tax relief, such as some business losses (see page 145), retirement annuity contributions (see page 206) and some business reliefs (see page 293). Reliefs and allowances are summarised in Table 1.2 on page 11, but note that if you claim more than £50,000 in tax relief overall the government plans to cap the amount you can claim. This only applies to reliefs that do not already have a limit (so relief for pension contributions or enterprise investments is not affected).

After deducting these items and your allowances, the first £34,370 of your remaining income in 2012–13 is taxed at the basic rate of 20 per cent, income between £34,371 and £150,000 is taxed at the higher rate of 40 per cent, and anything over £150,000 at the additional rate of 50 per cent. Rates of tax for 2012–13 are the same as in 2011–12, but the basic-rate limit has been reduced from its 2011–12 level of £35,000. For the purposes of working out which tax rate applies, your earnings or pension are taxed first, then savings interest and finally any share dividends. See Example 1.1 on page 9, while Figure 1.1 on page 8 gives you a simple calculator. Your total tax at each rate is then added up, and finally you can deduct:

- any tax you have already paid
- any extra tax relief you can claim, such as married couple's allowance if either partner was born before 6 April 1935. See page 80.

Keeping up with inflation

Tax allowances and bands are automatically increased in line with inflation each year, unless a decision is made to change them by a different amount. Until April 2012, they rose in line with the Retail Prices Index (RPI); but they now generally rise in line with the Consumer Prices Index (CPI), which tends to increase more slowly. The government also plans to freeze the age-related allowance at 2012-13 rates, and abolish it for people who turn 65 after 5 April 2013. However, the basic personal allowance had a big rise of £1,000 last year, and has increased by a further £630 in 2012, while the blind person's allowance will continue to increase by RPI until 2016.

On a low income?

There have been big rises in the basic personal allowance – the amount of income people under 65 can have tax-free. For 2012–13 it is now £8,105, while people aged 65 and over can already have at least £10,500 tax-free. So check your tax carefully, and if your income is below your allowances see page 189 for whether you can have savings interest paid tax-free.

Even if you are a taxpayer, you may qualify for a reduced rate of tax on your savings income. This applies if your non-savings income (e.g. from a job or pension), after deducting your allowances, is less than £2,710 in 2012–13 (£2,560 in 2011–12). If so, any savings income within the £2,710 band is taxable at 10 per cent instead of the normal 20 per cent. See Boris in Example 1.1 on page 9, and page 183.

Income above £34,370?

Although the higher-rate threshold is £34,370, this is the level after deduct-ing your allowances – so in 2012–13 someone under 65 can have income of £34,370 + £8,105 = £42,475 before paying higher-rate tax. The higher-rate threshold for 2012–13 was reduced from its 2011–12 level of £35,000 to compensate for an above-inflation increase in the basic personal allowance.

If you are above the higher-rate threshold, you will have extra tax to pay at 20 per cent on savings interest and 22.5 per cent on share dividends (see Chapter 11). You will also have to pay an extra 10 per cent tax on capital gains you make (see Chapter 14). Furthermore, from January 2013 you will start to lose your child benefit once your or your partner's income rises above £50,000 (see page 55). See below for how you may be able to keep below the threshold.

Cutting higher-rate tax

You may be able to bring yourself below the threshold for paying higher-rate tax or losing child benefit by paying into a personal pension or giving to charity by Gift Aid, and if you are married see page 80 for tips. HMRC gives basic-rate tax relief on the payments direct to the pension company or charity. But it gives you higher-rate tax relief by adding your payment, plus the basic-rate tax relief, to the basic-rate tax band so that less income is taxed at the higher rate. So if Barry, from Example 1.1, paid £2,040 a year into his pension (£2,550 after adding basic-rate tax relief, see page 207), his basic-rate band would be £34,370 + £2,550 = £36,920 and he would pay no higher-rate tax at all.

Income above £100,000?

Your personal allowance is cut by £1 for every £2 above £100,000 and 50 per cent tax is due on income above £150,000. You will also have additional tax to pay on share dividends, although until April 2013 (when the top rate of tax falls to 45 per cent) you get 50 per cent relief on pension contribu-tions (within limits, see Chapter 12) and on Gift Aid payments. Consider taking professional advice.

Figure 1.1: Income tax estimator for 2012–13

This will give you a rough idea of your tax. It is not precise by any means, for example it does not cover capital gains tax, National Insurance or married couple's allowance for older couples, which could reduce your tax bill by up to £771 (see page 80). And it does not work if your taxable income is £100,000 or more.

Add up your before-tax income, including earnings, pensions, business profits, rents and savings interest (but not share dividends). Do not include tax-free income.	**1** £...................
Add together: ■ personal allowance of £8,105 (or £10,500 if 65-plus, £10,660 if 75-plus, reduced if your income is £25,400 or more). See page 80 ■ blind person's allowance (£2,100). See page 50 ■ business losses and other full-relief deductions (see page 5).	**2** £...................
Take away **2** from **1**	**3** £...................
If 3 is less than £2,710, multiply: ■ non-savings income included at **3** × 20% ■ savings income included at **3** × 10% Your tax is the total of **4** and **5**. If you have a savings account which pays interest with tax taken off, you may be able to claim tax back.	**4** £................... **5** £...................
If 3 is more than £2,710, work out the tax due on **3**: ■ the first £34,370 at 20%* (but if you pay personal pension contributions and Gift Aid donations, first increase the £34,370 by adding your payments plus the basic-rate tax relief on them – this gives you any higher-rate tax relief you are due, see page 208) ■ the rest by 40%	**6** £................... **7** £...................
If you had 40% tax to pay at **7**, work out extra tax on share dividends: ■ share dividends plus tax credits × 22.5%. See page 193	**8** £...................
Add up **6**, **7** and **8** to find your estimated tax bill. Remember that unless you are self-employed, most of this tax will be deducted directly from your pay, pension or savings interest.	**9** £...................

*Or 10 per cent on any interest in the starting-rate band.

Example 1.1: Which tax rate in 2012–13?

■ Bob is aged 30 and earns £25,000 from his job in IT. The first £8,105 is his personal allowance which is tax-free. The remaining £16,895 is all taxed at 20%.

■ Barry is also aged 30 but he earns £45,000. The first £8,105 is his personal allowance which is tax-free. The next £34,370 is all taxed at 20%, leaving £45,000 − £8,105 − £34,370 = £2,525 which is liable to higher-rate tax of 40%.

■ Betty is a pensioner aged 70. She has pension income of £10,000. This is all within her personal allowance (£10,500) so it is all tax-free. She can receive a further £500 (from savings interest, for example) without paying any tax.

■ Boris is also a pensioner aged 70, with pension income of £11,000 and savings interest of £1,000. The first £10,500 of his pension is tax-free; the remaining £500 is taxed at 20%. But all his savings interest is taxed at 10%, because his total taxable income (£12,000 − £10,500 = £1,500) is less than £2,710.

Example 1.2: Calculating your tax

In 2012–13 Belinda earns £43,000, and receives savings interest of £800 (£1,000 before tax) and share dividends of £900 (£1,000 including a 10 per cent tax credit).

Earnings and interest	£44,000				
Personal allowance	−£8,105	No tax			
Taxable	£35,895				
In basic-rate band	−£34,370	×	20%	=	£6,874
In higher-rate band	£1,525	×	40%	=	£610
Dividends in higher-rate band	£1,000	×	22.5%	=	£225
Total					£7,709

Because all of Belinda's basic-rate band has been used on her earnings and interest, she has extra tax on her share dividends. However, 20% tax was deducted from her interest (£200) and £7,000 from her pay, so she owes only £7,709 − £200 − £7,000 = £509.

Table 1.1: Checklist of tax-free income

Families	Tax credits and some other state benefits (see page 51)
	Child benefit (technically tax-free, but see page 55)
	Some payments as a foster carer, or shared lives carer (see page 51)
	Maintenance and alimony (see page 54)
	Payouts from some insurance policies (see pages 51, 77 and 194)
Employees	Some benefits and expenses paid by employers (see page 92)
	Some payments on leaving a job (see page 111)
	Some payments to government employees (see page 92)
Pensioners	Pension credit and some other state benefits (see page 72)
	Some pensions and pension lump sums (see pages 72 and 210)
People receiving compensation	Some damages and compensation for personal injury
	Compensation or insurance payouts for loss or damage to goods (but see page 225)
	Interest on damages for personal injuries or death
	Interest on a tax refund
	Compensation paid on the dormant accounts of holocaust victims
People not resident in the UK	Overseas income if you are not resident in the UK (see page 168)
	Interest on British Government Stock if you are not ordinarily resident (see page 171)
Other	Betting winnings, including Premium Bonds and lottery winnings
	Income from savings and investments in some special government schemes, such as ISAs (listed on page 185)
	Rental income under the Rent-a-Room scheme (see page 156)

Rates and allowances for 2013–14

This book concentrates on the 2012–13 tax year. However, in the 2012 Budget the government announced that for 2013–14 the personal allowance will rise to £9,205 and the higher-rate tax threshold will fall to £32,245. This means that if you were born after 5 April 1948 you will pay higher-rate tax if your income is above £41,450 – if you were born before that the threshold is higher.

Table 1.2: Allowances, credits and reliefs

Who can claim?	*Which relief?*
Anybody (except some non-residents and some people with overseas income, see page 177)	Personal allowance (see pages 50 and 80)
People who were born before 6 April 1948	Higher age-related allowance (see page 80)
People who were born before 6 April 1935 (or whose spouse, ex-spouse or civil partner was)	Married couple's allowance and relief for maintenance or alimony payments (see Chapter 6)
People looking after a child	Child Tax Credit (see Chapter 5) and child benefit (see page 55)
Blind people	Blind person's allowance (see page 50)
Contributors to a pension scheme	Relief for pension contributions (see Chapter 12)
Employees	Relief for some expenses (see Chapter 7)
Investors in Venture Capital Trusts, Enterprise Investment Schemes and Community Investment Schemes	Income tax relief for money invested (see page 199)
People giving to charity (whether cash, investments or land)	Various reliefs for donations to charity (see Chapter 13)
People with some types of loan	Business loans (see Chapter 8)
	Loans to buy property to rent out (see Chapter 9)
People with overseas income	Foreign tax credit relief (see Chapter 10)
	10% deduction from foreign pensions (see page 169)
	Remittance basis (see page 173)
Sole traders, partners	Relief for some business expenditure (see Chapter 8)
	Relief for business losses (see page 145)
Working people on modest incomes	Working Tax Credit (see Chapter 5)

National Insurance contributions

National Insurance is effectively a tax on working, but it also earns you some important state benefits, including state retirement pension. The government is looking at how the administration of income tax and National Insurance could be integrated, but this is likely to be a slow and challenging process.

There are several types of contribution:

- If you are an employee, you pay employees' Class 1 contributions on your earnings.
- If you are an employer, you pay employers' Class 1 contributions on your employees' earnings, and Class 1A and possibly Class 1B contributions on taxable benefits you give your employees. An employee does not pay National Insurance on employment benefits.
- If you are self-employed, you pay Class 2 contributions at a flat weekly rate of £2.65 in 2012–13 (up from £2.50 in 2011–12) as well as Class 4 contributions on your profits.
- If you have not paid enough Class 1 or Class 2 contributions to qualify for a full state pension, you can pay voluntary Class 3 contributions at a flat weekly rate of £13.25 in 2012–13 (£12.60 in 2011–12). (See below and HMRC form CA5603 *Application to pay voluntary National Insurance contributions.*)

You do not have to pay National Insurance if you are over state pension age or if your income is less than £7,605 in 2012–13 (£7,225 in 2011–12), or for Class 2 contributions less than £5,595 in 2012–13 (£5,315 in 2011–12). And if you are liable to pay more than one class of contribution (because, say, you are self-employed as well as having a job), there is a maximum payment. Ask for HMRC forms CA72A (*Application for deferment of Class 1 National Insurance*) or CA72B (*Application for deferment of Class 2 and/or Class 4 National Insurance*).

- For details of contributions for employees, see page 118.
- For details of contributions for self-employed people, see page 148.

Check your National Insurance record

Your entitlement to state retirement pension and some other state benefits is reduced if you haven't paid National Insurance for enough years. Mistakes by your employer or HMRC may also affect your record. To check, contact HMRC's National Insurance Contributions and Employer Office or get a State Pension Forecast from the Pension Service (addresses in the Fact file). If you have not paid enough in one year, you can make Class 3 contributions to boost your entitlement, but you must normally act within six years of the year in question (you have longer if you reach state pension age before 6 April 2015). The number of years' payments needed to qualify for a full pension has been reduced, and you get credits for some periods not earning so make sure it is worth paying extra. There is a voluntary National Insurance contribution planner on the website of the Pensions Advisory Service that may help you decide (see the Fact file).

Student loan repayments

Repayments on student loans taken out after August 1998 are collected by HMRC along with your tax. These loans are known as 'income-contingent' because your repayments are related to your level of income.

The Student Loans Company notifies HMRC when you leave university. If you have a job, your employer will be required to deduct the repayment along with your PAYE; otherwise, it will be collected through your tax return. The repayments normally start in the April after you have finished your course.

The loans are repaid at a rate of 9 per cent of your income above an annual threshold, which was £15,000 for the 2011–12 tax year, increasing to £15,795 from 6 April 2012, but is £21,000 for courses starting from September 2012. No repayments are due if your income is below this figure, and taxable employee benefits, such as a company car, and investment income of £2,000 or less are ignored in calculating your income. More details are available on the government website, www.direct.gov.uk/studentfinance.

■ For more about how student loan repayments are deducted from pay, see page 121.

Capital gains tax

This is a tax on gains you make when you dispose of an asset such as investments, land, property, businesses and valuables. You pay tax on the proceeds of the transaction, after deducting the original cost, any expenses and various exemptions and reliefs.

In practice, however, most people do not have to grapple with capital gains tax because the first slice of taxable gains made in each tax year is tax-free. The tax-free amount is frozen at £10,600 in 2012–13, the same amount as in 2011–12.

All capital gains above the annual tax-free amount are taxed at 18 per cent, or 28 per cent if your gains plus your total taxable income take you above the higher-rate threshold for income tax. Entrepreneurs selling a business may qualify for a 10 per cent tax rate.

■ For more information about capital gains tax see Chapter 14.

Inheritance tax

This is a tax on the value of what you leave when you die (your estate). Tax may also have to be paid during your lifetime if you make a gift to some types of trust, or if you are a trustee. Most other lifetime gifts are 'Potentially Exempt Transfers', which means that they will be counted as part of your estate only if you die within seven years of making them. However, the first slice of your estate is tax-free, and some gifts are completely tax-free. The tax-free amount was £325,000 in 2011–12 and has been frozen at that level until 2015. However, married couples and civil partners can claim to transfer the unused tax-free band of the first person to die to the survivor.

The rate of tax is 40 per cent, but it is reduced to 36 per cent if you leave 10 per cent or more of your taxable estate to charity on your death.

■ For more about inheritance tax, see Chapter 15.

Value Added Tax (VAT)

VAT is added to the price you pay for most goods and services. The stand-ard rate is 20 per cent. A few items are taxed at zero or 5 per cent. Traders hand over the tax to HMRC – but can deduct VAT paid on things that they have bought for their business.

As a private individual, opportunities to save VAT are limited. The main exception is if you buy from a small business with an income below the threshold for registering for VAT (a gardener, say). Disabled people can also buy some goods VAT-free (see HMRC leaflet VAT Notice 701/7 *VAT reliefs for disabled people*).

■ For more about VAT if you are in business, see Chapter 8.

Record-keeping

The law requires you to keep records if you may need to complete a tax return (see page 28). You must keep records for at least 22 months from the end of the tax year to which they relate, or for five years and ten months after this date if you are self-employed or let property. You need to keep them longer if you received a late tax return, or if your tax office is enquir-ing into your return. (See HMRC booklet RK BK1 *A general guide to keeping records for your tax return*.)

If you don't need to complete a return, there is no legal requirement to keep records, but it is wise to do so in case you get a return later on, or you want to claim a tax repayment. As you can claim repayments up to four years in arrears (see page 37), it makes sense to keep records for at least that long.

There are some records that you might need to keep for longer – for example, records relating to purchases of assets like property and invest-ments (see page 236), records to show how much of your private pension lifetime allowance you have used (see page 215) or details of time spent overseas if there is any chance that you might be able to claim to be non-resident (see page 170). People in business will also need to keep records to back up other tax returns, for example VAT returns or Employer returns.

The law does not generally tell you exactly what types of record you must keep, but suggestions are in the HMRC booklet mentioned above, and examples are given at the end of each chapter. You should keep most original documents that show how much tax has been deducted (such as tax vouchers, certificates of tax deducted and the P60 your employer gives you each year). Most other records can be kept electronically (on a computer, say, or a storage device such as a disk, memory stick or network drive), provided that your system captures all the information on the document (back and front) and can reproduce it in legible form.

2

How tax is collected

Wherever possible, tax is collected 'at source', by deducting it from income before it is paid. If it is not possible to collect all your tax this way, or your tax affairs are complex, you will need to fill in a tax return and you may need to pay tax in instalments called 'payments on account'. This chapter explains how to check that the right amount of tax is being deducted and what happens if you get a tax return.

Top tips

- Check your tax code, which tells your employer how much tax to deduct.
- Don't assume that the right amount of tax has been deducted under PAYE. After each tax year, check the total deducted and contact your tax office if you think it is wrong.
- Be particularly careful if you see the letters 'BR' in your tax code. This should be only a temporary measure unless you have more than one job or pension.
- If you get a form P800 *Tax Calculation* stating that you owe tax, don't panic – see page 21.
- If you get a tax return but also have income taxed through PAYE, tax you owe up to £3,000 can be collected by adjusting your tax code – but only if you send your return in by 31 October (or 31 December if filing by internet).
- If you have to make payments on account, and your income is rising, be careful to put enough cash aside to meet the January payment.

How does HMRC know what income you have?

Your tax office will get most of the necessary information from your employer or pension payer. However, HMRC has other sources of information, for example:

- Banks and building societies must tell HMRC how much interest they have paid in the tax year to each customer.
- Businesses can be asked to give details of payments to non-employees.
- The Department for Work and Pensions passes on details of taxable state benefits.

You may also need to give information to your tax office. For example, you must tell HMRC immediately if you start up in business. You risk a penalty if you do not do so by 31 January after the end of the tax year in which you start up. Even if you are not sent a tax return, you are legally required to tell your tax office by 5 October 2012 if, in the 2011–12 tax year, you had any new source of taxable income that it does not already know about, or if you became liable to higher-rate tax on taxed investment income, or if you made a taxable capital gain. The tax calendar on page 264 summarises key milestones in the tax year.

HMRC prefers to collect all your tax at source. But if it finds out something about you that suggests this will not be possible – being self-employed, say – it will put you on its list for getting a tax return.

A tax return is not just a form to fill in: it brings you within a separate system of paying tax, with its own strict timetables, record-keeping requirements and penalties for non-compliance. This is called 'self-assessment', because you are responsible for working out the tax payable, although you do not have to do the sums yourself. See page 27 for an explanation of how your tax is collected under self-assessment.

HMRC tries to avoid bringing people within self-assessment unnecessarily. But one positive aspect of filling in a tax return each year is that your tax liability is properly calculated – and filling it in can be quite straightforward if you use one of the computer programmes now available, or HMRC's own online service. There is a step-by-step guide to filling in your tax return in Part 3 of this book.

Even if you do not get a tax return, your tax office may send you forms from time to time, so that it can check various aspects of your tax.

Checking your tax

Always check your tax after the end of the tax year. There are simple working sheets that will give you a rough idea in the notes to the tax return (short or long versions). You can get these from the HMRC Orderline on 0845 900 0404 or download them at www.hmrc.gov.uk/sa/index.htm. If you just want an estimate of your tax see page 8.

How tax is collected at source

There are two main ways of collecting tax at source:

■ By requiring financial organisations to deduct tax from some types of savings and investment income.
■ By deducting it from your pay or private pension, through the PAYE system (no tax is deducted from state pensions, although in many cases they are taxable).

Tax deducted from savings

Tax deducted at source from savings and investment income is usually at 20 per cent (10 per cent on dividends). This means that:

■ If your income is low, you may be able to claim tax back (but not the 10 per cent deducted at source on dividends). You will have to fill in a Tax Repayment form (form R40, described in Chapter 20). You may be able to have the income paid before tax instead (see page 189).
■ Higher-rate taxpayers may have more tax to pay on savings income. This is collected through PAYE if you have income from a job or pension, in which case you will see an entry on your coding notice (explained below). If it is not, you will have to fill in a tax return (see page 27).

PAYE

PAYE (Pay As You Earn) is a way of spreading your tax bill over the tax year by deducting tax from every salary or pension payment. Your tax office tells your employer (or the pension payer) how much of your pay to give you tax-free. It does this by giving you a 'tax code'. Using special tables, your employer can then work out how much tax to deduct from the rest of your pay.

PAYE is normally cumulative. It takes into account the amount of pay and tax deducted since the start of the tax year, so that the correct proportion of your annual basic-, higher- and additional-rate tax liability is deducted on each pay day. If your income goes up, more tax will be deducted; if your income goes down, too much tax may have already been deducted and the excess tax will be refunded in your pay packet. After the end of each tax year your PAYE is reconciled and you may get a form P800 *Tax Calculation* form if you have paid too much or too little tax.

PAYE applies to income tax, but your employer also has to deduct National Insurance contributions and, possibly, student loan repayments.

Changes to watch out for

PAYE has been essentially unchanged since it was introduced in 1944, but in 2009 HMRC introduced a new computer system which brings together all your PAYE and National Insurance details. The process of transferring people's records to the new system unearthed many errors in existing files and HMRC has issued millions of P800 *Tax Calculation* forms to people on PAYE who may have overpaid or underpaid tax in earlier years. However, the catching-up exercise is nearly complete, although you will still get a P800 form if the end-of-year PAYE reconciliation shows you have paid the wrong amount of tax.

More change is on the horizon. Currently, your tax code is set for a year at a time (although mid-year changes are possible) and employers send an end-of-year report to HMRC. However, there are plans to require employers to provide 'real time' information to HMRC each time they pay you, making it easier to keep tax codes up-to-date. A staged introduction is proposed, starting in 2013. The government is also looking at merging the operation of income tax and National Insurance, although this is unlikely to take effect until 2017.

If you get a P800 tax calculation form

Check it carefully, even if it says you are due a refund. It is an estimate, not a formal tax assessment, and it may be wrong. Does it show all your sources of income and deductions you can claim? Are the figures right – especially your personal allowance? If you are not sure, contact HMRC as shown in the Notes sent with the form.

If it is correct, but you owe tax, follow the guidance on page 37 onwards – you may be able to ask HMRC to waive the tax if it was its fault, and HMRC should get your employer to pay if it was their mistake. You can ask for time to pay, or ask HMRC to collect amounts under £3,000 through PAYE. The government has also said that HMRC will not ask you to repay amounts owing from 2009–10 or earlier years under £300, or underpayments that arose because a state pension or other state benefit was not taken into account. However, this does not apply for tax owed for 2010–11 or later years. There is helpful advice (including sample letters) on the website of the Low Incomes Tax Reform Group at www.litrg.org. uk under 'PAYE underpayments' or see page 43 for other sources of help.

How your tax code is worked out

Your tax code shown on your payslip will look something like this: 810L. This is all your employer sees – not how the code is made up.

Your tax office may send you a P2 coding notice, which explains how it has arrived at your code for the next tax year. To work out your tax code, your tax office starts with the total allowances (and other reliefs) you are entitled to. So, you will usually see a personal allowance of £8,105, but people aged 65 and over might get a higher allowance and also a married couple's allowance (there is more about this in Chapter 6). See Figure 2.1 on page 23 for other examples of possible allowances.

But your tax code is also used to collect tax underpaid from previous tax years, or tax on non-cash items such as a company car, or on other income that has nothing to do with your job, such as a state retirement pension, property income or untaxed interest. From January 2013 it may also be used to claw back child benefit from people with incomes above £50,000 (see page 55). The tax is collected by reducing your allowances. You can ask your tax office not to do this, but it does not have to agree. If it does you will probably have to complete a tax return and pay tax in a lump sum (see page 27).

The number in your tax code is simply the value of all your allowances, minus any deductions, with the final digit knocked off (the PAYE tables round in your favour):

- If your allowances come to more than the deductions, you will have some allowances left to set against your pay or pension. This means that you get some pay tax-free (see Example 2.1 opposite and Example 6.4 on page 87).
- If your deductions come to more than your allowances, you get no tax-free pay. The extra deductions are treated as additional pay for the purposes of working out how much tax to deduct. You will see a letter K in your code (see Example 2.2 on page 25). However, not more than 50 per cent of your pay can be taken in tax this way – any extra tax will usually be collected through your tax return.

The letter in your code is a shorthand way of telling your employer how to work out your tax. For example, L or Y codes help your employer to adjust your code to account for Budget changes. The letter in your code is:

- L if you get only the basic personal allowance
- P if you get the full personal allowance for people aged 65 to 74
- Y if you get the full personal allowance for people aged 75 and over.

However, in some cases you get no allowances, and all your pay from that particular job is taxable. With an 0T code, you get no allowances and are taxed at the relevant tax rates, while a BR, D0 or D1 Code means that all your pay from this job or pension is taxed at the basic rate, higher rate or additional rate respectively (used for second jobs, for example).

The T code is used for any special cases not covered by the codes above, or if you ask your tax office to use it (e.g. because you do not want your employer to know what allowances you get).

Note that if your personal allowance is reduced because your income is over £100,000, or if you are aged 65-plus and losing age-related allowance because your income exceeds £25,400 (see pages 78 and 81), your PAYE code should show the reduced allowance based on your estimated income.

Figure 2.1: Possible coding notice entries

Your tax allowances   *Deductions*

- Personal allowance
- Married couple's allowance
- Blind person's allowance
- Maintenance payments
- Loan interest paid (if it qualifies for tax relief)
- Job expenses
- Personal pension relief or charity gifts relief for higher-rate taxpayers only (other taxpayers have already had full relief by paying less to the pension company or charity – see pages 207 and 218)

- State pensions and benefits
- Other pensions not taxed at source
- Jobseeker's Allowance
- Taxable incapacity benefit or Employment and Support Allowance
- Benefits and expenses provided by your employer (e.g. car or car fuel benefit)
- Part-time earnings/tips/commission
- Other items of untaxed income (e.g. property income, interest)
- Tax underpaid in earlier years
- Higher-rate adjustment for taxed investment income

Allowances minus deductions gives the number in your tax code

Example 2.1: **If allowances are more than deductions**

Patrick earns £15,000 a year working in the maintenance department of his local council. He has his personal allowance of £8,105, and he is also eligible to claim tax relief of £100 for tools he provides. His total allowances are £8,105 + £100 = £8,205. However, his tax office also wants to use his PAYE code to collect tax on untaxed interest he receives of £50 a year. This is deducted from his allowances, and means that he should receive £8,205 – £50 = £8,155 in tax-free pay during 2012–13.

His PAYE code is 815L, which tells his employer to give him £8,155 ÷ 12 = £680 of tax-free pay each month: 20% tax is deducted from the rest.

Figure 2.2: PAYE Coding Notice (see Example 2.2)

 **HM Revenue & Customs**

PAYE Coding Notice
Tax code for the year 2012-13

025038:00006251:001   846

MISS H HARPER
10 GRANGE ROAD
FULFORD
TAXSHIRE
TX3 4HQ

Please keep all your coding notices. You may need to refer to them if you have to fill in a tax return. Please quote your tax reference and National Insurance number if you contact us.
HM Revenue & Customs
CUSTOMER OPERATIONS
GRAYFIELD HOUSE
5 BANKHEAD AVENUE
EDINBURGH
EH11 4AE

Phone	0845 302 1409
Tax reference	491/G7070
National Insurance number	CE 00 00 30 A
Date	2 March 2012

Dear MISS H HARPER

Your tax code for the year 6 April 2012 to 5 April 2013 is K21

You need a tax code so GIVEUS ABREAK LTD can work out how much tax to take off the payments they make to you from 6 April 2012. It is important that you make sure that we have got your tax code right. The **Notes** will help you do this. If you contact us we will need your National Insurance number and tax reference. Please keep your coding notes; you may need them if we send you a tax return.

Here is how we worked it out:

your personal allowance		£8105
car benefit	-£4100	
property income	-£2770	
reduction to collect unpaid tax £580	-£1450	-£8320
tax is due on		£215

We turn £215 into tax code K21 to send to GIVEUS ABREAK LTD. They should use this code to take off the right amount of tax each time they pay you from 6 April 2012. We tell GIVEUS ABREAK LTD what your tax code is but we do not tell them how it is worked out

Before the tax year starts

PAYE coding notices are usually sent out in January or February for the tax year starting in April – before the Budget.

The rates of state pensions and benefits and the next year's allowances are usually announced in time to be incorporated into your tax code for the coming year. The letters in the code allow your employer to make automatic adjustments for some Budget changes. If you are affected by other Budget changes, or if your own circumstances change, you may be sent a new tax code after the start of the tax year.

If your tax code includes an allowance for an item on which you get tax relief (such as a pension contribution) or a deduction for other taxable income (such as untaxed interest), your tax office has to estimate the amount, based on information from your employer or from your last tax return. You may be sent a Tax Review form (P810) to check the figures.

► Example 2.2: **If deductions are more than allowances**

Halina is a 40% taxpayer. Her coding notice for 2012–13 (shown in Figure 2.2 opposite) includes her personal allowance of £8,105.

Halina's tax office is using her tax code to collect tax on the rent she receives from letting out her holiday cottage (£2,770) and some unpaid tax. The unpaid tax is £580, but the amount deducted is £1,450 because, when multiplied by her top rate of tax, this will collect £1,450 × 40% = £580. She also has a company car with a taxable value of £4,100. Her total deductions are £8,320.

Halina's deductions come to more than her allowances (£8,320 – £8,105 = minus £215). Her tax code is K21 which means that each month her PAYE is calculated as if she received £215 ÷ 12 = £18 more pay than she actually does.

At the end of the tax year

By 31 May following the end of the tax year, your employer must give you a form P60 telling you how much pay you have received, how much tax has been deducted and what your tax code was. (If you leave your job, your employer must give you a form P45 with this information.) By 6 July, your employer must also give you a form P11D or P9D with details of your taxable expenses and benefits (if you had any).

If you get a tax return, you will need this information to fill it in. But the information is copied to your tax office, and if you do not get a return it will check your tax bill for the year and:

- If too much tax has been deducted, set the overpayment against any other tax you owe. You should be sent a cheque for the rest – though not if the amount is £10 or less.
- If you have underpaid tax, adjust your tax code for a future tax year to collect the tax (but see Chapter 3 if the underpayment arose because of an HMRC mistake). For example, tax underpaid in 2011–12 will usually be recovered through the 2013–14 tax code. You can ask for the amount collected to be limited to the amount of your PAYE bill for the current year (with the rest collected through the next year's code), or less in case of hardship. You will be asked to make a repayment direct to HMRC if the amount is above £3,000, or if you no longer have income taxed under PAYE.

When a job ends

When you leave a job, your old employer must give you a form P45 which tells you (and your new employer) how much pay you have received in the tax year so far, how much tax you have paid, and what your tax code was. This will enable your new employer to deduct the right amount of tax.

If you do not have a P45 – perhaps because this is your first job – your new employer will ask you to fill in a form P46. This is sent to your tax office, unless you are earning less than £107 a week in 2012–13, this is your only or first job and you have not been receiving a pension or certain taxable benefits. Your tax office will try to trace your records so that it can give you your proper code. If it can't, it will send you a form P91 asking for details of your previous jobs. Until a correct code is issued, your employer will usually give you the 'emergency' code or code 0T (see opposite).

If you are not going to a new job, but claiming Jobseeker's Allowance or Employment and Support Allowance, the P45 is given to the Jobcentre Plus which will keep track of your tax and give you any rebate due. If you are unemployed but not claiming these benefits, you may also be entitled to a tax rebate. You can use repayment claim form P50 (from tax offices or the HMRC website), but you must wait four weeks after leaving your job before returning it.

Avoid the 'emergency' code

If your employer does not know what your tax code is, you will be taxed on the 'emergency' code of 810L in 2012–13, or on code 0T or BR. Codes 0T and BR give you no allowance, while the emergency code gives you only the basic personal allowance for someone aged under 65. Unless this is your first job, the emergency code may also ignore any tax-free pay built up before you started your new job. So it is in your interests to give your new employer your P45 or, if you do not have one, to make sure your employer gives you a form P46 to fill in.

More than one job or pension

If you have more than one job or pension, you will probably get a separate tax code and coding notice for each, but your allowances will be given against the main source of income. If any allowances are left over, you will see them in your code for the second source.

Your tax office may instruct whoever pays your second income to deduct tax without giving you any allowances or at just the basic rate or higher rate, using a 0T, BR or D0 code, or at the additional rate of 50 per cent for high earners (code D1). If, as a result, too much of your income is taxed, you may see an adjustment.

How tax is collected through a tax return

Although, for many people, PAYE will collect all the tax due, it cannot deal with people who do not have a job or private pension. They will need a tax return. There are also some people who can pay the bulk of their tax through PAYE, but not all, or whose affairs are sufficiently complex for HMRC to need to carry out a full review. They may get a return as well as being taxed under PAYE.

Who gets a tax return?

Tax offices review taxpayers' records in January or February each year to decide whether to send a return the following April.

You will always get a tax return if you are a paid director of a limited company, self-employed or in partnership, or if you are an employee or pensioner with an annual income of £100,000 or more, or with investment income of £10,000 or more (before tax).

You usually also have to submit a tax return if you have untaxed income, e.g. from investments, property or from overseas, although it is sometimes possible to collect the tax by adjusting your tax code, if you have one.

You may also have to deal with a tax return if you are aged 65 or over and get a reduced age-related allowance (see Chapter 6), or if you have taxable income but none of your income is taxed under PAYE, or if you parted with an asset which might be liable for capital gains tax.

The full tax return is six pages long, with extra pages depending on your circumstances. However, there is a simplified four-page short return for people with relatively straightforward affairs, such as some employees and pensioners and self-employed people with turnover under £73,000 in 2011–12. Both the full and the short tax return are covered in Part 3 of this book.

Filing your tax return

Tax returns are normally sent out in April, to collect information for the tax year just ended. For the 2011–12 tax year, the deadline for sending in a paper tax return (short or full versions) is 31 October 2012. But you can file online, and if you do this the deadline is 31 January 2013. There is more about dealing with your tax return in Part 3.

If you are filing online, the tax due will be worked out for you automatically. If you are sending in a paper return, you can work it out yourself (HMRC can supply a guide) but otherwise HMRC will do it for you in time to pay any tax due on 31 January 2013 provided that you get your return in by 31 October. If you miss the October deadline, HMRC will still send you a tax calculation but possibly not by 31 January.

Tax return or PAYE?

If all your tax is collected through PAYE you may not get a tax return and if you do not, you don't have to meet the deadlines for filling in forms and paying tax. The downside of not getting a return is that you have to check your tax code carefully and remember to tell HMRC if you get a new source of income, and you are likely to pay tax sooner. You also need to make sure that you have reclaimed any tax you are owed, such as tax deducted from a savings account if you are a non-taxpayer, as there is no automatic trigger for tax claims if you do not get a tax return. If you would prefer to deal with your tax through a tax return, ring the Self assessment helpline on 0845 900 0444 and ask for form SA1.

Getting a tax return, and rather you didn't? It depends on what type of income you have, and how much. The criteria used for sending out returns are shown on the HMRC website at www.hmrc.gov.uk/sa/need-tax-return.htm. If you don't think you meet the criteria for getting a return, contact HMRC and get your previous year's tax return in early, so that the information is logged before your tax office decides whether or not to send you a return.

Self-assessment statements

HMRC opens a tax account for everyone who is sent a tax return. You will get a statement of your account when there are changes to the items on it, or when a tax payment is due.

- If HMRC owes you money, you can ask to be sent a refund. Otherwise, the money is credited to your account.
- If you owe HMRC money, it will normally be collected by adjusting your tax code, if you have income taxed under PAYE and you owe less than £3,000 for the 2011–12 tax year (up from £2,000 for 2010–11 and previous years). But you must send in your return by 31 October 2012, if you are sending in a paper return, or file online by 31 December 2012.
- If you miss the deadline, or you opt not to have the tax deducted through PAYE, or the amount owed is over £3,000, you must pay the tax by 31 January 2013.

Interest is payable on amounts owed. The rate varies, but in March 2012 the interest HMRC paid on accounts in credit was only 0.5 per cent, whereas it was charging 3 per cent on late payments.

Payments on account

Unless the bulk of your income tax can be collected at source through PAYE, you have to pay tax in a lump sum, and you may also have to make 'payments on account'. These are twice-yearly payments of tax due on 31 January and 31 July in advance of your final tax bill. But they apply only to income tax and Class 4 National Insurance contributions – capital gains tax is paid in one lump sum on 31 January following the end of the tax year.

Payments on account – a summary

If you are liable to make payments on account for the 2011–12 tax year:

- The first payment on account was due on 31 January 2012. This is half your tax bill for 2010–11 not met at source, unless you opt to pay less (see opposite).
- The second payment on account is due on 31 July 2012.
- If these two payments come to less than your total tax bill for 2011–12, a final, balancing payment will be due on 31 January 2013 (unless it is under £3,000 and can be collected through your tax code). If they come to more than your tax bill for 2011–12, you will be due a repayment instead, which can either be paid out to you or set against your first payment on account for the 2012–13 tax year.

Each payment on account is half of your previous year's income tax bill (excluding tax deducted at source). However, you do not have to make payments on account if either of the following applies:

- more than 80 per cent of your tax bill for the previous tax year was met from tax paid at source *or*
- the tax *not* deducted at source was less than £1,000.

So you are unlikely to have to make payments on account if you are an employee or pensioner, and your pay or pension is your main income.

> ## Example 2.3: **Calculating payments on account**

Sam is a self-employed plumber. His tax bill for 2010–11 was £8,000, including his Class 4 National Insurance contributions. He made no taxable capital gains. Sam's payments on account for 2011–12 are £8,000 ÷ 2 = £4,000 each, which he pays in January 2012 and July 2012. However, 2011–12 turns out to be a good year and Sam's tax bill comes to £10,000. He has a further £10,000 − £8,000 = £2,000 to pay by 31 January 2013.

On 31 January 2013 Sam must also make his first payment on account for 2012–13. This is half his tax bill for 2011–12, that is £10,000 ÷ 2 = £5,000. The total tax due on 31 January is therefore £2,000 + £5,000 = £7,000.

> ## Planning your tax payments

The final payment for one year coincides with the first payment on account for the next. If your income is rising year on year (or if you pay less tax at source, or expect to pay capital gains tax), you need to be careful to put enough cash aside to meet the January payment. If you are having difficulty paying tax due on a previous year's profits, see page 39.

Reducing your payments on account

If your taxable income is falling, you can claim to reduce each payment on account to half of your anticipated tax bill (ignoring capital gains tax). You can claim in your tax return, online or by completing form SA303 that should come with your self-assessment statement.

Your tax office will not 'approve' your claim – you simply go ahead and pay the reduced amount – but your claim may be rejected if you have not given a valid reason for reducing your payment. Note also that:

■ If your tax bill turns out to be more than you anticipate, you will have to pay interest on the difference between the full payment and the amount you actually paid, from the date the payment was due – and at a higher rate than you receive if you have overpaid tax.

■ If you make a fraudulent or negligent claim to reduce your payments on account to less than they realistically should be, HMRC can charge you a penalty of up to the extra tax that should have been paid.

Example 2.4: **Claiming to reduce your payments on account**

Sam had an unusually good year in 2011–12 (see Example 2.3 on page 31) and his tax bill of £10,000 means that he should make payments of account for 2012–13 of £10,000 ÷ 2 = £5,000 in January and July 2013. However, he was off work in September 2012 after an accident. He thinks this will bring his tax bill for 2012–13 down to about £7,000. In his tax return for the 2011–12 tax year he makes a claim to reduce his payments on account to £7,000 ÷ 2 = £3,500.

How to pay

If you have tax to pay, you will normally be sent a statement with a payslip attached. You can use this to pay at your bank or building society or at the post office, or send it with a cheque to HMRC's Accounts Office (the address is on the back of the payslip). However, HMRC encourages you to pay electronically, by using your debit or credit card over the phone, or via BillPay on the HMRC website, or by internet or telephone banking. Note though, that there is a charge for credit card payments (1.5 per cent over the telephone, 1.4 per cent online). You can also pay by direct debit, either in a lump sum or through a weekly or monthly budget payment. See HMRC factsheet TH/FS7 *Paying your tax – what you need to know*, or the HMRC website at www.hmrc.gov.uk/payinghmrc, or phone 0845 366 7816.

You can still pay if you haven't got a payslip, but check the HMRC website or phone the number above to make sure you provide all the necessary information. Note that HMRC has changed its bank, so make sure you use the right account details, or the payment may not go through.

Whichever method you use:

■ Make the payment a few days before the due date to give it time to go through (a cheque payment is treated as received on the day HMRC receives your cheque). You can now use the 'faster payments' system online or over the telephone, but check first if your bank puts any limits on the amount you can pay this way. You cannot use a post-dated cheque unless you pay early and it is dated on or before the due date, or unless you have a prior arrangement with your tax office.

■ Include your unique taxpayer reference (see page 45). Also write it after 'HM Revenue & Customs' on any cheque.

■ Keep proof of payment or proof of posting. HMRC does not provide receipts unless you send a letter requesting one with your payment.

If you are having difficulty paying a tax bill, see Chapter 3.

What to tell HMRC

Whether or not you get a tax return, you should tell your tax office about:

■ A change of address, or leaving the UK to live abroad.

■ Starting to work for yourself. See page 151.

■ Regular pension contributions or gifts to charity, if you are a higher-rate taxpayer. These will be picked up through your tax return but if the amounts are substantial and you are on PAYE you might want to notify your tax office earlier so that you can be given higher-rate tax relief through your tax code as soon as possible.

In addition, if you do not get a tax return you should contact your tax office:

■ If you have a new source of taxable income unless all your income is taxed under PAYE or has tax taken off at source (e.g. savings interest) and you are not a higher-rate taxpayer, or if you have made taxable capital gains. You must do this by 5 October after the end of the tax year in question.

■ If you have allowances or income in your tax code which vary in amount (such as property income or untaxed interest). You may receive a Tax Review form (P810) every so often, asking the questions necessary to adjust your code.

■ If you want to claim tax relief on work expenses. You may be sent a claim form P87 or a Tax Review form (P810).

■ If you need to claim tax back (because too much tax has been deducted from investments). You may need to fill in a Tax Repayment form (R40, covered in Chapter 20) or form R85 to get your interest paid without tax taken off (see page 189).

If you are claiming tax credits, there are some other changes you must tell HMRC about – see page 67 – and see Chapter 6 for what to tell your tax office if you or your spouse or partner have retired or are approaching 65.

Record-keeping

Make sure you keep your coding notices, payslips and P60s and (if you get one) your P11D, P9D, or P45. Your employer can give you a duplicate of your P60 if you lose it, but is not allowed to give you a duplicate P45, though your tax office should have the information from the employer's regular returns. Also keep a copy of any completed forms you send your tax office, records of any tax payments you make and tax deducted from savings income, copies of any correspondence and notes of any phone calls.

If you get a tax return, you must keep adequate records to support your tax return. Also keep all your statements of account and photocopies of everything you send HMRC.

■ For specific documents relating to people in different situations, and with different types of income, see the end of each chapter in Part 2.

■ For how long to keep your records, see page 15.

3

Troubleshooting

What happens if things go wrong? This chapter covers what you can do if you have a problem with your tax or are having difficulty paying a tax bill and tells you where to get further help.

Top tips

- Make a note of your taxpayer reference or National Insurance number. It will save time if you quote it in correspondence or in phone calls to your tax office.
- Keep a record of any phone calls to HMRC offices, including the date and time and the name of the person you spoke to.
- If you have to complain because your tax office has made a mistake or been slow, make a note of any costs you incur – you may be able to claim them back. Keep receipts, if possible.
- HMRC will sometimes waive tax if you are faced with a late and unexpected tax bill as a result of an HMRC error – check if Extra-Statutory Concession A19 applies to you.
- Don't be afraid to ask your tax office for help. As well as your own tax office, there are general enquiry centres and specialist helplines.
- If you make a genuine mistake, you should not be penalised if you can show that you took 'reasonable care' to get things right, including seeking help if you were unsure.
- If you have neglected your tax affairs you may be able to get back into the system without heavy penalties by making a voluntary disclosure – see page 41.

Your rights ...

All HMRC offices have targets for customer service. If HMRC fails to meet a service commitment, or you are dissatisfied with its service, you can complain. HMRC has also published 'Your Charter', which requires it to:

1. Respect you
2. Help and support you to get things right
3. Treat you as honest
4. Treat you even-handedly
5. Be professional and act with integrity
6. Tackle people who deliberately break the rules and challenge those who bend the rules
7. Protect your information and respect your privacy
8. Accept that someone else can represent you
9. Do all it can to keep the cost of dealing with HMRC as low as possible.

... and your responsibilities

HMRC's Charter states that – as well as being honest and respecting HMRC staff – you are expected to take 'reasonable care' to get things right, for example by seeking help if you do not understand something or cannot pay a tax bill, keeping accurate and up-to-date records, telling your tax office if your circumstances change, and providing correct and complete information when asked.

What's the problem?

You may think that HMRC has charged you too much tax, been slow or inefficient or just made a mistake. Here's what to do if you want to:

■ Appeal against an HMRC decision. The appeals procedure is laid down by law, and covers things such as your tax assessment, a penalty, a claim for tax relief and a tax credits award.

■ Complain about shoddy treatment – follow the complaints process
   described overleaf. There is an independent Adjudicator if you are still
   dissatisfied.
■ Claim a tax repayment – if you get a tax return, fill in page TR5 to
   claim a repayment, otherwise it will stay in your tax account and be
   set against future tax liabilities (see Chapter 17). If you do not get a
   return and think you might have overpaid tax, contact your tax office.
   If you have a job or pension you may get a repayment through your
   employer or you may be sent an R40 claim form – see Chapter 20.
■ Get help if you cannot pay a tax bill – see page 39.

How to appeal

When you receive a formal notice of an HMRC decision, it will say if you
have a right of appeal, and should include information about how to appeal
and an appeal form.

If you appeal, your tax office will try to settle it by agreement. You can
ask to have your case reviewed by a different officer from the one who made
the original decision. If you still disagree, the case will go before a tax Tribunal which will make a decision. The decision of the Tribunal is final on a
point of fact, but can be challenged in the courts on a point of law. See
factsheet HMRC1 *HMRC decisions – what to do if you disagree*.

Act quickly, because you usually have only 30 days from the date of the
decision in which to appeal, unless you can give a good reason for any delay.
Be prepared to pay any disputed tax in the meantime – you may be able to
postpone paying it, but interest will usually be added from the date the tax
was due if your appeal is unsuccessful.

If you make a mistake

If you have paid too much tax because of a mistake in your tax return, for
example you forgot to deduct an expense, you can correct it without question within one year and ten months of the end of the tax year. After that –
or if you did not complete a return – you can still claim back tax within four
years of the end of the tax year in question, so by 5 April 2016 for claims
relating to 2011–12. Note that these limits do not override specific time
limits for making claims in a tax return, such as claiming a business loss.

If HMRC makes a mistake

You should not face an unexpected bill if you keep your tax affairs in order and give HMRC the necessary information. If your tax office then tells you that something has gone wrong and you have paid too little tax – for example, you have received a form P800 showing tax due from an earlier year (see page 21) – HMRC may waive the tax, under Extra-Statutory Concession A19. This applies only if you were told about the arrears more than 12 months after the end of the tax year in which HMRC received the relevant information, and if it was reasonable for you to think that you had paid enough tax. The 12-month rule may be waived if there were repeated failures. If HMRC says that you are not eligible for Concession A19, ask for a full explanation, and if you still think you should qualify consider complaining. For advice and sample letters see the website of the Low Incomes Tax Reform Group at www.litrg.org.uk.

How to complain

If you have a disagreement with HMRC, check whether you have a formal right of appeal. If you do, it is usually better to follow this route rather than HMRC's complaints procedure in order to avoid missing the time limit for appealing, which is only 30 days. But if you can't appeal, you can still complain about things like mistakes, unreasonable delays or being given wrong or misleading information.

If you want to complain, first give the person you are dealing with a chance to put things right. Write 'Complaint' clearly at the top of any letter. If you have no joy, ask for it to be reviewed by the Complaints Manager. HMRC factsheet C/FS *Complaints* gives more information.

If you are still dissatisfied, contact the independent Adjudicator, whose services are free. You must normally do so within six months of receiving a final decision from HMRC. See leaflet A01 *The Adjudicator's Office for complaints about HM Revenue & Customs and the Valuation Office Agency*. The Independent Police Complaints Commission also has a role in overseeing HMRC's complaints system and investigating serious complaints such as misconduct of HMRC staff.

If all else fails, you may be able to complain to the Parliamentary Ombudsman. However, the Adjudicator cannot handle complaints that have already been investigated by the Ombudsman. Complaints to the Ombudsman must be made through an MP within 12 months of the cause for complaint arising.

While a complaint is under way, HMRC may agree not to pursue the tax you are disputing during the investigation, but interest will build up on any tax that turns out to be due.

Keep track of costs

If your complaint is upheld, you can claim any reasonable costs – such as postage, phone calls, travelling expenses, professional fees and interest on overpaid tax – you have had to pay as a result of an HMRC mistake or delay, so keep receipts. You can claim earnings lost as a direct result of having to sort things out. You may also be entitled to compensation for worry and distress.

Can't pay your tax?

If you are facing a tax bill that you cannot pay, your tax office has the right to start enforcement proceedings such as court action. It can also collect tax debts through PAYE on your job or pension if you have one. But it will often put off taking these steps if you get in touch as soon as possible, explaining any financial difficulties or other factors such as illness, or unusual business or family problems, and giving information about your finances. You might be able to negotiate 'time to pay' in instalments. But you will have to send in any outstanding tax returns, and give full details of your anticipated income and expenditure. The charity TaxAid has a useful leaflet and videos about tax debt on its website at www.taxaid.org.uk/guides/tax-debt and see HMRC factsheet TH/FS6 *Problems paying your tax – what you need to know*.

If you have an agreed payment plan in place it will mean that you avoid the penalties normally payable on tax unpaid 30 days and 6 months after the due date. But interest will still be clocking up on the amount owed and if you miss any payments HMRC may start enforcement proceedings. HMRC also has the power to set a repayment due from one tax (such as VAT) against some other types of tax you owe. Be realistic about your chances of paying off the debt, and get help early (see page 44 for charities that may help). HMRC may decide not to pursue the debt at all if, say, you are chronically ill, have no assets and few means and things are unlikely to improve.

Business Payment Support Service

HMRC has a service for individuals and businesses struggling to pay tax as a result of the economic conditions. Staff can discuss options such as time to pay, and give you a quick decision. They might allow extra time to pay if you think that you will make a loss in the current year that could reduce the tax you owe. There is a support line on 0845 302 1435.

Compliance checks

'Compliance checks' include enquiries into tax returns, investigations where fraud or negligence is suspected and inspections of records and business premises.

Checks on tax returns

If you have to complete a tax return, HMRC has one year after receiving it within which it can start a formal 'compliance check' (see page 268). A check does not necessarily mean that HMRC thinks something is wrong with your return – some are chosen at random. But you can still be investigated after the one-year period if it suspects fraud or negligence, or if you have not supplied full and accurate information.

Other checks

HMRC may also start an investigation if it suspects you have failed to declare taxable amounts. If this happens, co-operation is your best bet, but there are limits on what HMRC can ask for and what it can do. There is a range of compliance factsheets, listed in the Fact file, that set out what powers HMRC has to ask for information and documents and visit business premises (but not your home, unless you run your business there).

For the worst cases of tax evasion, HMRC can start criminal proceedings which could result in an unlimited fine or a prison sentence. However, HMRC is more likely to impose a penalty. Tax evaders may also be entered on the Managing Deliberate Defaulters Programme, and subject to special scrutiny for up to five years. There is a Tax Evasion Hotline on 0800 788 887 to report people you suspect of evasion.

If you have neglected your tax affairs, you may be able to get back into the system without heavy penalties by making a voluntary disclosure – see the guidance on the website of the charity TaxAid at www.taxaid.org.uk. Also watch out for special disclosure campaigns aimed at particular trades, such as electricians. These offer favourable settlement terms for a limited period. Contact HMRC's Campaigns Voluntary Disclosure helpline on 0845 601 5041, but consider taking professional advice first.

Penalties

If an investigation finds that you owe tax, you will have to pay what is owed, plus interest, plus a possible penalty. The penalty is a percentage of the tax you owe, as shown below, and the same penalties apply to virtually all taxes administered by HMRC (but not tax credits). There is no penalty if you made a mistake, providing you took reasonable care, or if no tax is due. But failing to tell HMRC if you realise you have made a mistake, or if it has under-assessed the tax you should pay, counts as a careless error.

Table 3.1: Penalties

Kind of error	Penalty range (%)*
Careless	0–30
Deliberate but not concealed	20–70
Deliberate and concealed	30–100

* Higher penalties may apply to overseas income and gains.

Disclosing any inaccuracies or undeclared income or gains will substantially reduce any penalty, particularly if the disclosure is unprompted. You can also appeal against a penalty, and if your only error was a failure to take reasonable care HMRC may agree to 'suspend' it for up to two years provided you comply with any conditions it imposes. See HMRC's range of compliance factsheets, in particular CC/FS6 *Compliance checks – What happens when we find something wrong* and CC/FS7 *Compliance checks – Penalties for errors in returns or documents*.

HMRC also has the power to publish the name of anybody who is penalised for deliberately dodging tax of over £25,000.

Tax avoidance

Tax *planning* is perfectly legitimate. But tax *avoidance* is a grey area, and can lead to HMRC challenges, so take care if an adviser or employer offers you a special 'tax-saving' scheme, particularly if there are high set-up fees, or you would have to pay money up-front. There are many 'anti-avoidance' rules and the Disclosure of Tax Avoidance Schemes regime requires 'promoters' of some schemes to notify HMRC, and the people who use them to make an entry in their tax returns (see page 298). The government also intends to introduce a general 'anti-abuse' rule in 2013.

In doubt about the tax treatment?

HMRC will not help with tax planning, but you can ask for information about its interpretation of recent tax law, and its internal guidance manuals are published on its website at www.hmrc.gov.uk/thelibrary/manuals.htm. If, after a transaction, you want HMRC to check your valuation of an asset for capital gains tax purposes, you can use form CG34. See the 'Clearances and approvals' section of the HMRC website at www.hmrc.gov.uk/cap.

Getting help

Help from HMRC

- *Pros*: Free, and HMRC staff have access to your tax records.

■ *Cons*: Service levels are suffering as HMRC is being asked to do more for less. No help with tax planning.

Your first port of call is likely to be your tax office. If you are an employee or receive a pension, this will be that of your employer or main pension payer. If you change jobs you will be transferred to a new tax office. Self-employed people are dealt with by a tax office in their area.

If you become unemployed, you stay with your existing tax office. But if you do not have a job or pension and have claimed tax repayments in the past, your records may find their way to the HMRC office in Leicester that specialises in repayments.

These days your records are held on various computer systems and you don't necessarily need to contact your own tax office. If you need help about something specific to you, phone the telephone number given on any relevant paperwork. For general queries look in the phone book under 'HM Revenue & Customs'. This also gives addresses of HMRC enquiry centres that can arrange face-to-face meetings. You can ask tax offices to call you back to save on phone bills and if you are housebound you can arrange for a home visit. Facilities for people with particular needs are on the 'Accessibility' page of the HMRC website.

There are also specialist HMRC offices covering, for example, tax credits, National Insurance and non-residents, which have their own helplines. HMRC helplines, leaflets and useful web pages are listed in the Fact file.

Frauds and scams

Fraudsters frequently pretend to be from HMRC in order to get personal information, for example by encouraging you to click through to a replica of the HMRC website to claim a rebate. HMRC will never ask for your login, bank or credit card details in a phone call or email. Known scams are listed on HMRC's website. To check that a phone call is genuinely from HMRC, call HMRC yourself using the phone number on any correspondence.

Problems contacting HMRC?

In July 2011, the chairman of HMRC apologised publicly for poor service standards, including problems getting through to tax offices. HMRC is making more call centre staff available at busy times, but it is worth keeping a note of every call attempt you make, including the date and time (to help track down HMRC recordings of the call). And if you are unreasonably refused a special service, such as a home visit, remind HMRC staff of the commitments in 'Your Charter' (see page 36). If problems persist, consider a formal complaint.

Help from a professional

- *Pros*: Independent. Good professionals can do the legwork for you, provide help with tax planning and negotiate with your tax office if necessary. Advice could pay for itself.
- *Cons*: Cost. Variable standards. You are still responsible if things go wrong – though you might have a claim against your adviser.

Many accountancy and law firms offer tax services. Lists of firms specialising in particular areas are available from their professional body (see the Fact file). Alternatively, you can go to a specialist 'chartered tax adviser', with the 'CTA', 'ATII' or 'FTII' qualifications awarded by the Chartered Institute of Taxation. A lower-level qualification is run by the Association of Tax Technicians (ATT). ATT members who meet requirements such as having insurance and up-to-date knowledge are described as 'Registered with the Association of Taxation Technicians as a Member in Practice'.

If you want someone to deal with HMRC on your behalf, you need to give your tax office authorisation to treat that person as your 'agent'. If you are using a professional agent, the agent will organise it; if you want a friend or relative to help you, you need to write to your tax office giving them permission.

There are also two charities – TaxAid and TaxHelp for Older People – that offer free advice to people who cannot afford to pay an accountant or tax adviser. Their details are in the Fact file.

What to look for in an adviser

Anyone can set themselves up as a tax adviser. Look for professional accountancy qualifications, or those from the Chartered Institute of Taxation or Association of Tax Technicians, and check that an adviser has up-to-date expertise that is relevant to your needs. Make sure that you get a letter of engagement explaining their fees and what they will do for you.

Record-keeping

See Chapter 1 for the records the law requires you to keep. However, you should always aim to keep records to back up any complaint or enquiry. If HMRC does investigate you, it will help your case if you can show that your affairs are in order. As well as copies of letters and emails sent and received, keep a note of any telephone conversation with HMRC, including the number you rang, the person you spoke to, the date and time. Also keep records of tax paid. If you make a payment or file a tax return online, make sure you receive an email that says the transaction has gone through.

Keep reference numbers handy

When you contact HMRC, you will be asked for your reference number and may be asked security questions to check that you are who you say you are. A ten-figure 'unique taxpayer reference' (UTR) will be on the front of your tax return, if you get one. Tax offices can also track your records down if you quote your National Insurance number.

Part 2
Planning to save tax

4

Tax as a family

Everybody, including children, is entitled to their own personal allowances and is taxed as an individual. However, there are some special tax rules for married couples and civil partners, and state benefits are worked out on a household basis. This chapter covers the tax rules for couples and children, an allowance for blind people, and how state benefits are taxed.

Top tips

- From January 2013, you will lose child benefit if your income is above £50,000. A pension contribution or Gift Aid donation could help, see page 55.
- Living with someone without being married? You do not benefit from the favourable rules for married couples, so check the tax rules for joint property and make a will.
- Married or not, you can save tax by giving investments to the partner who pays the lower rate of tax – but unmarried couples should watch out for inheritance tax or capital gains tax. See Chapters 14 and 15.
- You can claim blind person's allowance for any tax year in which you had evidence of blindness, even if you weren't registered until the following year. See page 50.
- Over the past two years there has been a big rise in the amount of income people aged under 65 can have before they pay tax, to £8,105 in 2012–13. If you are on a low income, are claiming state benefits, or are a student working part-time, check your tax carefully – the tax estimator on page 8 may help.

How your family affects your tax

Tax credits and other state benefits are worked out on the basis of your household income – see Chapter 5 for more information on tax credits. This is not the case for income tax, National Insurance, capital gains tax and inheritance tax. These taxes treat individuals separately, although there is some special treatment for married couples, summarised on page 52. Same-sex couples who have registered as civil partners are treated in the same way as married couples.

Income tax allowances

All UK residents, whatever their age, qualify for a personal allowance of at least £8,105 in 2012–13 (£7,475 in 2011–12). Your allowance is the amount of income you can have before you have to pay tax. People aged at least 65 may get a higher allowance (see Chapter 6), and blind people may get an extra allowance (see below).

Note that if your income is above £100,000, you will lose £1 of your allowance for each £2 above £100,000, until your income reaches £116,210 in 2012–13 (£114,950 in 2011–12), at which point the allowance is reduced to zero.

Blind person's allowance

This is an extra allowance of £2,100 in the 2012–13 tax year (£1,980 in 2011–12). You automatically qualify if you are registered as blind or severely sight-impaired (but not partially sighted) with the local authority. You can claim for the year before you were registered, provided that you had evidence of blindness, such as an ophthalmologist's certificate.

In Scotland or Northern Ireland, where there is no system of registration, you will qualify for the allowance if your eyesight is so bad that you are unable to perform any work for which eyesight is essential.

The tax relief is worked out in the same way as for the personal allowance – an extra £2,100 of your income is tax-free. The allowance is not reduced however high your income is, but if your income is too low for you to use up all your allowances, you can transfer any unused allowance to your husband or wife or civil partner, even if they are not blind.

Tax-free income for families

Tax-free state benefits for older people are covered in Chapter 6.

If you have children
- Child benefit (but see page 55), Child Tax Credit and Guardian's Allowance.
- Additions to benefits paid because you have a child.
- Educational allowances, scholarships and bursaries (such as the Education Maintenance Allowance, if it is still available where you are studying).
- Maternity Allowance and adoption allowances (but not statutory maternity pay).
- Most income as a foster carer or shared lives carer (see HMRC help sheet 236 *Qualifying care relief*). This includes adult placement carers, staying put carers and certain kinship carers.

Looking for a job
- Jobseeker's Allowance above the taxable maximum (see page 56).
- Some employment grants, e.g. New Deal training allowance.
- Return to work credit, Job Grant and in-work credit.

Bereavement
- Bereavement payment (a lump sum state benefit on bereavement).
- Insurance payouts from a protection-type life insurance policy, such as whole life insurance, term insurance or a family income benefit policy (but see page 194 for policies with an investment element).

Sickness and disability
- Income-related Employment and Support Allowance (see page 56).
- Payouts from a personal accident insurance policy, income protection policy, sickness or unemployment policy, unless the insurance was paid for by your employer. If so, any payment counts as employment income, see page 97.
- Disability living allowance, payments from the Independent Living Fund and disabled facilities grants.
- Incapacity Benefit if you previously claimed invalidity benefit before April 1995.

■ Industrial injury benefits (except industrial death benefit pension).

■ Pensions and benefits paid because of death, injury or disability in the Armed Forces (but some dependants' benefits are taxable). (See HMRC help sheet 310 *War Widow's and dependant's pensions*.)

Other

■ Maintenance and alimony.

■ Working Tax Credit and Income Support (unless on strike).

■ Council tax benefit, housing benefit and payments under the Armed Forces Council Tax Relief scheme.

■ Christmas bonus and cold weather payment made with some benefits.

■ Social fund payments.

■ Housing grants.

Couples

These are the main rules if you are married or in a civil partnership:

■ You each have your own personal allowance (£8,105 in 2012–13, more if 65-plus), but you can also claim married couple's allowance if either of you was born before April 1935 (this is covered on page 80).

■ You can transfer unused married couple's and blind person's allowance between you (but not personal allowance).

■ You can also transfer possessions, money and investments between you without incurring a tax bill. Such gifts are exempt from inheritance tax, and there is no capital gains tax until the recipient parts with the asset. But you can claim capital gains tax relief on only one home between you (see page 231).

■ If you own an investment jointly, married or not, you are normally each taxed on half of the income from it. Married couples who contributed unequal proportions to the investment can, instead, opt to have the income taxed in line with the proportion invested, by asking their tax office for Form 17. However, you cannot use this for bank accounts or life insurance.

But it's not all good news. To stop couples exploiting the rules too much, there are many 'anti-avoidance' rules which target couples. These particularly apply to family-owned businesses and capital gains tax. We alert you to the main traps throughout the book.

Couples who are living together do not benefit from any of the favourable rules for married people, but may still be caught by anti-avoidance rules. It is particularly important that people who have children, who own a home or a business together, or who might be liable to capital gains tax or inheritance tax, consider the implications for their tax and child benefit, make a will, and if necessary take professional advice (see Chapter 3).

Example 4.1: Saving tax by transferring investments

Harry and Harriet are married. Harry earns £50,000. He saves as much as he can in a tax-free cash ISA each year, but he still has taxable savings interest of £2,500, on which he pays tax at 40% – £1,000. Harriet has a part-time job paying only £6,000, leaving £8,105 – £6,000 = £2,105 unused allowance in 2012–13. If Harry puts his taxable savings into Harriet's name, she will pay no tax on £2,105 of the income, and only 10% on the remaining £395 (£39) – an immediate tax saving of £961. What's more, Harriet can move the money into her own ISA, so that the whole amount will be tax-free. However, to be effective Harry's gift must be a real gift, with no strings attached.

Being widowed

When somebody who is being taxed under PAYE dies, their P45 is sent to their tax office. If their widow or widower is entitled to a spouse's pension from an employer's or private pension scheme, the pension scheme will notify the widow or widower's tax office, and will pay the pension with tax deducted either as before, or at the basic rate from the whole amount, until a new tax code is issued. You may be sent a *Bereavement benefit coding* form (P161(W)) to help your tax office decide what your new code should be.

Divorced or separated?

For income tax purposes, couples are treated as separated if there is a court order or written deed to that effect, or if they are living apart and the separation is intended to be permanent. Any maintenance or alimony you receive is tax-free; any you pay does not qualify for tax relief unless either you or your ex-spouse were born before 6 April 1935 (see page 84). However, transactions on divorce – such as a lump sum payment to an ex-spouse – are exempt from capital gains tax or inheritance tax. For the capital gains tax rules, see HMRC help sheet 281 *Husband and wife, civil partners, divorce, dissolution and separation*. If you are claiming tax credits remember to tell HMRC's Tax Credit Office when you split up, whether or not you are married (see page 67).

Children

Children are taxed the same way as adults. They have their own personal allowance which means that the first slice of their income is tax-free but they pay tax on any income above that. However, children are normally non-taxpayers, so if yours have savings accounts make sure you register for the interest to be paid gross – i.e. without tax deducted. (See page 189.)

Note that, to stop parents investing in their children's names purely to use their allowances, any income arising from gifts to your own child is taxed as yours, unless it comes to less than £100 a year (per parent per child). If this is likely to affect you, choose a tax-free investment for your child (see Chapter 11). The rule doesn't apply to gifts from grandparents.

Having a baby

Maternity and paternity pay, including statutory maternity, paternity or adoption pay, is taxable and your employer will deduct PAYE and National Insurance. If you do not have the right to return to work after the birth, your employer will give you a P45. Any payments made after receiving your P45 will have tax deducted, so you may be able to claim a tax refund.

When your child is born you can claim child benefit and may also be entitled to Child Tax Credit and other benefits (see page 64). Child benefit is administered by HMRC, which has a helpline on 0845 302 1444.

Warning: child benefit changes

From 7 January 2013 anyone who has income above £50,000, or who is living with a partner who does, will lose £1 of child benefit for every £100 of income above £50,000. If your income is above £60,000 you will lose all your child benefit. If both partners have income above £50,000, the higher income is used.

You still get paid the full benefit, and it is (technically) tax-free, but a special income tax charge will be made through your tax return or PAYE code. You can opt not to get the benefit at all, but don't do this if your income might fall. Your income is calculated after pension contributions, business losses and Gift Aid, so you may be able to save your benefit by making a pension contribution or Gift Aid donation.

Child Trust Fund

The government has stopped issuing Child Trust Fund vouchers. It has introduced a 'Junior ISA' instead (see page 187), but this does not qualify for any contribution from the government.

If your child already has a Child Trust Fund, the money in it will stay there until they reach 18, and you can change the type of account, or move it to a different provider. The accounts are tax-free (in the same way as ISAs, see page 185), and other people can contribute a total of up to £3,600 a year into a child's account (£1,200 a year before 1 November 2011).

Students

Students who are working pay tax like anyone else, but you can earn up to £8,105 a year before paying income tax. If you work only during the holidays, you can fill in form P38(S) to have your wages paid without income tax – no National Insurance is payable on income below £146 a week.

However, you can't use form P38(S) if you have a part-time job in term time or if you study overseas. Each job will be treated as a new job and tax and National Insurance may be deducted, as described in Chapter 2. You may be able to claim a tax refund, or you may be one of the people who gets a form P800 *Tax calculation* suggesting that you owe tax (see page 21). There is a tax checker at www.hmrc.gov.uk/calcs/stc.htm.

Claiming state benefits

The government is planning to replace all working age benefits and tax credits with a single Universal Credit, starting in 2013. But currently there is a range of benefits, many of which are tax-free (as listed on page 51). The state retirement pension is the main taxable state benefit – covered in Chapter 6. Other taxable benefits are:

- Statutory sick pay and statutory maternity, adoption or paternity pay.
- Bereavement allowance, widow's pension, widowed mother's allowance or widowed parent's allowance.
- Industrial death benefit pension. This is no longer available to new claimants, but may still be paid to existing claimants.
- Jobseeker's Allowance. The taxable amount is capped: in 2012–13, the maximum taxable amount is £56.25 a week for a single person aged 18 to 24, £71 a week for a single person aged 25 or over, and £111.45 for a couple both aged 18 or over.
- Carer's Allowance paid to people who spend at least 35 hours a week caring for a disabled person.
- Incapacity Benefit unless you previously claimed invalidity benefit for this disability and have claimed continuously since 12 April 1995.
- Employment and Support Allowance. Any ESA you get on the basis of the National Insurance you have paid ('contributory' ESA) is taxable, but means-tested ('income-related') ESA is not.

Although the income is taxable, it is generally paid out with no tax deducted. However, the following state benefits get special treatment:

- Incapacity Benefit. If you receive taxable Incapacity Benefit and have no other income taxed under PAYE, the Department for Work and Pensions (DWP) deducts tax before paying you.
- Jobseeker's Allowance and Employment and Support Allowance. Tax is not deducted, but you must give your P45 to the Jobcentre Plus, which will give you a statement of the taxable amount at the end of the tax year. Any tax you owe is normally collected by adjusting your tax code when you get a new job. If you have paid too much you will usually get a refund from the Jobcentre Plus or your new employer.

What to tell HMRC

Your basic personal allowance should be given automatically through either your tax return or, if you have income taxed under PAYE, your tax code. Check that 'personal allowance' appears on your coding notice (see page 21). If you have no income taxed under PAYE and do not get a tax return, you may be a non-taxpayer and should contact your tax office to check if you can claim back any tax deducted from savings interest.

To claim blind person's allowance, or transfer unused allowance to your husband or wife, complete page TR4 of your tax return, if you get one. See page 284 for what to enter. If you do not get a tax return, contact your tax office. If you are unlikely to use your allowance in future tax years, your tax office may adjust your partner's tax code to allow for the expected transfer. You can also transfer unused married couple's allowance (see page 83).

The DWP will tell your tax office if you are receiving taxable state benefits, and if you get a tax return you must enter the taxable amount on page TR3. Tax credits are not taxable, but if you are claiming them you must tell HMRC's Tax Credit Office about various changes (see page 67).

Record-keeping

These are the documents you should keep – see page 15 for how long.

- If you own any assets or investments jointly with someone else, a note of how much you each contributed, unless you are happy to be treated as if you contributed equal amounts.
- Records of any gifts of money or assets.
- Any correspondence relating to your children's Child Trust Fund.
- For blind person's allowance, notification that you are registered blind and/or an ophthalmologist's certificate.
- Any letters from the DWP or Jobcentre Plus showing how much taxable benefit you have received. If you claim Jobseeker's Allowance, Incapacity Benefit or Employment and Support Allowance, you should receive a statement of taxable amounts on either a P45 (when you stop claiming) or a P60 (at the end of the tax year).

5

Tax credits

Child Tax Credit and Working Tax Credit are state benefits administered by HM Revenue & Customs (HMRC). They do not affect your tax bill, but they are means-tested. Note that the government plans to replace tax credits and some other benefits with a single Universal Credit. The changes will be phased in between October 2013 and the end of 2017, but in the meantime, tax credits have become considerably less generous.

Top tips

- Claim even if you are not sure whether your income is too high and renew your claim each year. This will protect you if your income falls and may entitle you to other benefits (see page 64). From 6 April 2012 you cannot backdate a claim beyond one month.
- Once you have claimed you must tell the Tax Credit Office about certain changes (see page 67) within a month or risk being penalised, or having to repay credits.
- If your income is just at the level where you lose tax credits, paying a pension contribution or Gift Aid donation could reduce your income enough to qualify.
- Check the 'award notice' that tells you how much tax credit you will get – you should tell HMRC about any mistakes within one month of getting the notice.
- Joint claimants are both liable for overpayments – if one partner cannot or will not pay, the other may have to repay the whole amount, although HMRC will not insist on this if you co-operate and pay your half.

Can you claim?

In 2012–13, you can claim Child Tax Credit if you are responsible for a child aged under 16, or under 20 and completing non-advanced education or approved training. Working Tax Credit is for people who work at least 16 hours a week, and who have a child, or are disabled, or are aged 60-plus. Even if none of these apply, you can claim if you are aged at least 25 and work at least 30 hours a week. From April 2012, couples with children have to work at least 24 hours a week between them (with one partner working at least 16 hours) to qualify, unless one partner is disabled, ill, in hospital or in prison, or receiving Carer's Allowance.

If you are married, or living with someone as husband and wife (including same-sex couples), you have to claim jointly. If you have a child who lives with an ex-partner for some of the time, either decide between you who will claim tax credit for the child, or HMRC will decide.

Contact HMRC's tax credits helpline or see the HMRC website. A useful leaflet is WTC2 *A guide to Child Tax Credit and Working Tax Credit.*

How the credit is calculated

The maximum credit depends on how many 'elements' you can claim (listed in Table 5.1 overleaf). The basic element of Working Tax Credit in 2012–13 is £1,920, and the basic (or 'family') element of Child Tax Credit is £545, plus a further £2,690 for each child. You may also get extra elements: for example, a further £1,950 if you have a partner or are a lone parent. Note, though, that these are the maximum yearly amounts:

■ Tax credits are awarded on a daily basis, so for each day you get the maximum annual amount divided by 365 (366 in 2011–12).
■ Your award is reduced if your income is above a limit (see page 61).

If you qualify for Working Tax Credit and pay for childcare, you also get the childcare element of 70 per cent of your eligible costs in 2012–13. The maximum eligible cost is £175 per week for one child, £300 for more than one – so, the maximum weekly amount is £300 × 70% = £210. The care

Table 5.1: Tax credits – maximum annual amounts

Working Tax Credit	2011–12	2012–13
■ Basic element for:		
– people who work at least 16 hours a week and who have are lone parents, have a disability, or are aged 60+;		
– couples with children who work at least 24 hours a week between them (16 hours for one partner);		
– people aged 25+ and working at least 30 hours a week	£1,920	£1,920
■ Extra for couples and lone parents	£1,950	£1,950
■ Extra for people who work at least 30 hours a week (including couples with children who work 30 hours between them, provided one works at least 16 hours)	£790	£790
■ Extra for disabled workers	£2,650	£2,790
■ Extra for workers with a severe disability	£1,130	£1,190
■ Extra for people aged 50+ who have moved into employment from benefits in the last 3 months		
– working 16+ hours a week	£1,365	Abolished
– working 30+ hours a week	£2,030	Abolished

Working Tax Credit childcare element		
■ People paying for childcare		
Percentage of maximum eligible amount	70%	70%
Maximum eligible weekly amount for:		
– one child	£175	£175
– more than one child	£300	£300

Child Tax Credit	2011–12	2012–13
Child Tax Credit child element		
■ Amount for each child	£2,555	£2,690
■ Extra for each disabled child	£2,800	£2,950
■ Extra for each child with severe disability	£1,130	£1,190
Child Tax Credit family element		
■ Families with children	£545	£545

must be provided by a 'registered' or 'approved' person, such as a registered childminder. A relative does not qualify, except in the cases set out in HMRC leaflet WTC5 *Help with the costs of childcare*. You cannot claim for care that your employer funds – see page 93.

Means-testing and income limits

Your total credit is reduced, depending on your income – or, if you are married, in a civil partnership or living with someone as husband and wife or as civil partners, on your *joint* income. This is broadly the same as your income for tax purposes, but excluding:

■ Most taxable perks from your job, except the taxable value of some share-related benefits, a company car and car fuel, mileage allowances above set limits (see page 116), vouchers and cheap or free goods.
■ The first £300 of the total of your pension income, investment income, property income and foreign income.

If your annual income is above £6,420, you lose first Working Tax Credit, then the child element of the Child Tax Credit. If you only get Child Tax Credit, it is reduced once your income rises above £15,860. Note that in 2011–12 you started to lose the family element only when your income rose above £40,000, but from 6 April 2012 you lose it immediately after the child element. You lose 41 pence for each pound above the relevant threshold. See Table 5.2 and the examples overleaf.

Table 5.2: Tax credits – income thresholds and withdrawal rates

	2011–12	2012–13
First income threshold	£6,420	£6,420
First income threshold if only entitled to Child Tax Credit	£15,860	£15,860
Amount of credit lost for each £1 above first threshold	*41p*	*41p*
Second income threshold*	£40,000	Abolished
Amount of credit lost for each £1 above second threshold	*41p*	*41p*

*Or, if higher, the level at which your child element is reduced to nil.

Figure 5.1: Calculating Working Tax Credit (2012–13)*

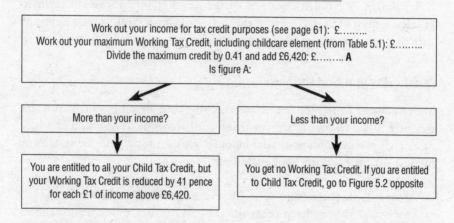

Work out your income for tax credit purposes (see page 61): £.........
Work out your maximum Working Tax Credit, including childcare element (from Table 5.1): £.........
Divide the maximum credit by 0.41 and add £6,420: £......... **A**
Is figure A:

More than your income?

You are entitled to all your Child Tax Credit, but your Working Tax Credit is reduced by 41 pence for each £1 of income above £6,420.

Less than your income?

You get no Working Tax Credit. If you are entitled to Child Tax Credit, go to Figure 5.2 opposite

*Note: this diagram assumes that you are entitled to the same tax credit 'elements' for the whole year. If not, the amount of tax credit has to be worked out on a daily basis.

Example 5.1: Calculating Working Tax Credit

Susie and Simon have two children and work full-time. For 2012–13 their initial tax credit award is based on their joint income for 2011–12 (£32,000). They pay £8,500 a year for childcare. In 2012–13 they are initially entitled to Working Tax Credit of:

Basic element	£1,920
Extra for couples	£1,950
Extra for people working 30+ hours	£790
Childcare: £8,500 × 70% =	£5,950
Total	£10,610

To work out their maximum income before their Working Tax Credit is reduced to zero, they divide £10,610 by 0.41, and add £6,420, to get £32,298. As their 2011–12 income was less than this they get some Working Tax Credit, but the amount is reduced by 41 pence for every pound above £6,420: £32,000 − £6,420 = £25,580 × 0.41 = £10,487. They get £10,610 − £10,487 = £123 Working Tax Credit, but their Child Tax Credit is not reduced. They get £2,690 for each child, plus £545 family element − £5,925 in total. Their total tax credits are £123 + £5,925 = £6,048 or £504 a month.

Figure 5.2: Calculating Child Tax Credit (2012–13)

Use the flowchart in Figure 5.1 first.

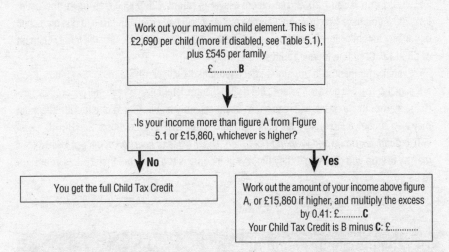

Work out your maximum child element. This is £2,690 per child (more if disabled, see Table 5.1), plus £545 per family
£...........**B**

.Is your income more than figure A from Figure 5.1 or £15,860, whichever is higher?

No

You get the full Child Tax Credit

Yes

Work out the amount of your income above figure A, or £15,860 if higher, and multiply the excess by 0.41: £..........**C**
Your Child Tax Credit is B minus **C**: £............

Example 5.2: **Calculating Child Tax Credit**

Like Susie and Simon from Example 5.1, Ahmed and Zahida work full-time, have two children and have childcare costs of £8,500, but their income is £38,000. They lost all their Working Tax Credit once their income rose above £32,298. They can claim Child Tax Credit of £2,690 for each child, plus family element of £545, i.e. £2,690 + £2,690 + £545 = £5,925. But this is reduced by 41 pence for each pound of income above £32,298 or £15,860 (whichever is greater): £38,000 − £32,298 = £5,702 × 0.41 = £2,337. This leaves them with Child Tax Credit of £5,925 − £2,337 = £3,588.

Tax credits cuts – it's still worth claiming

In 2011–12 you could usually get some Child Tax Credit if your income was below about £41,300. From 6 April 2012, the income level is about £26,000 if you have one child, £32,200 if you have two (though it can be higher if you have more children, a disabled child or you pay for childcare). This is because the £40,000 threshold for losing the family element of Child Tax Credit no longer applies.

Even if your income is too high to get anything, it's still worth claiming tax credits if you are eligible. You will get a 'nil award', but if your income later falls you can still get credits back to the start of the tax year, whereas a new claim can only be backdated one month. Claiming may also entitle you to other state benefits such as free NHS prescriptions. See HMRC leaflet WTC6 *Child Tax Credit and Working Tax Credit. Other types of help you could get.* HMRC staff may try to stop you claiming if they think your income is too high, but insist – it is your right to do so.

How to keep your income low

You can increase your tax credits by making a pension contribution or Gift Aid donation, as these are deducted from your income for tax credit purposes. You can also deduct business losses made in the same tax year, or unused losses from a previous tax year. But beware of making a taxable insurance gain (see page 196).

How awards are decided

When you first claim, HMRC will send you an 'award notice' showing what you are due – if you do not understand it, ask the tax credits helpline. More detailed calculations are available, but only if you ask.

At the start of each new tax year, your tax credits continue at the rate for the previous year on a provisional basis. In the summer you get a renewal pack to confirm your income for the previous year and check your personal circumstances. HMRC uses this to make an initial award based on the previous year's income, increased in line with inflation over the year – so your initial award for 2012–13 was based on 2012–13 tax credit rates and your current circumstances, but your 2011–12 income. After the tax year, when your actual income is known, your award may be recalculated.

If your income rises

The first slice of your extra income is disregarded. The disregard is £10,000 from 6 April 2011 and will fall to £5,000 in April 2013. So, if your actual 2012–13 income is:

■ not more than £10,000 above your 2011–12 income – your award is not recalculated (provided you have given HMRC the right information at the right time)
■ more than £10,000 above your 2011–12 income – your award is recalculated, using your actual income minus £10,000. You may have to repay tax credit. (See Example 5.3 overleaf.)

If your income falls

From 6 April 2012, the first £2,500 of any fall in income is disregarded. So, if your actual 2012–13 income is:

■ not more than £2,500 below your 2011–12 income – the fall is ignored for 2012–13. You won't get any extra tax credit in 2012–13.
■ more than £2,500 below your 2011–12 income – your award is recalculated, using your actual income minus £2,500 (see Example 5.3).

In both cases, your actual 2012–13 income will be used to work out your 2013–14 tax credits.

Changes during the tax year

If you expect your income to rise by more than £10,000, or fall by more than £2,500, you can ask during the year for the credit to be based on your estimated income. This avoids an underpayment or overpayment.

During the tax year you may stop living with a partner or start living with a new one. If so, you must tell the Tax Credit Office. Your award will stop and you will have to make a new claim. You must also tell the Tax Credit Office about some other changes (see page 67), and if so, although your credits will not necessarily stop, the amount you get may change.

Example 5.3: **Changes in your income**

Susie and Simon's tax credits for 2012–13 were initially calculated on the basis of the £32,000 they earned in 2011–12 (see Example 5.1 on page 62). In 2012–13 they can have an income of up to £32,000 + £10,000 = £42,000 without having their award recalculated. In May 2012, Susie's hours were cut, reducing their expected income for 2012–13 by £4,000 to £28,000. The fall was more than £2,500 so their tax credits were recalculated, but the first £2,500 of the fall was disregarded. Their new tax credit award assumed an income of £32,000 − £1,500 = £30,500. Their tax credits increased by £51 a month.

Have you started or stopped living with someone?

Your tax credit claim stops when your situation changes, so you may build up an overpayment. From 6 April 2012, any new claim cannot be backdated by more than one month, but you can claim a 'notional entitlement' of any tax credits you would have been entitled to between your old and new claims. This can reduce or eliminate your overpayment – but it's up to you to request it.

How overpayments are collected

You may receive too much tax credit because your income rises, or because your circumstances change, or because the Tax Credit Office has made a mistake. Any overpayments that are identified during the tax year will reduce your tax credits for the rest of the year. Overpayments from a previous tax year are usually collected by reducing future years' credit.

Up to a quarter of your tax credits can be used to pay off an overpayment, or the whole amount if you are entitled to only the family element of Child Tax Credit. People receiving the maximum award should lose no more than 10 per cent. You can ask to pay back less to avoid hardship.

▶ If you have an overpayment

You have several options – see the leaflet *Dealing with tax credit overpayments*, written by the Low Incomes Tax Reform Group and available from www.advicenow.org.uk.

If you think that HMRC has worked out your tax credits wrongly, appeal within 30 days, using the form in leaflet WTC/AP *What to do if you think your Child Tax Credit/Working Tax Credit is wrong*. If you agree you were paid too much, but don't think you should have to pay it back – for example, you told HMRC about a change but it did nothing – 'dispute' the claim. Use form TC846 *Tax credits overpayment*, and see HMRC leaflet COP26 *What happens if we've paid you too much tax credit?*

If paying back the money would cause you hardship, phone HMRC's Tax Credit Helpline immediately. It can suspend or reduce payments or write off the debt. You should also complain if you think HMRC has not acted properly. See page 38.

Adjusting next year's credits to collect an overpayment is not possible if you are no longer entitled to credits, or if joint claimants have split up, or if single claimants have started living with someone. HMRC can collect debts of up to £3,000 through PAYE on your job or pension if you have one. You can ask HMRC not to do this, but it can insist, and if it does agree not to collect it through PAYE you will have to pay in a lump sum or instalments instead. You can pay in 30 days or in 12 monthly instalments, or ask for a longer period to avoid hardship. Joint claimants who split up should arrange to cover any potential overpayments.

What to tell HMRC

To claim Working Tax Credit or Child Tax Credit, contact the tax credits helpline or get the forms from your tax office or Jobcentre Plus.

Changes will be picked up after the tax year through your Annual Review form, although if your income goes up during the year it's best to tell HMRC at once to avoid an overpayment. You must tell the Tax Credit Office within a month of the change if:

- you stop work or reduce your usual working hours to less than 30 hours a week, if you were working more than that, or to less than 16 hours or, for families with children, less than 24 hours between you. Temporary decreases may be ignored provided your normal working hours remain the same, and if you have been laid off or moved to part-time work your payments may not stop immediately – there is a four-week period of grace
- you stop being responsible for a child – your child leaves home, say, or is over 16 and leaves full-time education, or goes to university
- you marry, start living with someone (including a same-sex partner), split up or your partner dies
- you go abroad for longer than eight weeks (or 12 weeks if you go abroad because of an illness, family illness or bereavement)
- your childcare costs stop or go down by £10 a week or more over a four-week period.

The timescales for giving information are much shorter than for tax. If you fail to notify one of the changes listed above within one month of being aware of it, HMRC can charge penalties for delay of up to £300. You may also have a large amount to pay back, if the change means you have been overpaid.

Tell HMRC promptly if things change

If a change in your circumstances increases your right to tax credits (e.g. you have a baby), the increase is backdated to the date of the change only if HMRC is told within one month (possibly longer if waiting for the outcome of a disability claim). Make sure you ask for your claim to be backdated, because this doesn't always happen automatically. However, if you are not given the right amount because of an HMRC mistake that was not your fault, the increase can still be put into effect up to five years after the end of the tax year in question.

Changes that reduce your credit are always backdated, and you could end up having to repay a large sum if you don't notify HMRC as soon as possible.

HMRC can start a check on a tax credits claim up to a year after the annual review deadline (sometimes longer), so keep records of changes. And if you get a letter from the Tax Credit Office, always respond as requested or your credits might be cut.

Checking your Annual Review form

The Annual Review form that you receive at some point between April and June 2012 has two purposes – to finalise your award for 2011–12, and to renew your claim for 2012–13. It will be pre-printed with the information the Tax Credit Office has about you. If you received only the basic amount of tax credit (the 'family element') in 2011–12, all you need to do is to check that the information is still correct. If it is, you do not need to return the form and you will carry on getting tax credits. Otherwise, you should contact the tax credits helpline as soon as possible.

If you received more than the basic amount of tax credit, you will also get an Annual Declaration form asking about your income in 2011–12. You must provide details by 31 July 2012. If you do not, HMRC will send you a statement telling you to renew within 30 days. If you do not respond within 30 days, your credits will stop, you will have to put in a new claim (which cannot be backdated more than one month), you may have to repay any sums overpaid in the first part of the year, and you may be penalised. You should respond by 31 July even if you do not have all the information you need, for example because your business accounts are not finalised. If so, you can renew using estimates, but you must send the final figures in by 31 January 2013 at the latest, or the estimated figures will be used, and HMRC might decide to start a compliance check. If the estimates turn out to be wrong, you may get less credit than you are entitled to or, if you have understated your income, you may be penalised as well as having to pay back the excess credit. However, if you miss the 31 July deadline for a good reason (such as ill-health), HMRC will renew your claim provided you get your forms in as soon as you can, and before 31 January.

When completing the forms, note that:

■ You must return one Annual Declaration for each 'award period'.

(You may have had more than one award period in 2011–12 if, say, you split up with your partner and then claimed as a single person.)

■ You should enter your income for the whole of the 2011–12 tax year on each Annual Declaration, even if the 'award period' is shorter.

■ Photocopied forms are not accepted. If necessary, ask for a new form. Alternatively, you can renew your claim over the phone.

Record-keeping

There are no formal rules on keeping records, but information that you give in a tax credits claim can be used to cross-check your income tax. A reassessment of your income for tax purposes may also affect a tax credits award, so keep the following for the length of time described on page 15:

■ Records of any changes in circumstances, such as when you split up with a partner (see page 67).

■ Full records of childcare costs (see page 60).

■ Records of hours worked, if you don't work regular hours.

■ All correspondence relating to any tax credits claim.

■ Records of your (and your partner's) income for each year of claim.

■ Records of how much of your business losses you have set against your income for tax credit purposes.

■ Notes of any conversation with the tax credits helpline, including the date and time. Calls are recorded and it may be possible to trace them in case of disputes later on.

■ A copy of any claim and all your tax credit award notices.

■ Records of tax credit payments you have received.

6

....

Tax in retirement

S tarting to draw a pension, retiring or planning ahead? Tax can be complicated for pensioners, and major changes to age-related allowances announced in the 2012 Budget make it even more important to understand your tax. This chapter tells you how your tax might change in retirement, how to make the most of your allowances, and pitfalls to avoid.

Top tips

- Make sure your tax office knows in good time if you expect to start receiving a pension in the next few months so that they can sort out your tax code, if relevant.
- If you or your spouse or civil partner was born before 6 April 1935, remember to claim the married couple's allowance.
- If you were born before 6 April 1948, you should get an age-related personal allowance in 2012–13. Make sure you claim (see page 78).
- Born after 5 April 1948? You won't get age-related allowance, so see page 81 for how to minimise your tax.
- You can transfer any unused blind person's and married couple's allowance to your husband or wife, or registered civil partner (see page 83).
- Consider deferring your state retirement pension if drawing it would push you into a higher tax bracket or affect your age-related allowances (see page 73).

How much tax?

Pensions, including the state pension, are generally taxable, but if you turn 65 before 6 April 2013 you get a higher age-related allowance (see page 78). This means you can have more income tax-free and your tax bill is likely to go down. The allowance has been abolished for people who turn 65 after 5 April 2013, who will get only the basic personal allowance. However, there are a few types of tax-free income you might get once you have retired, covered in the list below.

Pension income is taxed at the same rates as income from a job. So in 2012–13 any pension income above your tax-free allowances is taxed at 20 per cent, or at 40 per cent if it falls within the higher-rate band. Most pensioners' incomes are too low for them to be affected by the 50 per cent additional tax rate on income above £150,000.

Tax-free pensions and state benefits for older people

- Pension credit. Note that the pension credit you get depends on your income after tax, so make sure the Pension Service is using the correct figure to work out your entitlement.
- £10 Christmas bonus paid with state pension.
- Attendance allowance (for people over 64 who need care).
- Cold weather and winter fuel payments for pensioners, and any one-off payment made alongside them.
- Council tax benefit and housing benefit.
- Payments from the Independent Living Fund and disabled facilities grants, and 'direct payments' for care (see page 77).
- Social fund payments.
- Pensions and benefits paid because of death, injury or disability in the Armed Forces (but some dependants' benefits are taxable). (See HMRC help sheet 310 *War Widow's and dependant's pensions*.)
- Most lump sums from a registered pension scheme, see page 210.
- Extra pension from an unregistered pension scheme if disabled at work.
- 10 per cent of an overseas pension.
- German and Austrian pensions for victims of Nazi persecution.

Taxable state pensions and benefits

When it comes to working out the taxable amount of a state retirement pension, the following additions to your pension are taxable:

■ Any addition for invalidity or for an adult dependant (but not a child).
■ The age addition you get if you are aged 80 or over.
■ Any additional pension from the State Earnings Related Pension Scheme (SERPS) or the State Second Pension.
■ Any graduated pension earned before SERPS was introduced.
■ Any increases paid by the Pension Service to uprate your guaranteed minimum pension if you are contracted out of the State Second Pension (see page 205 for what this means).

A state pension is taxed as yours if it is payable to you, even if you are a married woman claiming a pension on your husband's contributions.

In addition, you will also have to pay tax on any Carer's Allowance you get if you spend at least 35 hours a week caring for a disabled person. And if you are still getting industrial death benefit pension (which is no longer available to new claimants but may still be paid if your spouse died before 11 April 1988 as a result of an accident at work) this is also taxable.

Deferring your state pension

The state pension age is gradually being increased so if you have not yet retired, it is worth checking yours on the government website at www.direct.gov.uk/en/Pensionsandretirementplanning/StatePension/DG_4017919. However, you can choose to defer your state pension beyond state pension age. In return, you get a larger pension when you do start to draw it. This is taxable in the same way as other pension income. Alternatively, if you defer for at least a year, you can take the deferred amount as a lump sum. This will be taxable in the year you receive it, but it will not be taken into account when working out your age-related allowances (see page 78 and Example 6.1) or push you into a higher tax band. See Pension Service booklet SPD1 *State Pension Deferral – your guide*, from your Pension Centre.

You can also put off drawing your lump sum until the year after you draw your pension. This will save tax if you are a higher-rate taxpayer and expect to be a basic-rate taxpayer in future.

Example 6.1: A lump sum from deferring state pension

Iqbal carried on working after his 65th birthday and has deferred his state pension. In the tax year when he finally draws his state pension he earns £22,000. He doesn't need extra income so he decides to draw his deferred pension as a lump sum of £5,000, increasing his taxable income for the year to £27,000. Normally, a taxable income above £25,400 in 2012–13 means that the higher age-related allowance is reduced – but this does not apply to the pension lump sum. He gets the full allowance of £10,500. The same concession would apply had Iqbal been near the threshold at which higher-rate tax is payable – the lump sum would have been taxed at the basic rate even if most of it was above the threshold.

How the tax is paid

State pensions are always paid out before tax, even when they are taxable. The exception is the lump sum from deferring a pension, which will be paid with tax deducted.

HMRC's preferred way of collecting any tax due on state pensions and benefits is to adjust your tax code for another source of income taxed under PAYE, such as a private pension – see Chapter 2. This will mean that more of your private pension (or other income from which the PAYE is deducted) goes in tax. See Example 6.4 on page 87. If you do not have a source of income taxed under PAYE, you will be sent a tax return and the tax will be collected in a lump sum. See Chapter 16.

Tax on a private pension

In most cases, money you contribute to a pension is tax-free; money paid out, however, is usually taxable. This applies whether your pension comes from an employer's pension, personal pension plan or any other form of private pension. The exception is the lump sum that most pension schemes allow you to draw when you retire. This is tax-free, provided that you do not draw more than a quarter of your pension savings as a lump sum (see page 210). However, if you then invest your lump sum, the interest or dividends arising will be taxable like other investment income.

How the tax is paid

Income from a private pension is taxed in the same way as earnings from a job, whether you get a pension paid directly from the pension scheme, draw income from a pension fund or use your pension fund to buy an annuity (see page 210). Whoever pays the pension should deduct tax under the PAYE system, and HMRC will issue a tax code for you which tells them how much to deduct (see Chapter 2).

> ## A letter saying you've paid too much or too little tax?

After the end of each tax year, HMRC will reconcile the tax you have paid under PAYE and you may get a P800 *Tax Calculation* form, see page 21.

What happens when you draw your pension

If you are retiring on a private pension, you will receive a P45 or a letter notifying you of your pay and tax in the tax year to date. Your pension will be paid using your existing tax code until the end of the tax year or until your tax office reassesses your code. If you receive a P45, give it to the pension payer or you will be given only the basic personal allowance.

When you are getting near to state pension age you may be sent a *Pension coding* form (P161). This asks what sources of income you have, and how you expect this to change in retirement. It's important to fill it in and send it back as it will help your tax office get your code right when you retire.

Under your new code more tax may be deducted from your pension than you expect. This is because your code will also collect the tax on any state pensions, which are paid out before tax. But you may get a higher age-related allowance if you reach age 65 before 6 April 2013. See page 78.

Your previous employer may carry on giving some of the benefits you had before you retired, such as healthcare. If so, these benefits are taxed in the same way as for employees (see page 98).

Drawing a small pension in cash

When you take your pension, you will normally be given the option of taking part as a tax-free lump sum, as explained on page 210. However, if all your pension savings come to £18,000 or less you can take it all in cash, if your pension provider agrees. A quarter of the cash is tax-free, but tax is deducted under PAYE from the rest and you should get a P45 showing the amount. An 'emergency' code may be used to work out the PAYE, which makes it more likely that you will overpay tax (see page 27). If so, ask your tax office for form P53 to claim tax back – you don't have to wait until the end of the year.

Tax on other retirement income

If you are topping up your pension with other forms of income, this will be taxed in the same way as for younger people, although if your total income is low enough to fall within your tax-free allowances no tax will be due. Typical ways of topping up your pension might include:

■ Part-time work – if you are an employee, your earnings will be taxed under PAYE as if you had a second job (see page 27). If you set up your own business, see Chapter 8. However, once you reach state pension age you will not have to pay National Insurance contributions.
■ Redundancy pay and other lump sums on leaving a job – these may be tax-free, within limits. See page 111.
■ Payments if you have retired early because of ill-health – a private pension drawn early is taxed like any other pension, although any extra you get if your disability was caused by work is tax-free. Some state disability benefits are tax-free, but benefits based on your National Insurance contributions are usually taxable. See page 56.
■ Savings interest and other investment income – any income that is not

tax-free will usually be paid with tax deducted, but unlike pension income, a 10 per cent rate will apply to some or all of your interest if your total non-savings income is less than £2,710 above your tax-free allowances in 2012–13. So you may be able to claim tax back, or even get the interest paid tax-free if your total income is below your allowances. See pages 6 and 189.

■ An annuity not bought with a pension fund – a 'purchased life annuity' that you choose to buy is not taxed in the same way as a pension annuity. Part of the annuity income is tax-free. See page 193.

Equity release schemes

Equity release schemes such as lifetime mortgages and home reversions allow you to make use of part of the value of your home without having to move. Any lump sum you receive from releasing equity in your home is tax-free. However, if you then invest the lump sum, any income arising from it will be taxable in the normal way.

Some equity release schemes allow you to draw money in instalments, either as you need them or on a regular basis. These are treated as a return of your capital and are tax-free.

Note that if family and friends provide the funds for equity release, pre-owned assets tax may apply (see page 242). Get professional advice.

Paying for care

Most state benefits that you receive to help you pay for care are tax-free, such as payments from the Independent Living Fund or disabled facilities grants. However, if you are a carer receiving Carer's Allowance this is taxable, although no tax is deducted before you get it and in practice your income may be too low for you to have to pay any tax.

If your local authority is responsible for providing you with care at home, you may have the option of receiving 'direct payments' of cash to enable you to organise and pay for your own care. Even though these payments are not taxable as part of your income, if you employ someone to provide you with care you will be responsible for deducting tax and National Insurance from what you pay them like any other employer, although you may not have to file online (see page 150). The charity Age UK has a number of leaflets and factsheets on paying for care. See the Fact file for contact details.

You can take out insurance policies to pay for care. Payments from a long-term care insurance policy taken out before the need for care became apparent are tax-free, and so are payouts from a special annuity taken out to pay for care, provided they are paid direct to the care provider.

Claiming a higher tax-free allowance

Everybody gets a basic personal allowance (see page 50). This makes the first slice of your income free of income tax and will save you tax at your highest rate. Blind people get an extra allowance (see page 50).

For the 2012–13 tax year the minimum personal allowance is £8,105, up from £7,475 in 2010–11. However, if you are aged at least 65 at any point in the tax year – even if your birthday is the very last day – you are eligible for an increased personal allowance for the whole year, and it rises again once you reach 75. So, the rate for people aged 65 to 74 is £10,500 in 2012–13 (£9,940 in 2011–12), and for people aged 75-plus it is £10,660 in 2012–13 (£10,090 in 2011–12).

The extra age-related amount is gradually withdrawn, once your total income rises above a certain level known as the 'income limit' £25,400 in 2012–13 and £24,000 in 2011–12. It is withdrawn at the rate of £1 for every £2 of income above the income limit, until it is reduced to the basic personal allowance (£8,105 in 2012–13). And if your income is above a threshold of £100,000 the basic allowance is reduced too (see page 50).

Example 6.2 on page 80 shows how the allowance is worked out, and Table 6.1 shows the levels of income at which all age-related allowance is lost – so, for example, you lose all age-related allowance if you are between 65 and 74 and your income rises above £30,190 in 2012–13. See page 81 for ways of avoiding this.

Changes to age-related allowances

The government plans to abolish the age-related allowance for anyone who turns 65 after 5 April 2013 (that is, born after 5 April 1948). Instead they will get the basic personal allowance which will rise to £9,205 for 2013–14. People born before 6 April 1948 will still get an age-related allowance of

£10,500, and those born before 6 April 1938 will get £10,660, but the allowances will stay at those levels in future. Even if you are 65 by 5 April 2013, you will not get £10,660 when you reach 75.

What is 'income'?

When you are working out whether you are above the income limit for age-related allowances, you can deduct the following from your income (plus any basic-rate tax relief on pension payments or charitable donations):

■ Pension contributions you have paid.
■ Charitable donations and loan interest that qualify for tax relief.
■ Relief for business losses.

Table 6.1: Personal allowances for people aged 65 and over

Maximum age in tax year	Your income	Allowance in 2011–12
Under 65	Any income level	£7,475
65–74	Below £24,000	£9,940
	£24,000 to £28,930	£9,940 minus half of income above £24,000
	Above £28,930	£7,475
75+	Below £24,000	£10,090
	£24,000 to £29,230	£10,090 minus half of income above £24,000
	Above £29,230	£7,475

Maximum age in tax year	Your income	Allowance in 2012–13
Under 65	Any income level	£8,105
65–74	Below £25,400	£10,500
	£25,400–£30,190	£10,500 minus half of income above £25,400
	Above £28,930	£8,105
75+	Below £25,400	£10,660
	£25,400–£30,510	£10,660 minus half of income above £25,400
	Above £30,510	£8,105

Example 6.2: **Age-related allowance**

Harry, who is 70, can claim a maximum personal allowance of £10,500 in 2012–13. However, Harry's taxable income is £25,900, which is above the income limit of £25,400, so his personal allowance is reduced. To find the reduced amount, he checks whether he can deduct anything from his income. He makes charitable donations of £160 (£200 after adding back basic-rate tax relief), so his total income is £25,900 – £200 = £25,700.

His income is still £300 above the income limit of £25,400. His allowance is reduced by half of this: £300 ÷ 2 = £150. So his personal allowance is £10,500 – £150 = £10,350.

Tax planning as a family

If your taxable income is below your personal allowance, part of your allowance is wasted – you cannot transfer it to anybody else. You may be able to make better use of your allowances as a family by transferring income from higher-income family members to those with lower income, e.g. by putting investments in the name of a lower-income partner (see page 52 for how to do this). But watch out for the following:

- The transfer has to be a genuine gift, with no strings attached.
- The transfer may be liable to capital gains tax, or inheritance tax on your death, if the recipient is not your spouse or registered civil partner. See Chapter 13.
- Do not transfer shares in your own business without professional advice.

Married couple's allowance

You can claim this relief only if either you or your spouse was born before 6 April 1935 – that is, aged at least 77 in the 2011–12 tax year and 78 in the 2012–13 tax year. You must be living with your spouse, or, if not, neither of you must intend to make the separation permanent. Registered civil partners can also claim if they meet these conditions.

For couples who were married before 5 December 2005, the claim must be made by the husband unless they elect to have the higher-income partner claim (see page 83). For couples who meet the age conditions but got married on or after 5 December 2005, and civil partners, the claimant must be the partner with the higher income.

Making the most of your allowances

Now that the age-related allowance has been abolished for future pensioners and frozen for current pensioners, it's more important than ever to review your tax.

■ Invest in tax-free investments (see Chapter 11), or those which produce capital rather than income. These don't use up your allowance.

■ If you are close to the £25,400 income threshold above which age-related allowance is cut, but expect your income to drop, consider deferring any further income until it does – your state pension, say (see page 73).

■ Donations to charity through Gift Aid or pension contributions reduce your taxable income and so can increase your age-related allowances.

■ Beware of making a taxable gain on insurance bonds (see page 196). Even though basic-rate tax on the payout is settled by the insurance company, the gain counts as income for age-related allowances.

■ Plan your tax as a family – see opposite.

In 2012–13 the allowance is £7,705 for all eligible couples (£7,295 in 2011–12). However, unlike the personal allowance, you get relief at only 10 per cent of the full allowance, knocked off your tax bill at the end of the calculation. So an allowance of £7,705, say, is actually worth only £7,705 × 10% = £771 (the tax system rounds in your favour).

The amount of the allowance depends on the older partner's age, and the income of the claimant. Once the claimant's total income rises above the income limit of £25,400 (£24,000 in 2011–12), his or her age-related personal allowance is reduced. Then, when the personal allowance has been reduced to the minimum level (or if the claimant is under 65 and gets only the minimum allowance anyway), the married couple's allowance is reduced, by £1 for every £2 of excess income remaining, until it reaches the minimum of £2,960 (£2,800 in 2011–12). This is why, in Table 6.2, the income level at which married couple's allowance is reduced depends on the age of the claimant. However, provided that the claimant is aged at least 65 you will not lose any allowance in 2012–13 until your income is at least £30,190.

Table 6.2: Married couple's allowance if born before 6 April 1935

Maximum age in tax year	Claimant's income	Allowance in 2011–12
Claimant aged under 65, oldest partner born before 6 April 1935	Below £24,000	£7,295
	£24,000 to £32,990	£7,295 minus half of income above £24,000
	Above £32,990	£2,800
Claimant aged 65–74, oldest partner born before 6 April 1935	Below £28,930	£7,295
	£28,930 to £37,920	£7,295 minus half of income above £28,930
	Above £37,920	£2,800
Claimant born before 6 April 1935	Below £29,230	£7,295
	£29,230 to £38,220	£7,295 minus half of income above £29,230
	Above £38,220	£2,800
Maximum age in tax year	Claimant's income	Allowance in 2012–13
Claimant aged under 65, oldest partner born before 6 April 1935	Below £25,400	£7,705
	£25,400–£34,890	£7,705 minus half of income above £25,400
	Above £34,890	£2,960
Claimant aged 65–74, oldest partner born before 6 April 1935	Below £30,190	£7,705
	£30,190–£39,680	£7,705 minus half of income above £30,190
	Above £39,680	£2,960
Claimant born before 6 April 1935	Below £30,510	£7,705
	£30,510–£40,000	£7,705 minus half of income above £30,510
	Above £40,000	£2,960

Note, though, that you get the full allowance for a tax year only if you were married before 6 May in that year. In the year of marriage, you lose one-twelfth of the full allowance for each full tax month before the wedding (a tax month runs from the 6th of one month to the 5th of the next). So if you get married after 5 December 2012 but before 6 January 2013, say, you will lose eight-twelfths of the full allowance. You will be able to claim £7,705 × ⁴/₁₂ = £2,568.

The married couple's allowance is normally given to the claimant, but it can be allocated to the other partner. You can allocate half or all of the minimum allowance (i.e. half or all of £2,960), provided that you do so before the start of the tax year (in the year of marriage, you have until the end of the tax year). But whoever gets the allowance, if it turns out that his or her income was too low to make full use of it, the unused part can be transferred to the other partner after the end of the tax year (see Example 6.3 below), and this applies to all of the available married couple's allowance, not just the minimum.

Example 6.3: **Transferring allowances**

Elspeth and Roger are both 80. In 2012–13 Roger has a pension of £10,000 a year, but Elspeth has total income of £17,000. Roger's income is below his personal allowance of £10,660, so he has no tax to pay. Roger and Elspeth also qualify for married couple's allowance of £7,705. In the first instance, this goes to Roger because they married before 6 December 2005, but his income is too low to make use of it. He can transfer the whole allowance to Elspeth after the end of the tax year by ticking the relevant box in his tax return. They can also elect to have the allowance always paid to her in future. This will reduce her tax by £771. Roger cannot transfer the unused part of his personal allowance. However, they could save tax overall by putting some of Elspeth's savings in Roger's name so that all his personal allowance is used.

Married before 5 December 2005?

You can elect to be treated in the same way as people married on or after 5 December 2005 – so that the allowance always goes to the higher-income partner rather than the husband. This might be convenient if a husband's income is so low that he regularly transfers unused allowance to his higher-income wife, but don't make the election if her income is above the income limit of £25,400 because the allowance will be reduced. And, once you have made the election, you can't change your mind.

Allowances if you are widowed or divorced

On death, any married couple's or blind person's (but not personal) allowance still unused is transferred to the surviving partner for the rest of the tax year.

On divorce, or the dissolution of a civil partnership, the partner claiming the married couple's allowance continues to get it for the remainder of the tax year, plus – if either partner was born before 6 April 1935 – tax relief on maintenance paid under a legally binding agreement (see below).

From the start of the next tax year after being divorced or widowed, you are taxed as a single person. If you remarry in the same tax year as being divorced or widowed, and you were already getting married couple's allowance, you can continue to get it at the current rate for the remainder of the tax year. Alternatively, you can put in a new claim based on your new spouse's age, but you will only get one-twelfth of the allowance for each month of the new marriage.

If you live with someone without getting married, see page 53. It's particularly important to make a will, and see page 240 for inheritance tax implications.

Relief for maintenance or alimony

Provided that either you or your former spouse or former civil partner were born before 6 April 1935, you can get tax relief on the alimony or maintenance you pay, up to £2,960 in 2012–13 (£2,800 in 2011–12). The maximum is the same however many ex-partners you support. The rate of relief is 10 per cent, so the maximum tax saving is £2,960 × 10% = £296.

You must make the payments under a legally binding agreement, such as a written agreement, a court order or a Child Support Agency assessment – voluntary payments do not count. Legally binding agreements made in most European countries (listed in the notes to the tax return) also count. But be careful about the wording: to claim relief the payments must be for the maintenance of your ex-partner or any children aged under 21. Payments directly to a child do not qualify.

Note that tax relief stops on the date an ex-partner remarries.

What to tell HMRC

Make sure your tax office knows in good time if you expect to start receiving a private pension in the next few months so that they can sort out your tax code, if relevant. You may be asked to complete a *Pension coding* form P161 – if you are not, contact your tax office or download one from the HMRC website (see the Fact file). With state benefits, your tax office should not need notifying.

Also make sure HMRC knows if you are 65 before 6 April 2013, or married and born before 6 April 1935, so that it can give you the higher age-related allowances. There is space to give your age on the front of the tax return or form R40 *Claim for repayment*, but if you do not get a return, contact your tax office.

If you get a tax return, enter the taxable amount of any UK pension, state or private, and any taxable benefits, on page TR3 of the main return. Claim any blind person's allowance on page TR4. If you are entitled to married couple's allowance, or want to transfer unused allowances to your spouse or civil partner, you will need to complete the Additional Information pages (see page 289). However, pensioners often get the short version of the tax return which does not cover the transfer of allowances. You will need to contact your tax office.

Figure 6.1: PAYE Coding Notice (see Example 6.4)

 **HM Revenue & Customs**

PAYE Coding Notice
Tax code for the year 2012-13

025038:00006251:001   846

MR G PETROS
THE LARCHES
9 THE AVENUE
LONDON
SW25 2NR

Please keep all your coding notices. You may need to refer to them if you have to fill in a tax return. Please quote your tax reference and National Insurance number if you contact us.
HM Revenue & Customs
CUSTOMER OPERATIONS
GRAYFIELD HOUSE
5 BANKHEAD AVENUE
EDINBURGH
EH11 4AE

Phone   0845 302 1409

Tax reference   491/G7070

National Insurance   CE 00 00 30 A
number

Date   2 March 2012

Dear MR G PETROS

Your tax code for the year 6 April 2012 to 5 April 2013 is 333T

You need a tax code so Your Employer or Pension Provider can work out how much tax to take off the payments they make to you from 6 April 2012. It is important that you make sure that we have got your tax code right. The **Notes** will help you do this. If you contact us we will need your National Insurance number and tax reference. Please keep your coding notes; you may need them if we send you a tax return.

Here is how we worked it out:	
your personal allowance	£9735
married couple's allowance	+£3855
state pension	-£10257
a tax free amount of	£3333

We turn £3333 into tax code 333T to send to Your Employer or Pension Provider. They should use this code to take off the right amount of tax each time they pay you from 6 April 2012. We tell Your Employer or Pension Provider what your tax code is but we do not tell them how it is worked out

Notes

1   The law allows everyone who lives in the UK to receive some income before tax has to be paid – a "tax free amount" of income. That tax free amount starts from a "personal allowance" that depends on your circumstances. Our records tell us you are entitled to £9735.00 for this tax year. £9735 is the personal allowance for people who are 65 or more at 5 April 2012 with total income over £26930. But please read note 5 as well which tells you when to contact us if your income is likely to change.

Example 6.4: **Checking a coding notice if you are retired**

George is retired with a pension from his previous employer. His coding notice for 2012–13 (shown in Figure 6.1 opposite) includes his age-related personal allowance. The full allowance is £10,500, but George's allowance is reduced to £9,735 because his income exceeds the £25,400 limit for full age-related allowances (see page 78). The Note on the coding notice shows how much income his tax office thinks he has (£26,930).

George gets married couple's allowance of £7,705. This gives him £7,705 × 10% = £771 off his tax bill. But his coding notice shows £3,855, because when multiplied by his top rate of tax (20%) it produces the same amount: £3,855 × 0.20 = £771.

The notice also shows that the tax on George's state pension of £10,257 will be collected through PAYE on his employer's pension. To achieve this, the value of his state pension is deducted from his allowances: £9,735 + £3,855 – £10,257 = £3,333. This means that he can get £3,333 of his employer's pension tax-free each year, or £3,333 ÷ 12 = £278 each month. Tax is deducted from the rest.

The letter in George's code is T because he gets a reduced personal allowance (see page 78). His tax code is therefore 333T.

Checking your tax code

If you are entitled to age-related allowances, you should check that the tax code which tells your employer or pension company how much tax to deduct has given you the right amount. Your tax office will usually send you a coding notice in January or February each year which applies for the tax year starting in April. You will see:

■ The amount of your age-related personal allowance. If the amount is reduced because your income is above £25,400, you will also see a note of how much income your tax office thinks you will have.

■ Any married couple's allowance – but not the full amount. Because the allowance gives you only 10 per cent relief, whereas the allowances in your coding notice give you relief at your top rate of tax, the amount shown in your tax code is adjusted. To check it, multiply the amount shown by your top rate of tax. It should give the same result as the full allowance multiplied by 10 per cent. See Example 6.4.

■ The amount of your state retirement pension. Although this is taxable, it is paid out before tax. To collect the tax due, the amount of pension is deducted from your allowances, so that you get less tax-free pay from your employer's pension or other private pension. Check that the amount shown on your coding notice is correct and does not include any tax-free amounts (see page 72).

If any of the figures in your coding notice are not what you expect, contact your tax office at once. Your tax office will send you a new tax code if necessary.

A mistake that is not spotted may mean that you are eventually faced with a tax demand, or pay too much tax. HMRC will not realise that you have overpaid tax unless you point out the mistake.

Why you need to check your tax

In the past, mistakes often arose if you had more than one private pension, or were working at the same time as drawing a pension. If so, you might have a tax code for each source of income, issued by different tax offices. This problem should have been reduced by the introduction of a new computer system in 2009 which allowed HMRC to join up records of different sources of income. However, mistakes are still possible and you might receive a P800 form saying you owe tax after the end of the tax year. If so, see page 21 for what to do. The independent Office of Tax Simplification is also currently reviewing pensioner taxation and will come up with proposals during 2012 – although some of its work has been pre-empted by the government's decision to abolish age-related allowances for people born after 5 April 2013.

You may also be overtaxed because you have not been given all your allowances, or because you are paying too much tax on your savings. So check your tax and if you are not sure that it is correct, contact your tax office. You may also be eligible for a free 'tax health check' from the charity TaxHelp for Older People (TOP, whose address is in the Fact file).

Record-keeping

These are the main documents you should keep relating to age-related allowances or pensions. See page 15 for others to keep and for how long.

- Birth certificate, or other proof of age.
- Marriage certificate or civil partnership registration certificate.
- If claiming tax relief on maintenance payments, court orders or other legally binding agreements, and proof of amounts actually paid.
- The letter you receive from the Pension Service each year giving the value of your pension. If you are not sure how much is taxable, phone the Pension Service on 0845 301 3011 and ask for form BR735 for the relevant tax year.
- Letters from the Pension Service about any deferred state pension and any tax deducted.
- If you have a private pension, your P60 or other certificate received at the end of the tax year, showing the taxable amount and tax deducted.
- PAYE coding notices (P2), and records of any calls to HMRC about your tax code.

7

Income from a job

If you are an employee, your employer deducts tax before paying you and you usually get a tax return only if you are a director, have a high income or your tax is complex (see Chapter 2). Even if you don't get a tax return, you can't assume your tax is right.

Top tips

- Tax relief going begging? You may be able to claim a flat rate deduction for things like tools or special clothing (see page 115).
- If you regularly work from home, your employer can pay you £4 a week tax-free (sometimes more), to cover extra household costs (see page 113). If your employer does not pay you, you may be able to claim an expense deduction.
- Your pension contributions are deducted from your salary before working out your income tax, but National Insurance is worked out on salary before pension contributions. You save National Insurance if you sacrifice salary for higher employer's pension contributions (see page 118).
- Changing to a 'greener' company car could save tax, while paying for all your private fuel yourself could save up to £2,828 (more for very high earners). See page 105.
- If you use your own car for work, you can claim tax relief at the approved mileage rates even if your employer pays less (see page 116). And you can claim tax relief on home-to-work travel if you are working at a temporary workplace (see page 113).

Are you an employee?

There is often a grey area between being employed and being self-employed, as explained in Chapter 8. For tax purposes an 'employee' also includes:

■ Directors, including people who are directors of a company they own (see page 98).
■ Casual employees (although your employer may not have to deduct tax if your earnings are low – see page 150).
■ Part-time workers. If you have more than one job, you can be an employee for one, self-employed for the other – it is the nature of the work and your contract with the employer that count.
■ Agency staff. If a UK agency pays you direct, it is treated as your employer. If the firm for whom you are working pays you, it is treated as your employer. There are special rules for some types of worker, such as entertainers (see the 'Employment status' section of the HMRC website at www.hmrc.gov.uk/employment-status/).

A director or partner of your own firm?

If you are a director of a service company that you control, you may have extra tax to pay, if HMRC thinks that you are effectively an employee of a client for whom you are working (see page 98). The same may apply to some partners in a business partnership.

Tax-free income

You can start from the assumption that all your rewards for working are taxable – pay, expenses payments and employee benefits. However, you can claim tax relief on some 'allowable' expenses payments which you incur for work purposes and your employer may get a 'dispensation' from your tax office not to include them in your taxable pay (see page 112). Your employer may also agree with your tax office to pay the tax for you on some minor taxable benefits and expenses, under a 'PAYE settlement agreement'.

A few types of pay and perks, listed below, are completely tax-free provided various conditions are met. Your employer should ensure that what is offered meets the necessary conditions. Also see the HMRC guide 480 *Expenses and benefits. A tax guide* (available on the HMRC website).

Tax-free pay

- Your (and your employer's) contributions to a registered pension or life or sick pay insurance scheme (you still have to pay employee's National Insurance). (See Chapter 12 for more on pensions.)
- Donations to a payroll giving scheme (often called 'Give As You Earn').
- The first £30,000 of some payments on leaving a job (see page 111).
- Some payments from your employer if you are a full-time student at a university or technical college.
- Injury awards to members of the Armed Forces.
- Armed Forces operational allowance.

Tax-free expenses and benefits

- Subsidised meals at a staff restaurant (but not a cash account to buy food) and free tea and coffee, if available to all employees and not provided as part of a salary sacrifice or flexible pay deal.
- 15 pence a day in luncheon vouchers (until 6 April 2013).
- Loans of money, in some circumstances (see page 106).
- Some living accommodation (see page 107).
- Payments of up to £4 a week from your employer (£3 before 6 April 2012) for extra household costs if you regularly work from home under a contractual arrangement (not if you simply take work home in the evenings). Higher payments can be tax-free if you have supporting evidence (see page 113).
- Most relocation costs paid by your employer, up to £8,000 in total.
- A phone line at home, if your employer is the subscriber, you have a clear business need for it and private calls are kept to a minimum.
- Costs of a single mobile phone paid directly by your employer. HMRC has decided that this includes a BlackBerry or iPhone so you may be able to claim a refund if you have paid tax on one in the past.

- Eye tests and corrective glasses if you work at a computer screen.
- Medical check-ups (but not treatment).
- Treatment (or medical insurance) if you fall ill while working abroad.
- Workplace nurseries or playschemes.
- The first £55 a week of free childcare or childcare vouchers (but higher-rate taxpayers who first join their employer's scheme after 5 April 2011 get only £28, or £22 if liable to additional-rate tax). Care must be provided by an approved person, such as a registered childminder, not by a relative in your own home.
- Work-related training, including (in some cases) retraining costs met by your employer on leaving your job.
- Welfare counselling or redundancy counselling.
- Pension information and advice worth up to £150 a year.
- Long service (20 years) gifts and suggestion scheme awards.
- Non-cash gifts, worth under £250, if not from your employer.
- Staff parties costing less than £150 per head per year.
- Special staff sports and leisure facilities.

Childcare benefits can harm your tax credits

If your employer offers you free childcare or childcare vouchers, check the effect on your tax credits. You cannot claim tax credits for childcare costs met by your employer, so you could end up worse off, particularly if you give up salary in return for the perk. There is more information – and a calculator to work out if you would be better off with or without vouchers – on the HMRC website at www.hmrc.gov.uk/childcare/.

Tax-free travel expenses and benefits

- The cost of travelling for work (see page 113).
- Approved mileage allowance payments (see page 116).
- Parking provided at or near your work.
- Travel or overnight expenses if public transport is disrupted by strikes.
- Occasional taxis home if you are required to work after 9 p.m., and it would be impossible or unreasonable for you to use public transport.

- The travel expenses of your husband or wife if they have to accompany you on a foreign trip because of your health.
- Personal expenses such as newspapers and laundry if away overnight for work, up to an average of £5 a night in the UK, £10 a night overseas (if they come to more, the whole lot is taxable).
- Subsidised bus travel from home to your place of work.
- The loan of a bicycle and safety equipment used mainly for travel to work.
- Help for travel from home to work if you are disabled.
- Taking an emergency vehicle home, for emergency workers on call.
- Travel expenses of some directors, such as unpaid directors of some clubs.

Tax-free share perks

If your employer has given you free shares in the company, or the right to buy shares on special terms, this counts as a tax-free perk *provided* that it is done through one of the schemes below. (For taxable schemes, see page 108.) Dividends from the shares and capital gains when you eventually sell them are taxable in the normal way (see Chapters 11 and 14) unless otherwise stated. You can claim a capital loss if relevant (see page 227).

Your employer will tell you what sort of scheme you are in and what the rules are. See also the share schemes area of the HMRC website (www.hmrc. gov.uk/shareschemes/) and HMRC help sheet 287 *Employee share and security schemes and Capital Gains Tax*. Note, though, that the tax treatment of share schemes is currently being reviewed by the Office of Tax Simplification.

Approved share incentive plans. Your employer can give you free shares, or you can buy them. They are free of income tax and National Insurance provided that you keep them in the plan for at least five years (in most cases). There is no capital gains tax on free shares if you keep your shares in the plan until you sell them.

Enterprise management incentives. You have an 'option' to buy shares at a particular price at some point within ten years. The option is free of income tax and National Insurance provided that the price at which you can buy the shares is not below their market value at the time the option is granted, and provided that, if there is a 'disqualifying event' such as you leaving the company, you buy the shares within 40 days of the event.

Approved savings-related share option schemes. You have an 'option' to buy shares at a fixed price at a particular time, free of income tax and National Insurance. You can buy the shares only with amounts you have saved under a special Save As You Earn (SAYE) savings scheme, which pays a tax-free bonus at the end of the savings period.

Approved company share option plans give you an 'option' to buy shares at a fixed price at a particular time. The option is free of income tax and National Insurance provided that (in most cases) you buy shares no earlier than three years, or later than ten years, after receiving the option.

How the tax is worked out

This is how your taxable pay is worked out for income tax purposes (the rules for National Insurance contributions differ slightly, see page 118).

Step 1: add up taxable pay (listed on page 97). You can deduct any tax-free income (listed on page 92) and contributions to your employer's pension scheme.

Step 2: add extra taxable pay, for some directors and business partners. HMRC calls this a 'deemed employment payment' but it applies only if you are affected by the 'IR35' rules (see page 98).

Step 3: add the taxable value of employee benefits. If you get a perk which is not tax-free, there are special rules for working out the amount on which you are taxed (see page 98).

Step 4: add any taxable amounts from share schemes (see page 108).

Step 5: add any taxable lump sums. This includes some payments when your job changes or ends (see page 111).

Step 6: deduct expenses on which you can claim tax relief. HMRC calls these 'allowable expenses' (see page 112).

The result is your taxable pay from employment. After deducting your personal allowance (£8,105 for people under 65 in 2012–13) you pay tax on the remainder at 20 per cent, or 40 per cent if it is over the £34,370 threshold for higher-rate tax. Anybody earning over £150,000 has to pay 50 per cent tax on the excess in 2012–13 (see page 7).

The tax due is deducted from your income under PAYE, as described in Chapter 2. See page 117 for how to check your PAYE deductions.

Example 7.1: Working out taxable pay

Mindy is a personnel manager. Her salary in 2012–13 is £39,524 (excluding her pension contributions, which are tax-free). After deducting her tax-free personal allowance of £8,105, the remainder is taxed at 20 per cent. However, her company car and other benefits add £9,450 to her taxable pay, and push her over the higher-rate threshold of £34,370. She will pay tax at 40 per cent on £6,499 of the taxable value of her benefits.

Documents that make life easier

Your employer should send you a form P60 by 31 May after the end of the tax year and – if you received any taxable benefits and expenses – a P11D (or P9D) by 6 July. Keep them carefully, as they have all the information you need to check your tax and fill out a tax return. Employers may now send electronic P60s; if so, make sure to save it or keep a printout.

The national minimum wage

Employers must pay most employees at least £6.08 an hour, or £4.98 if aged 18 to 20, £3.68 if aged 16 or 17, or £2.60 for apprentices (excluding tips and some travel expenses). From October 2012, the rates are £6.19, £4.98, £3.68 and £2.65 respectively.

Taxable payments

■ Payments from your employer, such as salary, wages, fees, bonuses, commission and overtime – you are taxed on these when you receive them or become entitled to them, whichever is earlier.

■ If you are a director, amounts credited to your account in the company's books (normally taxable from the date they are credited).

■ Expenses payments, whether these are reimbursing you for amounts you have laid out, flat-rate expense allowances, or tickets etc. bought for you (don't worry – any expenses for which you can claim tax relief are taken away at Step 6). But expenses covered by a 'dispensation' are not taxable (see page 112). Taxable expenses payments are shown on the form P11D or P9D you get from your employer.

■ 'Honoraria' from any posts that count as employment rather than self-employment (this can be a grey area – see Chapter 8).

■ 'Golden hellos'.

■ Sick pay, maternity, paternity or adoption pay (but see 'Off work?' below).

■ Loans that have been written off by the lender.

■ Taxable amounts from a profit-sharing scheme.

■ Payments from someone other than your employer, received because of your job, for example tips. You can exclude goodwill entertainment and gifts (other than cash) costing the donor less than £250 a year.

■ One-off payments to compensate you for agreeing to changes in your terms and conditions of employment.

■ In most cases, income from working abroad, if you are resident in the UK for tax purposes – but see Chapter 10 for special rules.

Off work?

Maternity, paternity and adoption pay, statutory sick pay, and any sick pay from an insurance scheme paid for by your employer, are all taxable. However, if you pay the premiums for sick pay insurance yourself, the payouts are tax-free. Your employer will deduct PAYE and National Insurance from any taxable payments, but as these are likely to be less than your normal pay you may get a refund of some of the tax paid so far.

An employee of your own company?

If you are a joint or sole shareholder of a company for which you work, your salary is taxed like any other employee's, but you may also have to pay extra tax if the company hires out your services and HMRC thinks you are exploiting the special tax treatment of company shareholders in order to avoid tax. There are several pieces of legislation designed to stop this, as described on page 126, but if you would have been an employee of your client, had the company not existed, you will be caught by the 'IR35' rules (named after the press release in which the rules were announced).

If you are affected, instead of paying tax just on the pay or dividends you receive, you will have extra tax to pay on the additional amount received by the company or partnership for your services (see Example 7.2).

There is an HMRC IR35 helpline and a special area on the HMRC website (see the Fact file). You can also ask HMRC to give an 'opinion' on whether you are affected.

> Example 7.2: **The effect of IR35**

Hannibal is the only employee of his own company. In 2011–12 he worked on a software project, for which his client paid him £50,000. Hannibal took a salary of only £25,000. If HMRC thinks that he is effectively an employee, he is also taxed on an extra 'deemed' payment of £25,000 (minus a bit for the costs of running the company).

Employee benefits

Some perks are tax-free – see page 92. Others are taxable whatever your income. The tax on non-cash benefits is collected by adjusting your tax code (see Chapter 2). However, if you are lower-paid some perks may be tax-free, or favourably taxed (see opposite). Any perks your family gets as a result of your job count as yours, and if you receive a benefit from a former employer it is taxed in the same way as for employees.

Are you 'lower-paid'?

Employee benefits are tax-free for lower-paid employees, except for mileage allowances above certain limits (see page 116), living accommodation, free or cheap goods, vouchers, company credit cards and tokens (see rule 5 overleaf).

You are lower-paid if your total gross pay is under £8,500 a year. This includes any expenses and taxable perks (valued as if you earned £8,500 or more), but minus pension contributions and payroll-giving donations. If you are in a job for only part of the year, the annual equivalent of your pay is used – so if you earn £5,000 for six months, the annual equivalent is £10,000. And if you have more than one job in a year, the £8,500 limit applies to each job separately.

Directors count as lower-paid only if they earn less than £8,500 and:

- they (and others associated with them) control 5 per cent or less of the shares in the company *and*
- *either* they are full-time working directors, *or* the company is a charity or non-profit-making.

How employee benefits are valued – eight general rules

When it comes to working out the taxable value of your perks, there are special rules for some types. Otherwise, there is a set of general rules that apply in all other circumstances. There is a quick guide to the most common taxable perks in Table 7.1 on page 101, which will tell you where to find more detail. In practice, you will not have to do the sums yourself, because your employer should give you a form P11D or P9D after the end of the tax year, giving the taxable value. Tax-free perks are listed on page 92.

Rule 1: Cheap or free use of something. Tax-free if you are lower-paid or if it is used primarily for work, otherwise you pay tax on 20 per cent of the market value of the item (such as a television or motorbike) at the time when it was first provided as a perk, or on the rent or hire charge paid by your employer if greater, plus any running costs or other expenses met by your employer. (See HMRC help sheet 210 *Assets provided for private use*.) However, there are special rules for cars, vans and living accommodation.

Rule 2: Gifts of things previously used as a perk. For example, being given a television you have previously borrowed (see Example 7.3 on page 102). You are taxed on the market value of the asset at the time of the gift, or (if higher) the initial market value minus any amounts on which tax has already been paid under rule 1. However, if the item is a car, van, bike or living accommodation the market value is always used. (See HMRC help sheet 213 *Payments in kind – assets transferred.*)

Rule 3: Cheap or free services. Tax-free if you are lower-paid, otherwise you are taxed on the extra cost to your employer of providing the services (e.g. hairdressing at work). However, if the services are those your employer provides in their business the extra cost may be nil (e.g. free travel for rail company employees).

Rule 4: Cheap or free goods. If you are lower-paid, you are taxed on the second-hand value of the goods. If you are not lower-paid, you are taxed on either the second-hand value or, if higher, the cost to your employer. If you are given goods your employer makes, you are taxed on the materials and manufacturing costs, not the retail price.

Rule 5: Credit cards, tokens and vouchers. Spending on these is taxed as cash, unless the item is tax-free (see the list on page 92), or counts as an allowable business expense. You can exclude payments for a company car or van – you are taxed on these separately. Note, too, that for non-cash vouchers you are taxed on the cost to your employer, not the face value, and you are not taxed on any interest or subscription fee on a company credit card. (See HMRC help sheet 201 *Vouchers, credit cards and tokens.*)

Rule 6: If you pay for something. You can deduct from the taxable value of a perk anything you pay for it.

Rule 7: Restricted use. The taxable value is reduced if you have the benefit for only part of a tax year, or if it is shared with another employee.

Rule 8: If you use a perk partly privately, partly for work. You can claim a deduction from the taxable value for the work use of a perk.

Table 7.1: A quick guide to taxable employee benefits

	Taxable value	Taxable value if lower-paid
Chauffeur	Cost to employer (rule 3)	Tax-free
Childcare over tax-free amount (see page 93)	Cost to employer (rule 3)	Tax-free
Company cars	Taxed on up to 35% of car's price, and on up to £6,580 for free fuel in 2012–13 (see overleaf)	Tax-free
Company motorbike	20% of value, or rent if higher (rule 1)	Tax-free
Company vans	Taxed on a flat £3,000, plus £550 for free fuel (see page 106)	Tax-free
Educational assistance for your children	Rule 3 applies, unless help is 'fortuitous'	Tax-free
Free or cheap goods	See rule 4	Second-hand value
Free or cheap services	Cost to employer (rule 3)	Tax-free
Gifts of things previously borrowed	See rule 2	Second-hand value
Living accommodation, unless tax-free (see page 107)	Basic charge of rental/rateable value	Taxable
Loans of goods	20% of value, or rent if higher (rule 1)	Tax-free
Loans of money	Taxed on interest saved, but only if total loans are over £5,000 – lower amounts are tax-free	Tax-free
Mileage allowances	Covered under 'Expenses' (see page 116)	See page 116
Private medical or dental insurance for UK treatment	Cost to employer (rule 3)	Tax-free
Relocation expenses	The first £8,000 is tax-free (see page 92) – anything else is taxed in the same way as other perks of the same kind	See previous column
Vouchers, tokens and credit cards	Taxed on most spending on these	Taxable

> ## Example 7.3: **How the general rules fit together**

Ian's employer lends him a top-of-the-range home entertainment system. Each year, Ian is taxed on 20% of its market value at the time he first got it. This was £2,000, so the annual taxable amount is £400 (rule 1).

Eighteen months later, the company gives Ian the equipment for a token payment of £500. As he had it for only half of the second year, he is taxed on only half of the annual value: £200 (rule 7). The gift itself is taxed at either the current market value (£1,200) or, if higher, the initial market value minus any amounts on which Ian has already been taxed, i.e. £2,000 − £400 − £200 = £1,400 (rule 2). He is taxed on £1,400 minus the £500 he is paying, i.e. £900 (rule 6).

Company cars and free fuel

The taxable value of your company car is a percentage of its list price (even if it is second-hand or leased), with reductions if you have the car for only part of the year or pay something for it. The percentage on which you are taxed is between 5 and 35 per cent, depending on your car's carbon dioxide (CO_2) emissions.

The emission levels needed to achieve a lower percentage have fallen over the years and will fall again in 2013 and 2014, and the maximum charge will increase to 37 per cent in 2015. For current rates, see Table 7.2 on page 104. Diesel cars are charged 3 per cent more than petrol cars until 2016. However, the following cars get favourable treatment:

- Zero-emission (including electric) cars – tax-free until April 2015.
- Automatic cars driven by disabled employees use the same list price as the equivalent manual car and are treated as having the same CO_2 emissions.

If you get free fuel for private use, the taxable benefit is the same percentage as you pay on your car (i.e. up to 35 per cent) but using a set 'price' of £18,800 in 2011–12 and £20,200 in 2012–13. It will rise again in 2013–14. You can avoid this charge only if you repay the *full* cost of all fuel used for private journeys. The charge is reduced if you have free fuel for only part of the year – but not if you receive free fuel again in the tax year. (For more information and calculators, see HMRC help sheet 203 *Car benefits and car fuel benefits* and the 'Cars' section of the HMRC website, www.hmrc.gov.uk/cars/.)

The price of a car – the whole price

You cannot reduce a car's taxable value by excluding the cost of accessories if they were fitted before you got the car (except for disability equipment and mobile phones). Accessories fitted afterwards will also be added to the taxable value if they are worth more than £100 per accessory or set of accessories (e.g. alloy wheels).

Working out the taxable value of a company car

1. *Find its 'price'.* This is usually its list price when registered, including delivery charges, taxes, VAT and accessories, but not road tax or the car registration fee. You can deduct anything up to £5,000 you paid towards the cost of the car. The price of a classic car (at least 15 years old, worth at least £15,000 and worth more now than when first registered) is its market value.

2. *Find the approved CO_2 emissions figure.* Use this to find the relevant percentage in Table 7.2 overleaf. CO_2 emissions appear on your car registration document, if registered after 1 March 2001; if not, try the Car Fuel Data website of the Vehicle Certification Agency (www. vcacarfueldata.org.uk). For cars without an approved emissions figure see HMRC help sheet 203 *Car benefits and car fuel benefits*.

3. *Multiply the car's price by the percentage charge.* This gives its annual taxable value.

4. *Adjust if the car was unavailable for part of the year.* Multiply the annual taxable value by the number of days it was available, and divide the result by 365 (366 in 2011–12, a leap year). Gaps of under 30 days are ignored.

5. *Deduct anything you paid towards your private use of the car.* The result is your car's taxable value.

6. *Find the taxable value of any free fuel.* The taxable value is worked out

using the same percentage as for the car itself (from Table 7.2), but using a set 'price' for the fuel of £18,800 in 2011–12 and £20,200 in 2012–13. If the car was unavailable for part of the year, the charge is reduced as described in step 4 above. (See Example 7.4 opposite.)

Table 7.2: Taxable percentage of car's price

Approved CO_2 emissions g/km*	2011–12		2012–13	
	Petrol car %	Diesel car%	Petrol car %	Diesel car%
75 or less	5	8	5	8
76–99	10	13	10	13
100–104	10	13	11	14
105–109	10	13	12	15
110–114	10	13	13	16
115–119	10	13	14	17
120–124	10	13	15	18
125–129	15	18	16	19
130–134	16	19	17	20
135–139	17	20	18	21
140–144	18	21	19	22
145–149	19	22	20	23
150–154	20	23	21	24
155–159	21	24	22	25
160–164	22	25	23	26
165–169	23	26	24	27
170–174	24	27	25	28
175–179	25	28	26	29
180–184	26	29	27	30
185–189	27	30	28	31
190–194	28	31	29	32
195–199	29	32	30	33
200–204	30	33	31	34
205–209	31	34	32	35
210–214	32	35	33	35
215–219	33	35	34	35
220–224	34	35	35	35
225 or more	35	35	35	35

*Grams per kilometre.

Alternatives to a company car

A company motorbike or van might be a cheaper alternative. Pool cars – used by more than one person, and not usually left overnight at your home – are completely tax-free, as are bicycles used mainly for travel from home to work or between workplaces. Some employers give you the option of extra salary instead of a car.

Example 7.4: **How much tax on your company car?**

Graeme's company car has a price of £16,000, and a CO_2 emissions figure of 200. Table 7.2 shows that he is taxed on 31% of the price in 2012–13. The taxable value of his car if he has it for the whole tax year is £16,000 × 31% = £4,960.

Graeme changed his car in July 2012 for one with CO_2 emissions of 155 and a list price of £20,000 – an annual taxable value of £20,000 × 22% = £4,400.

The taxable value of the free fuel Graeme gets for his company car in 2012–13 is worked out at the same percentage as charged on the car itself but using a set 'price' for the fuel of £20,200. So, Graeme will pay tax on £20,200 × 31% = £6,262 on his old car if he had it for the whole year, and £20,200 × 22% = £4,444 on his new car.

Graeme has had his first car for 122 out of the 365 days in 2012–13, his second car for 243 days. The annual taxable values are adjusted as follows:

Car			Fuel		
£4,960 × $^{122}/_{365}$	=	£1,658	£6,262 × $^{122}/_{365}$	=	£2,093
£4,400 × $^{243}/_{365}$	=	£2,929	£4,444 × $^{243}/_{365}$	=	£2,959
Total	=	£4,587	Total	=	£5,052

Free fuel – is it worth it?

The tax charge on free fuel in 2012–13 can be up to £1,414 if you pay tax at 20 per cent, £2,828 at 40 per cent and £3,535 at 50 per cent. If you don't do much private mileage, consider paying for all your private fuel yourself, and negotiating a pay rise instead.

Company vans

A company van you use for private travel is always tax-free if you are lower-paid (see page 99). Zero-emission vans are also tax-free until April 2015. Any other van is tax-free if you use it for work and the only private use of it that you are allowed is to commute between home and work, with any other private use being insignificant. If you can use it for any other private travel, it counts as a taxable benefit, with a taxable value of £3,000, or £3,550 if you get free fuel for private use. The taxable value is reduced if the van is not available for the whole year, or if it is shared.

Free or cheap loans

A free or cheap loan is tax-free if:

■ your employer is in the loan or credit business, and you get your loan on the same terms and conditions as members of the public
■ *or* you could claim full tax relief on the loan (see page 293), with no deduction for personal use
■ *or* the total amount you owe throughout the tax year comes to £5,000 or less, excluding loans on which you can claim full tax relief. This exemption would normally cover season-ticket loans. If you go over the £5,000, the whole lot is taxable, not just the amount over £5,000.

▶ Example 7.5: **The value of a cheap loan**

Alberta works for a bank and gets a mortgage on preferential terms. She wants to know roughly how much this has cost her in tax in 2011–12. As the average 'official' interest rate for 2011–12 was 4.0%, and the average actual rate was 2.6%, the perk has saved her interest of 4.0% − 2.6% = 1.4%.

She finds the average loan outstanding by adding the amount outstanding at the beginning of the tax year (£31,000) to the amount outstanding at the end of the tax year (£29,500) and dividing by two. This gives an average loan of £31,000 + £29,500 = £60,500 ÷ 2 = £30,250. The taxable amount is £30,250 × 1.4% = £424.

The taxable amount is the difference between the interest you actually paid in the tax year (if any), and the interest you would have paid at the average 'official' rate of interest set by HMRC (4 per cent for 2011–12 and 2012–13). The official rate of interest is listed on the HMRC website (see the Fact file).

The taxable amount is usually worked out using the average interest rate paid over the year and the average loan outstanding. However, if the average figures would give an unrealistic answer (because you paid off most of the loan at the start of the year, say) either you or your tax office can opt to use the real figures worked out on a daily basis.

Low-cost alternative finance arrangements (see page 189) are taxed in the same way as free or cheap loans.

Free or cheap accommodation

Free or cheap housing is tax-free if it is necessary for you to live there to do your job properly, or it is customary for people doing your type of job (e.g. newsagents running paper rounds) and you are on call outside normal working hours. (See HMRC help sheet 202 *Living accommodation*.) This does not apply to company directors, unless they are 'lower-paid' and they are full-time working directors or they work for a charity or a not-for-profit company. But housing is tax-free for all employees if there is a security threat and they are living there as part of special security measures.

Otherwise you are taxed on any accommodation provided by your employer, however much or little you earn. You are taxed on a basic amount, plus an extra amount if the property cost over £75,000, minus anything you pay for the accommodation. Figure 7.1 overleaf shows how this works. If part of the property is used for business, or it was available to you for only part of the year, you can also deduct a proportion to account for this.

Note that if you could choose higher pay instead of free accommodation, you are taxed on the extra pay if this is more than the taxable value of the accommodation.

Figure 7.1: Tax on free or cheap living accommodation

You are taxed on whichever of the following is higher:

- the yearly rent, if the property is rented
- *or* the gross rateable value of the property (or an estimate agreed with your tax office if there is no rateable value); the rateable value is multiplied by $100/270$ if the property is in Scotland to account for differences in rating revaluations
- *minus* any rent you pay

plus (if the property cost over £75,000)

- the cost (or market value, if whoever provides the property has owned it for at least six years before you moved in)
- *minus* £75,000
- *multiplied by* the 'official' rate of interest, set from time to time by HMRC

plus (unless you are 'lower-paid')

- any expenses of the property paid by your employer, such as heating (tax-free for the lower-paid if the supplier's contract is with your employer)
- loans of furniture – see page 99. If the accommodation is tax-free (needed for your job, say), the maximum taxable amount is 10% of your taxable pay.

Share schemes

Over the years various governments have tried to encourage employee share ownership by introducing 'approved' schemes (see page 94). Benefits from approved schemes are taxable only if you breach the conditions in some way (e.g. by withdrawing benefits early).

Because of the restrictions laid down for approval, employers may prefer to give their directors and employees 'unapproved' shares or share options (an 'option' is the right to buy shares at a set price at some point in the future). Below we explain how unapproved share schemes are taxed.

However, HMRC is keen to stop tax avoidance schemes using shares – see page 298. The Office of Tax Simplification is also carrying out a review of the rules for 'unapproved' share schemes.

Free or cheap shares

The normal rule, if you receive free or cheap shares from an unapproved share scheme, is that you are liable for income tax and National Insurance contributions on the difference between what the shares are worth and the price you paid for them. The rules apply to a wide range of securities, such as loan stock, bonds, unit trusts and futures. (See the share schemes area of the HMRC website at www.hmrc.gov.uk/shareschemes/.)

To prevent employers reducing the taxable value of the shares by artificial schemes, you may also have a further tax bill (a 'post-acquisition charge') on benefits such as perks not available to other shareholders. A charge will also apply if schemes are constructed with restrictions or conversion options which can be used to increase their value later.

There is also special treatment for shares that were issued partly paid or paid for in instalments. And, in a few circumstances, shares are taxed as if they were employee benefits, rather than pay. If so, they may be taxed as if you had received an interest-free loan to buy them. (See HMRC help sheet 305 *Employee shares and securities – further guidance* and page 291.)

Share options or securities options

You might have to pay income tax and National Insurance contributions on an option to buy shares or securities:

■ When you use the option to buy shares ('exercise' it) through an unapproved scheme.

■ If you receive anything in return for cancelling the option – that is, agreeing not to exercise the option, or transferring it to someone else. You are taxed on the amount you receive, whether the scheme is approved or unapproved.

You are unlikely to have to pay tax at the time you are granted an option in an unapproved scheme.

With all taxable options, you are taxed on the difference between the market value of the shares and what you would pay for them using the option. You can deduct anything you paid for the option itself, plus any employers' National Insurance contributions which you may have agreed to pay on your employer's behalf.

How the tax is collected

Your employer must generally account for income tax and National Insurance on any taxable benefit you have received. Even if tax has been paid, you must complete the share schemes box in the Additional Information pages of the tax return. The notes to the Additional Information pages give a lot of helpful information about how share schemes are taxed.

Sheltering your shares

If you are likely to make a taxable capital gain when you sell your shares, check whether you can transfer them into an Individual Savings Account (ISA). See page 185. In some cases, transfers are free of capital gains tax, and shares in the ISA are tax-free when you eventually sell them. You may also be able to transfer shares into a personal pension fund. See HMRC help sheet 287 *Employee share and security schemes and capital gains tax*.

Taxable lump sums when you leave a job

These payments fall into three categories: always tax-free, always taxable and sometimes taxable. The notes to the Additional Information pages of the tax return include a calculator for working out the taxable amount.

Negotiate before you leave

Lump sums are a difficult area, and much depends on the circumstances. Before leaving, do your best to make sure that the deal is set up to produce the smallest tax bill for you. If the sum involved is large, or if you are a director, get professional advice.

Always tax-free

■ Payments from a registered pension scheme or a foreign government pension scheme.

■ Special contributions from your employer to a registered pension plan for you, within limits (see Chapter 12).

■ Lump sums paid on account of medical unfitness caused or aggravated by service in the Armed Forces.

■ Statutory redundancy pay; Armed Forces redundancy pay.

Always taxable

The following taxable payments will usually have tax and National Insurance deducted through PAYE like your ordinary pay:

■ Any payment under your terms of employment – e.g. holiday pay, bonuses or outstanding salary paid out in a lump sum – except those specifically referred to as redundancy pay or benefits.

■ Pay in lieu of notice (but this may be in the 'sometimes taxable' category if you were not entitled to this in your contract, and there was no custom of your employer making such payments), and pay where notice is given but not worked.

■ A non-contractual payment that your employer is accustomed to make or that you could reasonably have expected to receive.

■ Compensation for changes in the terms and conditions of your job.

■ Payment in return for agreeing to restrict your behaviour, e.g. not poaching your ex-employer's staff.

■ Lump sums from a non-registered pension scheme (see page 206), unless you paid the contributions, or your employer paid them but you paid tax on them at the time, or (in some cases) they come from an overseas scheme. Payments made because of an accident are also tax-free.

■ Contributions paid by your employer into a non-registered overseas pension scheme for you (with some exceptions, see the notes to the Additional Information pages of the tax return).

Sometimes taxable

Other payments and benefits, including non-statutory redundancy pay, compensation for loss of your job and genuine ex gratia payments, are potentially liable to income tax, but not usually National Insurance. When working out the taxable amount, you can deduct:

- Payments if your job ends because of injury or disability.
- Some or all payments if your job involved 'foreign service' (the notes to the Additional Information pages of the tax return will help you work this out).
- The first £30,000 in total of any 'sometimes taxable' payments. Note that statutory redundancy pay, while tax-free itself, must be included when working out how much of the payment is over £30,000.

Any taxable amount is treated separately from your earnings, and taxed as your top slice of income. This means that a one-off lump sum does not push your other income into a higher tax bracket.

Example 7.6: **Leaving a job**

Alphonso is made redundant, with redundancy pay of £40,000 and pay in lieu of notice. He is taxed on the pay in lieu of notice because this was in his contract. The first £30,000 of his redundancy pay is tax-free, and the remaining £10,000 is taxable at his highest rate of tax.

Tax reliefs you can claim

Expenses

You can deduct from your employment income expenses you incur for work, whether or not your employer reimburses you. The reimbursements are taxable (unless they fall within the list of tax-free expenses on page 92), so it is important to claim any possible deductions. But your employer may have a 'dispensation' from your tax office to ignore tax-free expenses. If so, the reimbursements are not included in your taxable pay and you cannot claim a deduction for them.

Any expenses you claim must meet quite stringent tests. To qualify for tax relief on non-travel expenses, you must incur them wholly, exclusively and necessarily in performing your duties. Table 7.3 on page 115 lists the main expenses that you might be able to claim.

Working at home

You can claim expenses for working at home only if you have to carry out all or part of the key duties of the job there, and have no choice about doing so, and if appropriate facilities are not available at your employer's premises or it is too far away. If these conditions are met, you can claim the extra cost (if any) of gas, electricity, metered water, business phone calls and internet access. You can claim £3 a week in 2011–12 without having to show what you spent, but you can claim more if you have records to back up your claim. This is expected to rise to £4 a week from 6 April 2012, although it has not yet been announced. Alternatively, your employer can pay you £3 a week, tax-free (£4 from 6 April 2012), or more if you can give your employer supporting evidence.

Travel expenses

If you have to travel for work, whether or not you are reimbursed, you can claim tax relief on travel expenses, such as fares, and the cost of 'subsistence', e.g. accommodation and meals arising from business travel.

There are two types of journey for which you can claim relief (in both cases, the travel must be 'necessary', not just for personal convenience):

■ Travel 'on the job', e.g. between two workplaces, or between appointments if you work at your clients' premises.
■ Travel to or from a place that you go to in order to do your job – but not ordinary commuting, or private travel to a place you do not have to attend for work purposes.

It is usually quite clear when the first type of journey applies, but the second can be tricky. Start by ruling out ordinary commuting, defined as any travel between a permanent workplace and home, or any place that is not a workplace. 'Permanent' can apply to an area, if you have no single permanent workplace and your work is defined by reference to a set area that you visit regularly – as area representative for Essex, say.

You *can* claim tax relief for travel between your home and a temporary workplace – somewhere you go to for a limited time or for a temporary purpose. But you cannot claim if you carry out, or expect to carry out, a significant part of your duties there over a period of 24 months, or as long as your job lasts if less than 24 months. HMRC interprets 'significant' as more than 40 per cent of your working time. See Example 7.7. There are more examples in HMRC guide 490 *Employee travel. A tax and NICs guide for employers*.

Example 7.7: Is it business travel?

Annie, Betty and Charlie are all full-time engineers based at head office in Reading. They are all sent to work on a contract in Norwich:

- Annie is sent to work full-time on a particular phase of the work expected to last about 14 months. Norwich counts as a temporary workplace, and she can claim tax relief on the cost of getting there, hotel bills and meals.
- Betty spends only three days a week in Norwich, but as this is more than 40% of her working week and her work there is expected to last for three years, Norwich is not a temporary workplace and she cannot claim tax relief.
- Charlie is also expected to be in Norwich for three years, but he spends only one day a week there. This is not a significant part of his duties so he can claim relief.

More generous rules for foreign travel

If you travel abroad for your work – and providing your employer pays the expenses or reimburses you – you can claim the cost of all journeys from anywhere in the UK. You can also claim two return trips each tax year (per person) for a spouse and children who accompany you, if your work keeps you abroad for 60 days or more. See Chapter 10 for the rules if you do all your work abroad.

Table 7.3: Non-travel expenses you might be able to claim

Books	If needed to do your job, not just to keep up to date. May have to claim capital allowances instead if costly and expected life of over two years.
Business entertaining	You can claim only if you work for: ◾ a non-trading organisation *or* ◾ a trading organisation which has not itself claimed tax relief on the payments (look for a tick in section N of your form P11D), and which has reimbursed you or provided a special entertaining allowance.
Capital allowances for cost of buying equipment necessary for your work, e.g. office equipment	All or part of the cost of things such as office equipment, but not cars, motorbikes or bikes. If you make a profit when you sell things on which you have claimed an allowance, there is a taxable 'balancing charge'. See HMRC help sheet 252 *Capital allowances and balancing charges*.
Employee liabilities and indemnities	Cost of meeting claims for your errors or omissions as an employee, or insurance to cover such costs.
Guide dog if blind	Cost of keeping and replacing a dog.
Home phone and internet access	May be tax-free, see page 92. If not, you can claim work-related share of call charges if a phone is necessary (e.g. for a health worker on call or if you are required to work at home). You cannot claim line rental costs, or the cost of an 'unlimited access' internet package, so get your employer to pay these direct.
Loan interest	Only if you can also claim capital allowances on the item you are buying, and the loan is repaid within three years.
Professional fees and subscriptions	Payments that are relevant to your work, or a condition of working (e.g. as a solicitor). Ask your professional body or tax office which fees qualify or see List 3 on the HMRC website.
Security measures	Special security measures that are necessary because of your job.
Cost of maintaining or replacing tools, special clothing (but not ordinary clothing worn at work)	Flat rate expense deductions have been agreed for workers in some industries, e.g. £120 for plumbers. You can claim more if you spend more. Ask the trade union or other similar body what you can claim (you do not have to be a member to claim).
Working at home	See page 113.

Using your own car, van or bike for work

Whichever way your employer reimburses you for work travel – flat-rate allowance, mileage allowance, or not at all – you are entitled to the same amount of tax relief, worked out using HMRC-approved mileage rates. These 'approved mileage allowance payments' (AMAP) are shown in Table 7.4.

- If your employer pays you more than the approved rates, any excess is taxable pay – even if you count as lower-paid (see page 99) – and will be shown on your P11D or P9D.
- If your employer pays you the approved rates the amount will not appear on your P11D or P9D, but you cannot claim any tax relief.
- If your employer pays you less than the approved rates, you can claim tax relief on the difference, using form P87 *Tax relief for expenses of employment*. You need to keep a log of business mileage.
- If you carry other employees or volunteers on business travel your employer can also pay you a tax-free allowance of up to 5p per passenger per mile, but you cannot claim tax relief if you are paid less than 5p.

The AMAP rates are designed to take account of the capital cost of buying a car. You cannot claim any additional tax relief to cover the cost of buying or renting the car, or for depreciation.

Note that if you have a company car but no free fuel, and your employer either reimburses you for your business mileage or pays you no more than an 'advisory' rate set by HMRC, this is tax-free. But you cannot claim tax relief if your employer pays you less than the advisory rate.

An HMRC factsheet *Using your own vehicle for work* is available, and also see the HMRC website at www.hmrc.gov.uk/mileage.

Table 7.4: Approved mileage allowance payments

Business mileage in tax year	First 10,000 business miles 2011–12 and 2012–13	Each mile over 10,000 miles 2011–12 and 2012–13
Cars and vans	45p	25p
Motorcycles	24p	24p
Bicycles	20p	20p

Checking your PAYE

How PAYE works is explained in Chapter 2, but this is how you can make a very rough check of the tax shown on your payslip.

First deduct from the gross pay for the week or month as shown on your payslip any contribution to a pension plan or payroll giving scheme (which will also appear on your payslip) – you pay no income tax on these. Next check the tax code shown on your payslip. If it shows a number, put a zero on the end of the number (i.e. multiply by 10) and divide it by 52 (if you are paid weekly) or 12 (if paid monthly). Then:

■ If your code has a K in it – *add* the result to your gross pay (the K code means that your tax office is using your code to collect tax on employee benefits or other income received before tax).

■ For all other letters – *deduct* the result from your gross pay (because this is the allowance you can have tax-free).

Multiply the figure you get from the sums above by 20 per cent – this is the tax a basic-rate taxpayer should pay. If you are a higher-rate taxpayer, you will have an extra 20 per cent to pay on taxable income above £34,370 in 2012–13 (divided by 12 if paid monthly, or 52 if paid weekly) or 30 per cent on income above £150,000.

You might not have a number in your code (see page 22). The most likely alternatives are codes 'BR' or '0T', which mean that you get no allowances. If so, check that your allowances are deducted from other income (such as another job or business income), or you will pay too much tax.

Example 7.8: **Checking tax deducted**

Zebedee received gross pay of £1,800 for the month of July 2012, after deducting his pension contributions. His tax code is 810L. He puts a zero on the end – 8,100 – and divides by 12. This means that the first £8,100 ÷ 12 = £675 of his pay each month (rounded in his favour) is tax-free. He pays 20 per cent tax on the rest: £1,800 – 675 = £1,125 × 0.20 = £225.

Keeping below the tax threshold

No income tax is payable if your earnings are below £156 a week, £675 a month, or £8,105 in 2012–13, and no National Insurance is payable if they are below £146 a week, £634 a month or £7,605 a year. However, you will still qualify for important state benefits, such as the state retirement pension, if your earnings are over £107 a week, £464 a month, or £5,564 a year in 2012–13 (up from £102 a week, £442 a month, or £5,304 a year in 2011–12).

Checking your National Insurance contributions (NICs)

You have to pay Class 1 NICs on your earnings, unless you are under 16 or over state pension age. However, employers still have to pay contributions for employees over state pension age.

Class 1 NICs are not affected by your tax code, because there is no adjustment for individual allowances and deductions. You do not have to pay NICs on most employee benefits – although your employer does – but there is no deduction for pension contributions you make. Also, unlike income tax, National Insurance is not worked out on an annual basis. Each pay period (e.g. week or month) is treated separately – so if your earnings dip below the earnings threshold in one earnings period, you cannot carry the unused amount forward to the next period.

You do not pay NICs on the first £146 you earn each week (£634 a month, £7,605 a year) in 2012–13. Above that, you pay 12 per cent on pay up to £817 a week (£3,540 a month, £42,475 a year), and 2 per cent on any pay above that. See Table 7.5. Your employer pays more – 13.8 per cent on all your pay above the earnings threshold. But both your and your employer's payments are reduced if you are a member of an occupational pension scheme that is still 'contracted-out' of the state second pension. This means that your employer's scheme takes on responsibility for building up extra pension for you, see page 205, but it now applies to very few schemes.

You can use Figure 7.2 on page 120 to check the amount shown in your payslip, unless you are contracted-out, a woman paying reduced-rate contributions, or are claiming a deferral (see page 121).

Table 7.5: Class 1 National Insurance contributions 2012–13

Earnings	Employee	Employer
First £146 weekly, £634 monthly, £7,605 annually	**Nil**	**Nil**
Next £671 weekly, £2,906 monthly, £34,870 annually	**12%** (reduced to 10.6% on earnings between £146 and £770 if a member of an occupational pension scheme 'contracted out' of the State Second Pension)	**13.8%**, reduced if employer offers a 'contracted-out' pension
Anything above £817 weekly, £3,540 monthly, £42,475 annually	**2%**	**13.8%**

Example 7.9: Checking your National Insurance

Amina received total pay of £3,000 for the month of July 2012. To check the National Insurance on her payslip, she deducts the first £634, which is the amount below the earnings threshold: £3,000 − £634 = £2,366. As this all falls below the upper earnings limit of £3,540, she pays 12 per cent National Insurance, which works out at £2,366 × 0.12 = £284. (See Figure 7.2 overleaf.)

In December Amina receives commission that brings her earnings up to £4,000. As this is above the upper earnings limit she pays 12 per cent on the amount between the earnings threshold (£634) and the upper earnings limit (£3,540), i.e. £2,906 × 0.12 = £349. She pays 2 per cent on her remaining earnings of £4,000 − £3,540 = £460, i.e. £9. Her December contributions are £349 + £9 = £358.

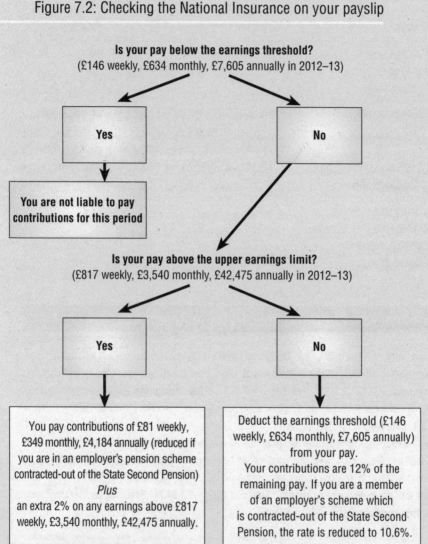

Figure 7.2: Checking the National Insurance on your payslip

Is your pay below the earnings threshold?
(£146 weekly, £634 monthly, £7,605 annually in 2012–13)

Yes

No

You are not liable to pay contributions for this period

Is your pay above the upper earnings limit?
(£817 weekly, £3,540 monthly, £42,475 annually in 2012–13)

Yes

No

You pay contributions of £81 weekly, £349 monthly, £4,184 annually (reduced if you are in an employer's pension scheme contracted-out of the State Second Pension) *Plus* an extra 2% on any earnings above £817 weekly, £3,540 monthly, £42,475 annually.

Deduct the earnings threshold (£146 weekly, £634 monthly, £7,605 annually) from your pay. Your contributions are 12% of the remaining pay. If you are a member of an employer's scheme which is contracted-out of the State Second Pension, the rate is reduced to 10.6%.

More than one job?

You could end up paying contributions at the full rate of 12% on each job, even though overall your income is above the limit on which this rate is payable. If you expect to pay contributions on earnings of at least £817 a week from one job (or combination of jobs) throughout the 2012–13 tax year, you can ask to defer some contributions, by filling in form CA72A *Application for deferment of payment of Class 1 National Insurance*. You can settle up, or get a refund, when it is clear, at the end of the tax year, what you have earned.

Married women paying reduced contributions

If you are a married woman who opted for reduced National Insurance contributions, the rate you pay is currently 5.85%. These contributions do not entitle you to a state pension in your own right and you should consider switching to the full rate. (Details are on the HMRC website at www.hmrc.gov.uk/ni/reducedrate/givingupright.htm.)

Saving tax on pension contributions

You pay National Insurance on your own contributions to a pension, but not on your employer's contributions. You may save money by giving up some of your salary in return for a higher employer's pension contribution. This won't work if you pay and your employer reimburses you – if your employer is paying into a personal pension for you, the pension application form should state that these are your employer's contributions.

Checking your student loan deductions

Repayments on student loans may also appear on your payslip. The Student Loans Company tells your employer to deduct them – they will not appear on your PAYE coding notice. Student loan repayments are based on the same earnings (i.e. excluding employee benefits) as NICs, but they are not due on the first slice of income. This is £15,000 in 2011–12, increasing to £15,795 in 2012–13 (£304 weekly, £1,316 monthly), but £21,000 for courses starting in September 2012. The repayments are 9 per cent of anything above these figures.

Like NICs, student loan repayments are non-cumulative and each pay period is treated separately. If, at the end of the year, you have paid too much, you can get a repayment from the Student Loans Company, so keep your payslips in case you want to query something.

Coming to the end of your student loan?

HMRC collects student loans, but only tells the Student Loans Company (SLC) the amount collected after the end of the tax year, which can lead to overpayments. To avoid this, you can opt out of having the repayments collected under PAYE for the last 23 months of your loan and pay them by direct debit instead, by contacting the SLC on 0845 0738 891. If you are taxed under self-assessment, tell your tax office if you are near the end of your loan.

What to tell HMRC

As an employee, you are unlikely to get a tax return unless you are a director or a minister of religion (of any faith), or if your income is high or you have untaxed income. Your employer should give your tax office the information that it needs. But you should tell your tax office if things change (see page 20) or if you have a new source of taxable income not taxed under PAYE, or if you want to claim tax relief on work expenses and do not get a tax return.

If you get a tax return you will need to fill in a separate set of the Employment supplementary pages for each employer *unless*:

■ all your employment income is from overseas and it is not taxable in the UK (see Chapter 10)
■ *or* you are a director who received no payment in any form, or held a position such as honorary secretary and received only expenses.

Even in the two cases above, you need to say that you were an employee on page TR2 of the main tax return, and explain in 'Any other information' at the end of the return why you have not filled in the Employment pages.

You will also have to fill in the Additional Information pages if you have received any taxable benefits from a share scheme, or if you received a lump sum, or if you are claiming an exemption for foreign earnings (see page 174). And if you have left your job but received sickness benefit paid for by your ex-employer, enter the taxable amounts in the main tax return.

Record-keeping

Here are some of the key records you should keep in addition to those shown on page 15.

Your pay and expenses
■ Your payslips, P60 or P45 as evidence of your taxable pay, and your P11D or P9D showing taxable benefits and expenses.
■ A note of any tips or gratuities, or any other taxable pay. Record these as soon as you get them, rather than estimating them later.
■ Correspondence relating to any lump sum payment.
■ Copies of expense claims and foreign travel itineraries.
■ Records of business mileage; VAT receipts for motoring expenses.
■ Receipts, credit statements and other purchase records. If you have to give these to your employer, keep copies of your expense claims.
■ Notes of cash payments for which you have not got a receipt.
■ Household bills to back up a claim for the costs of working at home.

If you received share-related benefits
■ Any related correspondence from your employer.
■ The price you paid for your shares or options, and the relevant dates.
■ The market value of the shares at relevant dates, such as when you received them (or options to buy them) or exercised an option to buy.
■ A copy of each share option certificate or exercise notice.
■ Notes of any benefits received, or alteration in the rights or restrictions attached to your shares.
■ A note of any tax you have already paid on the benefit.

8

Tax if you are self-employed

As the 'job for life' moves towards extinction, more people are experiencing self-employment for at least part of their working lives. However, becoming self-employed also means taking responsibility for sorting out your own tax, and organising your cashflow. The Office of Tax Simplification has recommended changes to make tax simpler for the smallest businesses, which the government intends to implement.

Top tips

- You must notify HMRC as soon as you start your business (see page 151).
- Get a good record-keeping system in place from day 1. Also keep records of your costs before you start trading – you can claim these as a business expense.
- See page 145 for guidance on choosing your accounting period. The simplest option is to end it on 31 March.
- In January after the tax year in which you first make a profit, you may have to pay some tax in advance, as well as tax owed so far. Put cash aside to meet the bill.
- Struggling to pay tax? HMRC has a Business Payment Support Service (see page 40).
- If you make a loss you can set it against other taxable income (see page 145).
- Remember to claim the VAT portion of any expense if you are not VAT-registered. If you are registered, the Flat Rate Scheme may save you VAT (see page 128).
- If you work from home, you can claim some household expenses (see page 133).

Are you self-employed?

This chapter affects you if you are self-employed, either as a sole trader or in a partnership. If you are a director of your own company, you are also 'in business', but strictly speaking you are an employee of the company and your tax is covered in Chapter 7. The company has its own tax return and is subject to corporation tax – not covered in this book.

This chapter does not affect you if receive odd bits of freelance income but have not set up in business to do this. Income of this type is taxed separately and should be reported under 'Other UK income' in the tax return (see page 279). However, if you regularly receive such income – from frequent eBay trading, say – or the amount is substantial, you might be regarded as trading. If in doubt, contact your tax office.

Sole traders

A 'sole trader' is what you are if you simply start up on your own, without creating (or buying into) a partnership or setting up a company (a separate legal entity). The whole of any profits or losses counts as your income, on which you are liable to pay income tax and Class 2 and Class 4 National Insurance contributions. You may also have to pay capital gains tax (see Chapter 14) on profits from disposing of or transferring business equipment or property, although there are special tax reliefs for businesses.

Partners

As a partner, you have a share in the partnership's profits or losses, and in any capital gains, as set out in the partnership agreement. The partnership has its own tax return, but is not itself taxed – you pay income tax and National Insurance on your share of profits as if you were a sole trader. And you can make your own choices about how you use your share of any losses – your choices may be different from those of other partners.

Sole trader, partner or company?

Many people working for themselves do so as a company or partnership. A key reason is that you can pay yourself in the form of either a salary or dividends (with a company), or alter the profit-sharing agreement (with a partnership), to benefit from differing tax and National Insurance rules.

For example, National Insurance is not due on dividends the company pays you. The company pays corporation tax, not income tax, on its profits, and the tax rate for small companies is 20 per cent on profits up to £300,000.

The right legal structure for your business depends on your individual situation. Take professional advice, but do not be driven by tax considerations alone – companies have to meet many more legal requirements than sole traders. Note, too, that the Office of Tax Simplification has recommended a simpler basis of calculation for sole traders with a low turnover, which the government intends to take forward in 2013. Other disadvantages of incorporation are:

- If you provide services through a company or partnership that you control, you may be treated as if you received extra pay. There are two types of company that might be caught: 'personal' service companies that are affected by what are known as the IR35 rules (see page 98) and 'managed' service companies provided by an outside business.
- In an attempt to stop businesses shifting income between business partners in order to reduce the overall tax bill – for example, if you pay dividends to a family shareholder who plays no direct role in the business – HMRC may use what is called the 'settlements' legislation to tax the income as yours (see HMRC help sheet 270 *Trusts and settlements – income treated as the settlor's*).

To start with, it's up to you to decide whether you are self-employed, but HMRC can review this at any time and may decide later on that you are not self-employed, but an employee of your client, liable to PAYE and employee's National Insurance. Note that you can be employed for one piece of work and self-employed for another.

There is no simple definition of self-employment, but there have been many court cases and a number of 'tests' have developed. (See Table 8.1 opposite, but it is the overall picture that counts, and each test cannot be looked at in isolation.) You cannot sidestep the tests by stating in a contract that you are not an employee – it is the nature of the work that counts. You can ask your tax office for a written decision about your 'employment status', and you can appeal if you disagree. (See HMRC factsheet ES/FS1 *Employed*

Table 8.1: Tests for self-employment

These suggest employment	*These suggest self-employment*
Control Your client has the right to tell you at any time what to do, or when, and where and how to do it	**Right to subcontract** You can choose whether to do the work yourself or hire (and pay) someone else to do it for you
Location You work at your client's premises, or at a place or places he or she decides	**Providing your own equipment** You supply the main items needed to do your job
Payment You are paid by the hour, week or month, receive overtime pay and benefits (e.g. sick pay or expenses) and work set hours or a given number of hours a week or month	**Risking your own money** You bear the cost of overheads, for example by working on a fixed price, or paying for your own skills training for use in future work
Part and parcel of the organisation You have staff management responsibilities, for example	**Risk of losses** You have to correct unsatisfactory work in your own time and at your own expense
Right of termination Either you or your client can end the contract by giving a set period of notice, even if there is no breach of contract	**Personal factors** You may be, for example, a skilled worker working for several clients in a year
Long periods working for one client	**No right to work and pay** Your client has no obligation to provide work or pay when no work is available

or self-employed for tax and National Insurance contributions.) There is an interactive 'employment status indicator' on the HMRC website, and a factsheet, TH/FS14 *Paying tax if you buy and sell things from home.*

Should you register for VAT?

You have to register if your turnover over the previous 12 months (excluding exempt sales) rises above £77,000 from 1 April 2012, or you expect it to do so in the next 30 days. If you are not UK-established, but sell in the UK, you must register whatever your level of turnover from 1 December 2012. The standard rate of VAT is 20 per cent, and a few goods and services are exempt, zero-rated, or chargeable at 5 per cent. Contact the VAT helpline on 0845 010 9000 and see leaflet VAT/FS1 *What you need to know about VAT* or the Business Link website at www.businesslink.gov.uk.

Even if you do not have to register, you may choose to do so voluntarily, because it allows you to reclaim the VAT on things you buy for the business. However, it will put up your prices for private customers (business customers should be able to reclaim the VAT you charge). Note that if your products are exempt (e.g. health services) you cannot reclaim VAT.

If you register you must file a VAT return each quarter, showing the VAT you have charged your customers ('output tax') and the VAT you have paid on your business purchases ('input tax'). Your input tax is deducted from your output tax and you pay the balance over to HMRC (which administers VAT). If your input tax comes to more than your output tax, you get a refund. Online filing and electronic payment are compulsory for almost all VAT-registered businesses from April 2012.

There are several schemes to simplify matters for small businesses:

- *Annual Accounting* – you pay instalments towards an annual VAT bill. At the end of the year you submit a single return and any balance due.
- *Cash Accounting* – with this scheme, you account for VAT on the basis of payments you receive and make, rather than on invoices you issue and receive, so you don't pay VAT until your customers pay you.
- *Flat Rate Scheme* – this allows businesses with turnover below £150,000 to charge the full rate of VAT but pay less to HMRC, ranging from 4 per cent to 14.5 per cent of turnover depending on the trade, with a further 1 per cent reduction in the first year of VAT registration. If you do this, you cannot reclaim VAT on the things you buy.
- *Retail Schemes* – to simplify paperwork if you sell direct to the public.
- *VAT margin schemes for second-hand goods, art and antiques* – you account for VAT on the difference between the purchase price and the selling price.
- *Bad Debt Relief* – if a customer fails to pay you.

Flat rate VAT – a simpler way

Many businesses will save VAT by using the Flat Rate Scheme (see the ready reckoner on the HMRC website) and, if you keep your books on a VAT-inclusive basis, it is simpler.

How income tax on your business is worked out

You are taxed on your business profits (or losses) for a 'basis period'. Normally, your basis period is the accounting period ending in the tax year in question. So if you make up your accounts to the end of December each year, say, in the 2011–12 tax year you pay tax on your profits for the period from 1 January 2011 to 31 December 2011. HMRC help sheet 222 *How to calculate your taxable profits* explains basis periods, and see page 139.

Working out your taxable profits

You must work out your profits on an 'earnings' basis – i.e. income is included in your accounts from the date it is earned, not when you receive it, and expenses on the date you incur them, not the date paid. However, the government is looking at allowing small businesses to use a cash basis, that is the date of receipt or payment.

■ *Step 1: add up your business income*, i.e. the turnover from your trade or profession. There is no tax-free income to ignore, but exclude sales of capital items. If you take things from stock for your own or your family's use, this counts as a sale.

■ *Step 2: deduct your business expenses*, adjusted to take account of any expenses in your accounts not allowed for tax, such as depreciation on cars and business equipment (see overleaf).

■ *Step 3: deduct your annual investment allowance or capital allowances –* you can claim these instead of depreciation (see page 136).

The result of steps 1 to 3 is your net business profit (or loss) for an accounting period for tax purposes. But you may need to adjust this:

- *Step 4: adjustments if your basis period is not the same as your accounting period.* This may affect you in the first year or so you are in business or in your final year of trading (see page 139 for how it works).
- *Step 5: deduct losses from previous years* – the result is your taxable profit for a basis period. See page 145 for more about losses.
- *Step 6: add on any other taxable business income.* This includes business start-up allowances (such as the New Enterprise Allowance) and incentives received if you take a lease on business property.

The result gives you your taxable income from self-employment, which is taxed at 20 per cent, or 40 per cent on any amount above the higher-rate threshold of £34,370 in 2012–13. If your taxable income is above £150,000 you will have to pay 50 per cent tax on the excess in 2012–13.

A partner in a partnership?

Steps 1 to 3 all take place in the partnership's tax return. The business profits (or losses) are then shared out according to the partnership agreement, and the adjustments covered in steps 4 to 6 are made in your own tax return. Joining a partnership counts as starting in business, and leaving counts as closing down.

Work in progress for service businesses

You should include in your profits an amount for unbilled work, valued at its full selling price. Say you are working on a job for which you will charge £12,000 and at your year end you have spent half the time you expect to spend on it overall. You must add £6,000 to your profits for the year just ending. See HMRC help sheet 238 *Revenue recognition in service contracts*.

What expenses can you deduct?

The law concentrates on what you *cannot* do rather than what you can – in particular, you cannot deduct expenses which are not 'wholly and exclusively' for your trade. However, there are many expenses that HMRC commonly accepts. These are called 'allowable' expenses. There is useful guidance on the HMRC website in the *Business Income Manual.* The government is also looking at a simplified expenses system for business use of a home or car by small businesses.

If an expense is partly for business, partly private, you can usually claim a proportion in line with the business use. For example, you can claim some expenses for using your car or home for work. Table 8.2 overleaf summarises the main items, but there is more detail in the notes to the Self-employment or Partnership pages of the tax return.

The following do not count as allowable expenses:

■ The cost of buying or improving fixed assets, or depreciation (you can claim annual investment allowance or capital allowances, see page 136).
■ Costs and fines for breaking the law (a VAT penalty, say).
■ Business hospitality – you can claim the cost of entertaining staff, but not if this arises as part of business hospitality (e.g. if an employee takes a customer out to lunch, the whole cost is business hospitality).
■ The non-business part of any expense.
■ Tax (except employer's NICs and, if you are not VAT-registered, VAT).
■ Your own pay, pension contributions and NICs.
■ Charitable and political donations.

Raw materials and goods bought for resale

If you make or sell things, the cost of raw materials and stock is a business expense, so you will need to carry out a stock-take at the end of each accounting period. You should value your stocks (including your work in progress) at their cost to you or, if lower, the amount they would fetch. Include things that you have received but not yet paid for.

To work out what you have used during the period:

■ take the value of your stock and work in progress at the start of the period
■ *add* anything you bought during the period
■ *deduct* what you have left at the end of the period.

Table 8.2: Summary of business expenses you can deduct from turnover

Advertising and promotion	Newspaper advertisements, mailshots, non-consumable gifts worth £50 or less per person in each tax year provided that they advertise your business
Bad debts	Amount of money included in turnover but written off at end of accounting period (not a general bad debts reserve)
Employee costs	See opposite
General administrative costs	Phone bills, postage, stationery, printing, office expenses, insurance, publications if necessary for work
Interest and other finance	See page 134
Legal and professional costs	Fees of accountant, solicitor, surveyor, stocktaker etc., professional indemnity insurance, costs of debt recovery (but not costs of buying or selling fixed assets)
Premises costs	See opposite
Raw materials and goods bought for resale	See page 131
Business costs of cars and other vehicles	See page 135
Other business travel costs	Rail, air and taxi fares, hotels, meals when away overnight on business. Lunches only if away overnight, or if you habitually travel on business, or on occasional trips outside your normal pattern of travel
Pre-trading expenditure	Allowable expenses from the previous seven years are treated as if incurred on the date you start trading
Research and development costs related to a trade (not a profession)	Excludes costs of acquiring rights to research – you may be able to claim capital allowances instead
Trade and professional subscriptions	Subscriptions to relevant associations. Also contributions to local enterprise agencies and other such bodies

Employee costs

You can deduct all the costs of hiring other people, whether they are permanent, temporary or casual staff, or subcontractors. This includes pay, pension contributions, employer's NICs and all other staff-related costs, such as employee benefits and training. However, you cannot deduct your own pay, NICs, benefits or pension contributions. You can claim the cost of your own training if this is to update your existing skills, but not to acquire a completely new skill.

If you take on an employee, you will have to comply with the requirements for operating PAYE (see Chapter 2). HMRC has a new employer helpline on 0845 607 0143 which you can use to register or get advice.

Employing family members

You can claim tax relief on the pay and National Insurance of a family member you employ, but you must be able to show that the work is needed for the business, the family member actually does it and is formally paid for doing it, and that you are paying a reasonable rate for the job (at least the National Minimum Wage, see page 96). Your employee can avoid tax and National Insurance if you pay less than £146 a week in 2012–13, but it is a good idea to pay at least £107 a week (the level at which they start to build up a benefit entitlement), to protect their right to state pension and some other benefits.

Premises

If you have business premises, you can claim rent, business rates, water rates, light, heat, power, maintenance and repairs (but not improvements), property insurance, security costs and so on. For leases of 50 years or less, you can claim part of any premium you pay. You cannot claim the cost of buying property, although you can claim mortgage interest and you may be able to claim an allowance for fixtures and fittings or for some types of property (see page 136). Note that if you set up in an Enterprise Zone you may qualify for benefits such as a cut in business rates – see www.businesslink.gov.uk.

If you work from home, you can claim the same types of expense (including mortgage interest and council tax), in line with the proportion of your home used for business. But HMRC says that when part of the home is being used for business then that must be the sole use for that part at that time. The basis for any claim should be explained – and records kept to support it. For minor use you can claim a reasonable estimate (up to £3 a week) without having to keep full records. HMRC has a section on working from home in the *Business Income Manual* on its website.

Using part of your home exclusively for work

If part of your home is used for business alone, with no private use, part of any gain when you sell the house is liable to capital gains tax (see Chapter 14).

Example 8.1: Using your home for work

Paul runs a software business from home. He has one of the eight rooms set aside as an office, and he claims one-eighth of his mortgage interest as a business expense. At the end of the tax year he asks his lender for a 'certificate of interest paid' and claims one-eighth of the interest shown (he can't claim capital repayments). He also claims the same proportion of his heating, lighting and council tax bills.

Interest and other finance costs

You can claim bank charges, credit card charges and overdraft interest. You can also claim interest on a loan to buy something you use in your business (or a proportion of the interest if you use it partly for business, partly privately). This includes hire purchase interest (but not capital repayments), finance lease rentals for under five years (for longer leases, see page 139) and alternative finance payments (see page 189).

Note that if you lease a car (but not a van) with CO_2 emissions above 160g/km (130g/km from April 2013) you can claim only 85 per cent of the lease payments. Different rules apply for leases starting before 6 April 2009.

Cars and other vehicles

You can claim the running costs of a vehicle you use for work, including fuel, servicing, repairs, road tax, insurance, rescue services, parking and congestion charges (but not fines). You cannot claim the purchase cost of the car as an expense, but see overleaf for allowances you can claim instead.

If you use the car for private purposes as well as for business, there are two methods of claiming vehicle costs, but you can only change between methods when you acquire a car. Whichever method you use, you can claim interest on a loan to buy the car, or other finance costs. The methods are:

■ you can claim a proportion of the costs, in line with the amount of business mileage you do, plus capital allowances (see overleaf)
■ *or* if your turnover is below the level at which you need to register for VAT (see page 127), whether or not you have registered, you can claim a mileage rate per business mile, shown in Table 7.4 on page 116. If so, you cannot claim allowances for the purchase cost of the car.

Example 8.2: **Claiming your car as an expense**

About 20% of Leah's mileage is for business. She can either claim 20% of the running costs of her car, plus a £612 capital allowance for the cost of buying it (see Example 8.4 on page 138), or, because her turnover is below the VAT registration limit, she can claim just the HMRC-approved mileage rate (45p per mile in Leah's case). In either case, she can also claim 20% of the interest on her car loan.

VAT on your expenses

Unless you sell only exempt goods or services, you can deduct the VAT you pay on most things you buy for your business.

If you are not VAT-registered you get your tax relief by deducting the VAT-inclusive cost of expenses and capital allowances from your turnover. If you are VAT-registered, your profits are usually worked out excluding VAT on both your income and your expenses. If you have opted for the Flat Rate Scheme, you can keep your books either way. But if your accounts exclude VAT, then any VAT you save by being on the scheme must be declared as taxable income on your tax return, otherwise you will get income tax relief on more VAT than you have paid – see page 306.

Investment and capital allowances

If you buy plant and machinery (capital assets) for use in your business, such as vans, tools, computers and office equipment, you can claim either annual investment allowance or capital allowances to deduct from your profits. Cars qualify only for capital allowances, and whichever allowance you qualify for, only a proportion can be claimed if an asset is used partly for private purposes. Note that these allowances are being reduced from 6 April 2012, so consider timing your spending to maximise them.

Annual investment allowance (AIA)

You can claim AIA of 100 per cent of the first £100,000 you spent on plant and machinery in the 2011–12 tax year, but the limit has fallen to £25,000 for 2012–13. If your accounting period straddles 5 April, you get part of the allowance for each period. So if your year end was 5 January 2012, you get $^{3}/_{12} \times$ £100,000 = £25,000 for purchases in the first three months (6 January to 5 April 2011) and $^{9}/_{12} \times$ £25,000 = £18,750 for later purchases.

You cannot claim AIA on cars (see page 138), although you can claim it on vans and motorcycles. Nor can you claim it on houses, shops or offices, but you can claim it on some 'integral features' of business premises, such as electrical, lighting and heating systems, water systems, lifts, thermal insulation and solar shading.

Capital allowances

Capital allowances apply to purchases before 6 April 2008, or later purchases for which you cannot claim AIA (e.g. cars), or if you have used up your AIA. The basic principle is that your capital expenditure is pooled, and you can claim a percentage of the pool each year as a 'writing-down' allowance. The percentage was 20 per cent of the pool (or 10 per cent on integral features of a building) in 2011–12, falling to 18 and 8 per cent from 6 April 2012.

Some purchases must be kept in separate pools, e.g. assets used privately as well as for business, and special rules apply to cars – see page 138,

HMRC help sheet 252 *Capital allowances and balancing charges* and the capital allowances section of the Business Link website at www.businesslink.gov.uk.

Be careful in the first year of business

If your accounting period is shorter or longer than a year, your AIA and writing-down allowance are increased or decreased in proportion. So if your first accounting period is shorter than a year, remember your AIA will be reduced (see Example 8.3). Either spread your spending over two years, or consider a longer first accounting period.

Example 8.3 Claiming annual investment allowance

Sam opens a shop in January 2013. He spends £30,000 on freezers, shelving units, tills and other equipment. He can claim 100% AIA on the first £25,000 of purchases in 2012–13, but he plans to end his first accounting period on 31 March 2013. This is only three months later, and would mean that he could only claim a quarter of the full allowance, i.e. £6,250, and capital allowances at 18 per cent a year on the rest. He could claim 100 per cent on the whole lot if he either extended his accounting period to 31 March 2014 (to benefit from the allowance for 2013–14) or delayed the bulk of his purchases until after 31 March 2013.

100 per cent allowances
In addition to your annual investment allowance (AIA), you can claim the following 100 per cent allowances (and see below for cars):

■ Business premises renovation allowance for renovating vacant business premises in disadvantaged areas.
■ Flat conversion allowance for the cost of converting flats over shops and other business premises (to be abolished after 5 April 2013).
■ Allowances for spending on environmentally friendly equipment (although this is under review) – there is a website at www.eca.gov.uk

listing items that qualify. If you have no profits to set against the allowance, you can claim a limited cash payment instead.

■ Research and development allowance.
■ Until April 2015, an allowance for buying unused zero-emission goods vehicles.

Cars

Purchases of business cars do not qualify for AIA, but until 31 March 2013 you can get a 100 per cent allowance for unused electric cars or cars with emissions of 110g/km or less. Other cars bought after 5 April 2009 qualify for 20 per cent allowances if they have emissions of 160g/km or less (130g/km from April 2013), and 10 per cent if their emissions are higher, reducing to 18 per cent and 8 per cent from 6 April 2012. See Example 8.4, but note that different rules apply for cars bought before 6 April 2009.

Example 8.4: **Capital allowances on a car**

Leah bought a car for £17,000 in May 2012. Her accounting period ends in March. As the car's emissions are 130g/km, the maximum allowance she can claim in 2012–13 is 18% – £3,060 in Leah's case. However, as her business mileage in the car is only 20% of the total mileage, she can claim only 20% of the full allowance: £3,060 × 20% = £612.

Small pools of capital expenditure

With capital allowances, you claim a percentage of your pool of expenditure in year 1, and a percentage of the remaining pool in year 2, and so on. This means that you can end up with a very small pool. If your pool is £1,000 or less, you can claim it all in one year - but you do not have to do so, if your profits are too low to benefit.

> ## Buying on credit

You can claim AIA and capital allowances for things bought with a loan or on hire purchase. You cannot claim them on items bought with a finance lease (the lessor gets the allowance, not you) unless the lease lasts at least five years, sometimes more – though you can claim the lease payments as an expense (see page 134).

Basis periods explained

Your profits are calculated for an accounting period, but you are taxed on your profits for a 'basis period'. After you have been in business for two or three years, the two periods will coincide. Until then, if your basis period is shorter than the period covered by your accounts, you pay tax on only part of the profits in your accounts. If it is longer, you add in part of the profits of the next set of accounts. This is done according to the number of days, weeks or months in each period. On your tax return you report your profits for the whole of your accounting period, but then make an adjustment as shown in Example 8.5 overleaf.

You may have to make similar adjustments if you change your accounting date.

If you are a partner in a partnership, you have your own basis period, which may differ from that of the other partners in the first year or so after you join. Otherwise, the rules are the same as for sole traders.

First tax year you are in business

Your 'basis period' is the period between the date you start up and the next 5 April. (See page 151 for what you need to do on starting up.)

Example 8.5: **Your first tax year in business**

Archie starts up on 5 January 2012 and ends his first accounting period on 5 January 2013. His basis period for 2011–12 is 5 January 2012 to 5 April 2012 – three months. However, as his accounts cover a 12-month period, he pays tax for 2011–12 on $\frac{3}{12}$ of the profits of his first accounting period. On his tax return for 2011–12 he reports his profits for the whole of his first accounting period, but then deducts an adjustment of $\frac{9}{12}$ of his profits.

Give yourself time to work out your profits

If your first accounting period ends just before 31 January (the last date for sending in your return, if you file online), you might have to work out your tax using provisional figures. HMRC allows this if – like Archie in Example 8.5 – your accounting period ends within three months of 31 January, but you will have to pay interest if you underestimate your tax.

Second tax year you are in business

Your basis period depends on the length of your first accounting period. If it is less than 12 months, you are taxed on 12 months' profits, beginning on the date you started (see Example 8.6 opposite). If it is 12 months or more, you are taxed on the profits of the 12 months up to your accounting date (see Example 8.7 on page 142). If you had no accounting period ending in the tax year, you are taxed on the profits of the 12 months from 6 April in one year to 5 April in the next.

Example 8.6: **First accounting period less than 12 months**

			2012–13 basis period						
		2011–12 basis period							
2010–11 basis period				Second accounting period					
	First accounting period								

| 30 Sep | 31 Dec 2010 | 31 Mar | 30 Jun | 30 Sep | 31 Dec 2011 | 31 Mar | 30 Jun | 30 Sep | 31 Dec 2012 |

First tax year (2010–11) | *Second tax year (2011–12)* | *Third tax year (2012–13)*

Belinda starts in business on 1 October 2010, and ends her first accounting period after 9 months, on 30 June 2011. Her basis period for her second tax year in business (2011–12) is the 12 months from the day she started up, i.e. 1 October 2010 to 30 September 2011. Her profits were:

1 October 2010–30 June 2011   £18,000
1 July 2011–30 June 2012   £40,000

To make up the profits of her 2011–12 basis period, Belinda is taxed on the 9 months' profit from her first accounting period (£18,000), and 3 months of the profits from her second accounting period – i.e. £40,000 $\times$ $^3/_{12}$ = £10,000. She will be taxed on £18,000 + £10,000 = £28,000.

Six months of these profits overlap with those included in the 2010–11 basis period (£18,000 $\times$ $^6/_9$ = £12,000), and three months overlap with those included in the 2012–13 basis period (£40,000 $\times$ $^3/_{12}$ = £10,000). These are called 'overlap profits' (see page 143) and in Belinda's case they amount to £12,000 + £10,000 = £22,000.

Example 8.7: **First accounting period 12 months or longer**

2012–13 basis period

2011–12 basis period

2010–11 basis period

Second accounting period

First accounting period

30 Sep	31 Dec 2010	31 Mar	30 Jun	30 Sep	31 Dec 2011	31 Mar	30 Jun	30 Sep	31 Dec 2012

First tax year (2010–11) | *Second tax year (2011–12)* | *Third tax year (2012–13)*

Andrew also starts in business on 1 October 2010, but he ends his first accounting period on 31 December 2011 – 15 months later – with a profit of £25,000. For the 2011–12 tax year (his second in business) his basis period is the 12 months up to 31 December 2011. The profits for this basis period are $^{12}/_{15}$ of the profits in his first accounting period – i.e. £25,000 × $^{12}/_{15}$ = £20,000. He must enter a negative adjustment of £25,000 − £20,000 = £5,000 in his 2011–12 tax return.

Three months of the profits in Andrew's 2011–12 basis period are also included in his 2010–11 basis period, i.e. £25,000 × $^{3}/_{15}$ = £5,000. These are 'overlap profits'.

Third tax year you are in business

From this tax year on, your basis period is the 12 months running up to your accounting date in that year – so if, for example, you make up your accounts to 30 September each year, your basis period for the 2011–12 tax year would be the period from 1 October 2010 to 30 September 2011.

Your accounting period ending in the third tax year may be longer than 12 months. If so, you will need to take just 12 months of this period's profits – so if the accounting period lasts 16 months, say, you multiply your profits by $^{12}/_{16}$.

Dealing with overlap profits

As the illustrations in Examples 8.6 and 8.7 show, when you start up in business some of your profits – 'overlap profits' – fall into more than one basis period. If you started in business before 6 April 1994, you may also have overlap profits that arose on the transition to self-assessment. You can claim 'overlap relief' for these profits – but only when you close your business or change your accounting date, by which time it may not be worth very much after taking inflation into account.

Overlap profits look as though they have been taxed twice. In practice, at the end of each tax year you will find that the number of months' profit on which you have been taxed, including the overlap period, is the same as the number of months in which you have been in business so far.

Note that if you make a loss in an overlap period, you cannot claim the whole loss in each overlapping basis period. Instead, part of the loss belongs to one tax year and the rest to the next tax year. (So if Belinda in Example 8.6 made a loss in her first accounting period, six-ninths of it would belong to 2010–11 and three-ninths to 2011–12.)

Keeping things simple

You have no overlap profits if you end your accounting period with the end of the tax year – which doesn't necessarily mean 5 April. If your accounting period ends on any date from 31 March to 4 April, you can treat it as ending on 5 April. The Office of Tax Simplification has recommended that HMRC makes 31 March or 5 April the default year end for new businesses.

When is your first tax bill due?

If you make any taxable profits in your first basis period (running up to 5 April), you will have to pay the tax on them by the following 31 January.

You may also have to start making payments on account on 31 January following the end of your first tax year in business, but as explained on page 30, you have to do this only if less than 80 per cent of your tax bill for the previous tax year was met from tax paid at source, and if more than £1,000 of your tax was *not* deducted at source. (See Example 8.8 overleaf.)

Planning your tax

Depending on your tax outstanding after the first tax year in business and when you end your first accounting period, you will have to start making payments on account anything from 10 to 22 months after the end of your first tax year in business. A long delay could mean a large bill to pay in one go, so plan ahead. (See Example 8.8.)

Example 8.8: **When do you first pay tax?**

Craig and Darren each started a business in October 2011, making a profit of £6,000 in 2011–12. Craig was unemployed for the first half of 2011–12, and his tax for the year is £430. He must send in his tax return and pay the tax by 31 January 2013, but he has no payments on account to make for 2012–13 because his 2011–12 tax was under £1,000.

Darren, however, was in a good job before he left to start up on his own, and his tax for 2011–12 comes to £4,370. He will have to make a payment on account for 2012–13 if less than £4,370 × 80% = £3,496 of his 2011–12 tax was paid at source and if the amount not paid at source is more than £1,000. His employer had deducted PAYE, but only £3,000, so on 31 January 2013, as well as paying the £4,370 – £3,000 = £1,370 tax outstanding for 2011–12, he must also start making payments on account for 2012–13. These are £1,370 ÷ 2 = £685, payable in January and July 2013.

For 2012–13 they again had the same profits and they each had a tax bill of £3,000, due on 31 January 2014. Darren had already paid £1,370 through his payments on account. But Craig had to pay the whole £3,000 in one go. At the same time, they both had to make their first payment on account of £1,500 for 2013–14:

		Craig	Darren
31 Jan 13	Outstanding tax for 2011–12	£430	£1,370
	First payment on account for 2012–13	–	£685
	Total tax to pay	£430	£2,055
31 July 13	Second payment on account for 2012–13	–	£685
31 Jan 14	Outstanding tax for 2012–13	£3,000	£1,630
	First payment on account for 2013–14	£1,500	£1,500
	Total tax to pay	£4,500	£3,130

> ## Choosing your accounting date

■ Depending on the date chosen, you may have a lot of overlap profits or none at all.

■ Overlaps work in your favour if your profits are rising, and against you if your profits are high in the first year and then drop.

■ The simplest option is to end your first accounting period at the end of a tax year; but ending your accounting period as early as possible in the tax year means that you have longer to work out your tax bill before you have to submit your return.

■ If your first accounting period is less than 12 months it will reduce the amount of annual investment allowance you can claim – see Example 8.3 on page 137.

When your business ends

You are taxed on your profits between the end of your basis period for the previous tax year and the date you stop trading or leave the partnership. If you have any profits when you close down, you can deduct any overlap relief brought forward. If you close with a loss, it is increased by the amount of any overlap relief.

Losses

If you make a loss, you must 'claim' it either by entering it on your tax return or by writing to your tax office. Then, if you do nothing else, the loss is carried forward indefinitely and used in the first year in which you have profits from the same business – even if those profits are not taxable because they are less than your personal allowances, say.

Alternatively, you may be able to claim relief immediately. You can set the loss against other income or gains of the same year (known as 'sideways' relief) or the previous year ('carry back'). Losses made in the first four years of starting up can be set against other income or gains of the previous three years, earliest year first. And if you make a loss in the year you close down you can carry it back against any profits from the same business made in the previous three years.

If you carry back losses, the tax saved is worked out using the rates of

Figure 8.1: Your choices for claiming a loss

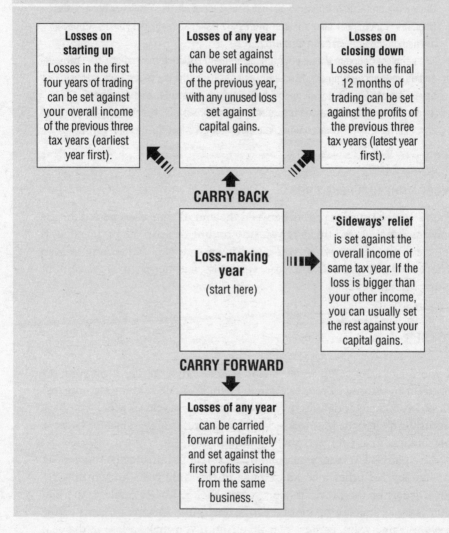

Losses on starting up
Losses in the first four years of trading can be set against your overall income of the previous three tax years (earliest year first).

Losses of any year
can be set against the overall income of the previous year, with any unused loss set against capital gains.

Losses on closing down
Losses in the final 12 months of trading can be set against the profits of the previous three tax years (latest year first).

CARRY BACK

Loss-making year
(start here)

'Sideways' relief
is set against the overall income of same tax year. If the loss is bigger than your other income, you can usually set the rest against your capital gains.

CARRY FORWARD

Losses of any year
can be carried forward indefinitely and set against the first profits arising from the same business.

tax that applied in the earlier year, and given as a credit against your self-assessment statement.

Your choices are summarised on Figure 8.1 opposite, and see HMRC help sheet 227 *Losses*. But note that if you do not spend at least ten hours a week (on average) running the business, you are restricted in the amount of losses that you can claim against your overall income. In the 2012 Budget, the government also said that it would cap some reliefs at £50,000 a year from April 2013. This is likely to include business loss relief.

If you are a partner in a partnership, any losses are shared out according to the partnership agreement, and can be used as each partner prefers.

Time limits for using your losses

It often makes sense to set your losses against other income or carry them back, rather than carry them forward against profits that may never arise. But this depends on your tax bill in the earlier and current years, and your likely profits in future.

If you want to carry back losses, or claim sideways relief, you must claim on your tax return (or tell your tax office) within 12 months of 31 January after the end of the tax year in which you made the loss, i.e. by 31 January 2014 for losses made in 2011–12. The time limit for claiming losses made in 2011–12 is longer – 5 April 2016 – if you just want to have your losses carried forward, or if your business ended in 2011–12 and you want the losses set against the profits of the previous three years.

Example 8.9: **Claiming a loss**

Anji made a loss of £5,000 in her first year in business and expects her profits for the next year to be low. She can carry her loss forward, or set it against the overall income of the current or previous tax years or the previous three tax years. Anji has some income from investments in the current tax year, but she will pay only basic-rate tax on this, whereas in the previous tax year (before she left her job to set up on her own) she was a higher-rate taxpayer. She will save most tax by carrying back her loss: £5,000 × 40% = £2,000.

Struggling in the economic crisis?

You may be facing a tax bill from a previous tax year even though you are expecting to make a loss this year. To ease the situation:

- see page 31 for how to reduce your payments on account
- see page 40 for HMRC's Business Payment Support Service, which may be able to give you further time to pay
- if you're really struggling to keep your business afloat, get help sooner rather than later – contact Business Debtline on 0800 197 6026.

National Insurance contributions

As a self-employed person, you may have to pay both Class 2 and Class 4 National Insurance contributions.

If you have a job as well as being self-employed, you may also have to pay Class 1 employees' NICs, but there is an overall maximum. You can apply to defer paying contributions. Details are given in HMRC forms CA72A *Application for deferment of payment of Class 1 National Insurance contributions* and CA72B *Deferment of payment of Class 2 and/or Class 4 National Insurance contributions*.

Class 2 NICs
These are flat-rate contributions of £2.65 a week in 2012–13 (£2.50 in 2011–12). When you start up in business, you should register with HMRC immediately. Payments are due on 31 January and 31 July, but you can pay by monthly or six-monthly direct debit. You will be sent a separate bill for any contributions between registering and the first direct debit. However, you do not have to pay once you are over state pension age.

If your profits are less than £5,595 in 2012–13, you can apply not to pay Class 2 contributions. But this could affect your right to state pension and some other benefits, so you may want to continue paying. (Full details are given in form CF10 *Self-employed people with small earnings*.)

Class 4 NICs

You do not have to pay Class 4 NICs for any tax year if, on the first day of that year, you are over state pension age. Otherwise, you pay a percentage of your profits. Table 8.3 shows the rates and thresholds payable in 2012–13; for 2011–12 rates and thresholds see page 355. So if your taxable profits are £46,875 in 2012–13, say, you would pay nothing on the first £7,605, 9 per cent on the next £34,870 (i.e. £3,138) and 2 per cent on anything over £42,475 (i.e. £46,875 – £42,475 = £4,400 × 2 per cent = £88). This comes to £3,138 + £88 = £3,226 in total.

Class 4 NICs are collected with your income tax through your payments on account and any balancing payment. If you have more than one business, the rate payable depends on the total profit from all your businesses (see HMRC help sheet 220 *More than one business*). If you are a partner in a partnership you pay Class 4 NICs on just your share of the partnership's profits. You do not have to pay them if you are a sleeping partner, contributing to, but not working in, the partnership.

Table 8.3: Class 4 NICs for 2012–13

Slice of taxable profits	Rate payable
First £7,605	Nil
Next £34,870	9%
Anything above £42,475	2%

Use your losses

You can use losses to reduce your Class 4 NICs. However, if you choose for income tax purposes to set your losses against non-trading income (which is not liable to Class 4 contributions), you will have unused losses for National Insurance purposes. You do not have to use them the same way as for income tax, and instead you can carry them forward to set against future profits when working out Class 4 NICs. (See Example 8.10.)

Paid too much National Insurance?

You may have paid too much National Insurance if, for example, you had losses from a previous year that you have not yet set against profits, or if you carried on paying even though you were over state pension age (see page 12). If you think you might have paid too much, contact HMRC's National Insurance Contributions and Employer Office (see the Fact file).

Example 8.10: **How losses can reduce Class 4 NICs**

Anji (from Example 8.9) had a loss of £5,000 that she set against her non-trading income of an earlier year – but this income wasn't liable to Class 4 NICs. So she still has the whole £5,000 available to reduce her profits for the purposes of Class 4 NICs in future years.

Thinking of taking somebody on?

You must deduct National Insurance once your employee's pay rises above £146 a week in 2012–13, and PAYE above £155 a week, although new businesses in some areas may qualify for a National Insurance holiday. The holiday applies to businesses that start trading after 21 June 2010 and before 6 September 2013, and to NICs due between 6 September 2010 and 5 September 2013. If you qualify, you can deduct up to £5,000 from the employer NICs that would normally be due in the first 12 months of employment, for each of the first ten employees you take on. The qualifying areas, calculators and other information are on the government business website at www.businesslink.gov.uk (search on 'NICs holiday').

Even if you don't have to deduct National Insurance, you must register as an employer with HMRC if your employee has another job, or if you provide any benefits, or if you pay more than the 'lower earnings limit' of £107 a week in 2012–13, as this will affect your employee's right to state benefits. Contact HMRC's helpline for new employers on 0845 607 0143.

What to tell HMRC

The most important thing is to register as self-employed, or a partner, as soon as you start trading. If you don't register by 31 January following the end of the tax year, and you have no reasonable excuse, you will have to pay a penalty unless you can show that no tax or National Insurance was due.

You can register using the form CWF1 (on the HMRC website), or online, or by phoning the helpline for the newly self-employed (0845 915 4515). HMRC has Advice Teams that run free local workshops (see the Fact file), and you may find leaflets SE1 *Thinking of working for yourself?* and SE2 *Giving your business the best start with tax* helpful. There is also a wealth of information and useful tools in the 'My New Business' area of the website www.businesslink.gov.uk.

Once you have registered, you should receive tax returns and will have to complete the Self-employment or Partnership supplementary pages – though probably only a short version if your turnover is below £73,000 over a full year and your affairs are simple (see page 303).

If you stop trading, phone HMRC's National Insurance self-employed helpline (0845 915 4655) and cancel your Class 2 National Insurance contributions.

Tax relief on pre-trading expenses

You can claim tax relief on business expenses incurred in the seven years before you formally start in business. You deduct the expenses from your turnover in your first trading period, so make sure you keep records of all possible expenses. If you register for VAT, you can also claim back VAT on some pre-registration expenses, but you will need a receipt showing the supplier's VAT registration number.

A partner in a partnership?

The partnership gets its own tax return which covers all the business profits received by the partnership. It also contains a 'partnership statement' that tells your tax office how the income and gains have been shared out between the partners. Individual partners also get Partnership supplementary pages for their own tax returns, covering their share of the profit or loss, and any adjustments claimed by them as individuals (e.g. losses).

Setting up your records

When you start up, spend some time getting your records set up to make filling in your tax return easy. Do get help to establish what expenses you can claim – as well as on accounting periods and whether you should set up a company or partnership rather than operating as a sole trader. Note that online filing of VAT returns, employers' PAYE returns and company tax returns is now compulsory for nearly all businesses.

Special rules for some trades

- Agriculture – see HMRC help sheets 224 *Farmers and market gardeners* and 232 *Farm and stock valuation*.
- Art and literature – see help sheet 234 *Averaging for creators of literary or artistic works*.
- Foster or adult care – see help sheet 236 *Qualifying care relief*.
- Construction – see leaflet CIS340 *Construction industry scheme* and the construction industry section on the HMRC website at www.hmrc.gov.uk/cis.

Record-keeping

You do not need to send a copy of your accounts to your tax office. But you must keep records to back up your entries, and you must keep all records for at least five years and ten months from the end of the tax year (so records for the 2012–13 tax year must be kept until 31 January 2019). See page 15 and HMRC factsheet TH/FS1 *Keeping records for business – what you need to know*. There are various tools to help you set up a record-keeping system on the 'Record-keeping (self-employed)' section of the Business

Link website. These guides have lists of records to keep (such as records of income and expenses, receipts and invoices), but don't forget:

■ if you are starting up, the date you registered as self-employed and a note of how you did so (or a copy of the registration form)
■ transactions between your business and your private finances (it is usually simplest to keep separate bank accounts)
■ bank statements showing business transactions
■ stock and work in progress at the end of the accounting period
■ cash transactions, such as till rolls and a daily note of tips received
■ payments to staff, including (if you are in the building trade) records of tax deducted from payments and a note of what you did to decide whether staff were employees or self-employed
■ business mileage in a car used both privately and for work (and running expenses if you are not using the HMRC-approved mileage rates)
■ any losses made and how much of them you have set against your profits for income tax, tax credits and Class 4 National Insurance purposes. Because your choices for how you use your losses are slightly different in each case, you can end up with different amounts of unused loss (see page 149).

If you keep your records on computer you must also keep your original paper records unless you copy them electronically (back and front) in a readable format.

9

Income from property

Whether you take in a lodger to help with your mortgage, rent out your home while working overseas, or own a buy-to-let property, if you make money from property – whether you own it or not – you'll usually be liable for income tax. And if you make a profit when you sell a property, there may be a capital gains tax bill, covered in Chapter 14.

Top tips

- If you take in a lodger, you pay no tax on the income you receive if you charge less than the Rent-a-Room limit (£354 a month or £177 if letting jointly).
- If you let out furnished holiday property, you may be able to claim relief under favourable rules. See page 158.
- You can claim tax relief on a mortgage to buy a property you let out, but not on a mortgage on your own home (unless you let out part of it).
- If you employ your partner or children to do the cleaning or gardening at the properties you let you can claim what you pay them as an allowable expense – you can't do this if you do the work yourself. But they must actually do the work and be paid at a realistic rate.
- There are tax advantages if you convert a flat above a shop to rent out before 1 April 2013 (see page 163).
- Living for a period in a property you let can reduce the capital gains tax when you sell – see page 231.

What tax is payable?

Income from land or property falls into the following broad categories:

■ Tax-free income from letting out a room in the home you are living in under the Rent-a-Room scheme (see overleaf).

■ Rental income from letting out land or property in the UK. This is lumped together, however many properties you have. You can deduct various outgoings, such as mortgage interest (see page 162).

■ Rental income from land or property abroad. This is taxed separately from UK rental income, although the taxable amount is calculated in broadly the same way (see page 176).

■ Trading income, if the way you make your money from the property counts as a trade, such as running a guest house. If so, the tax is worked out using the rules for self-employment. See page 157 and Chapter 8.

■ Furnished holiday lettings. Income from lettings in the UK or Europe may qualify for some of the advantages of trading income, although it is still taxed as property income (see page 176).

■ Income from investing in property through an investment fund. This is normally taxed as investment income, except for some payments from a 'Real Estate Investment Trust' or 'Property Authorised Investment Fund' which are taxed as property income (see page 198).

If you have any taxable property income (excluding trading income), it is added to your other non-savings income and taxed at 20 per cent, or 40 per cent if it takes your total income over the higher-rate threshold of £34,370 in 2012–13, or 50 per cent if it takes it over the additional-rate threshold of £150,000 a year (see page 5).

Capital gains tax

Capital gains tax may also apply when you sell land or property or give it away (to a child, say). The whole of any gain in the value of the property is potentially subject to capital gains tax although, if you sell at a loss to someone to whom you are not 'connected', you can use the loss to reduce other taxable gains.

You can reduce or eliminate the gain if you live in the property as your only or main home at some point. If so, you can claim 'private residence relief', depending on how much time you spent there and how much of the house you occupied. You don't lose any private residence relief if you just let a room to a lodger who shared your living space. But you may lose part of the relief if the part of your home you let was self-contained, or you made major structural alterations. If you made no structural alterations, you may also be able to claim 'lettings relief' (see page 233).

If you have two properties which you use as a home, you can nominate one as your main residence. You can choose which one, but there are strict time limits for doing so. See page 232.

Stamp duty

There is no stamp duty land tax to pay if you buy residential property worth less than £125,000, or non-residential property worth less than £150,000, or a new zero-carbon home. Otherwise, the tax is 1 per cent of the purchase price if the property is worth £250,000 or less, 3 per cent if it is worth £250,001 to £500,000, 4 per cent above £500,000, 5 per cent above £1 million and, from 22 March 2012, 7 per cent above £2 million. The government is also introducing special charges to stop people holding property in a company or investment scheme to avoid tax.

Tax-free income from property

Under the Rent-a-Room scheme, the first £4,250 of income each tax year from letting a room (or rooms) in your home is tax-free. This applies to owner-occupiers and those who sublet a room in a home they rent. If you share a home, the person who lets the room gets the whole exemption of £4,250. If two (or more) people share the rental income, or you rent out separate rooms in a joint home, each gets an exemption of £2,125.

If the money your lodger pays is more than the exempt amount that you're entitled to, the rest counts as income from a rental business and is taxable. So if you receive £5,000 in rent and are entitled to the full exemption of £4,250, you'll pay tax only on £5,000 − £4,250 = £750.

Rent-a-Room is usually the best option

Under the Rent-a-Room scheme, you cannot claim any expenses. You do not have to claim Rent-a-Room relief, but unless you have expenses of more than £4,250 (£2,125 if you let jointly) from letting a room in your home (which is unlikely in most cases), you will be better off – and have less paperwork to deal with – if you do claim. If you are just over the £4,250 threshold, get your lodger to pay some bills separately. If it is included in the rent, the money for bills counts as income and you'll have to pay tax on it.

Property classed as a trade

This receives advantages that do not apply to other rental properties. For example, you can claim investment and capital allowances for the cost of furnishing your property. You can also use losses from the property to reduce tax on non-property income, and claim 'entrepreneurs' relief' on selling up (see page 235) and business property relief from inheritance tax (see page 252).

The key requirement for your property to be classed as a trade is that you remain the legal occupier of the premises (whether or not you live there), retain control over them, and provide services or facilities to someone else. By contrast, if you allow someone to occupy your premises for payment, it counts as a rental business. The following count as a trade:

- using your home to run a guest house or B&B
- charging tenants (in a property you don't live in) for services – such as meals and laundry – which are well beyond the services normally provided by a landlord; for tax purposes, you should record these charges separately from the rents you receive even if the tenant pays you a single amount to cover rent and services
- farming and market gardening
- exploiting the natural resources on your land – this includes things like mining, quarrying and cutting timber from woodland.

> ## Rent-a-Room for traders

Although the income you get from using your home to run a B&B, guest house or small hotel counts as trading – rather than rental – income, you can still claim Rent-a-Room relief. (For more information, see HMRC help sheet 223 *Rent a Room for traders*.)

Furnished holiday lettings

Income from property that meets the 'furnished holiday lettings' test below is not trading income, but it gets many of the same advantages and is taxed separately from other rental income. It lets you claim trading loss relief for tax years before 6 April 2011 (see page 145), capital allowances (see page 136), and some capital gains tax reliefs, such as entrepreneurs' relief (see page 235). It is also classed as 'earnings' if you want to pay more than £2,880 a year into a pension (see page 208).

The Labour government planned to abolish this favourable treatment, but the Coalition government decided to keep it, although properties must meet a stricter test from 6 April 2012 (1 April for companies).

These rules used to apply only to property in the UK. But you can now claim them for qualifying properties in the European Economic Area and you can claim in arrears, provided that you do so within the time limit for making claims.

The furnished holiday lettings test
You can take advantage of the special rules for holiday property provided that the property is furnished and you meet all of the following conditions in the 12 months covered by the tax year. However, in the first year of letting, the 12 months runs from the date the property was first let; in the final year of letting the 12 months runs to the date of the last letting. Whichever time period applies, the property must:

- be available for letting at a commercial rent for at least 210 days (140 days before April 2012)
- actually be let on commercial terms for at least 105 days (70 days

before April 2012). If you have more than one property they can be let for at least 105 days on average (70 days on average before April 2012). If you meet the 105-day condition in one year and intend to meet it in future, you can elect to be treated as meeting it in each of the two following years, even if you do not. To claim this you must tell your tax office by 31 January after the end of the tax year

■ not have been rented out on longer-term lets (i.e. more than 31 days) for more than 155 days in total during the year.

Furnished holiday losses – it's not too late to benefit

If you make a loss on furnished holiday lettings in 2011–12 or any later year, your only option is to carry it forward and set it against future profits from your holiday lettings. However, if you made a loss in 2010–11 or earlier tax years, you can also claim to set it against non-property income, or possibly carry it back to previous tax years (as shown in Figure 8.1 on page 146). You must claim by 31 January 2013 if you want to do this with a loss made in 2010–11.

Other rental income

As well as rents, income from a rental business includes:

■ service charges, ground rents and (in Scotland) feu duties
■ income from caravans or houseboats that never go anywhere
■ income from sporting rights such as fishing and shooting permits
■ income from allowing waste to be buried or stored on your land
■ payments for allowing other people to use your property – e.g. to store things in your shed or as a location for a film
■ grants from local authorities or others for repairs (not improvements)
■ refunds of running costs you claimed previously as allowable expenses
■ payouts from rental guarantee insurance
■ lump sums you receive when you grant a lease of less than 50 years

Working out your taxable profits on rental income

All your rental income from property in the UK is lumped together, with the exception of any property that qualifies for special treatment as trading income or furnished holiday lettings. This means that if you have more than one property, you don't need to work out the profit (or loss) separately for each one. You can ignore income that is tax-free under the Rent-a-Room scheme (see page 156).

You don't pay tax on all the rental income you receive because you can deduct the expenses involved in letting your property. You cannot deduct 'capital expenditure', which includes the purchase price of the property and the cost of any improvements to it – although you may be able to claim an allowance for some capital costs (see page 163). You can also deduct losses made in previous years.

Tax is based on the profits from rental income due to you in a tax year even if you don't get some of the income until after the end of the tax year (see below) and even if your accounts cover a different 12-month period.

Below we explain how to work out your taxable profits, but full details are in the *Property Income Manual* on the HMRC website.

A simpler way of working out your profits

Strictly speaking, when working out your taxable profits, you should include rent (and other income from property) that is earned from the tenant's use of the property in a tax year – called the 'earnings basis' – irrespective of when you got the money. However, you may be able to work out your profits using the simpler 'cash basis' where you base your figures on the cash paid and received in the tax year if your gross rental income is less than £15,000 and you always use the cash basis when working out your profits.

Tell HMRC under 'Any other information' in your tax return if you are doing this, and beware – you might not be allowed to use the cash basis if it means that your profits are substantially lower than they would be if you had used the stricter earnings basis.

What expenses can you claim?

To be able to deduct the full amount of other costs, they must be incurred 'wholly and exclusively' in letting the property. If you incur an expense partly for private use (e.g. you use a holiday property for your own holidays or let friends and family use it rent-free), you can deduct only the proportion of the expense which relates to the commercial letting of it. So if you use the property for your own holidays for a month each year, you will be able to claim only $^{11}/_{12}$ of any expenses that do not arise wholly from the letting.

HMRC divides allowable expenses into six main categories.

Rent, rates, insurance, ground rents etc.
- rent if you lease a property which you then sublet
- buildings, contents and rental guarantee insurance (which provides cover against non-payment of rent)
- business rates, council tax, water rates, ground rents, feu duties (in Scotland), service charges (for flats)
- gas and electricity bills, less any amount your tenants contribute towards them

Repairs, maintenance and renewals
- repairs and maintenance, but not most improvements (see page 163)
- painting and decorating – inside and out
- other work necessary to prevent the property from deteriorating – e.g. stone-cleaning and damp treatment
- renewing and replacing moveable objects such as furniture, domestic appliances, cutlery and crockery. You can claim either the actual cost or a 'wear and tear' allowance. This is 10 per cent of the rent you receive, minus council tax and other bills that you, rather than your tenant, pay. You cannot claim a wear and tear allowance for furnished holiday lettings
- Until April 2015, Landlord's Energy Saving Allowance for the cost of draught-proofing, or insulating walls, floors, lofts or hot-water systems in residential property (up to £1,500 for each residence). You cannot claim for property on which you are also claiming Rent-a-Room relief, or for furnished holiday lettings

Wear and tear advantage

The advantage of choosing to claim a wear and tear allowance rather than deducting the cost of replacement items is that you can make the deduction every year even if you haven't replaced anything. It also makes record-keeping simpler. But once you have chosen the way in which you are going to get tax relief on renewals, you can't change your mind.

Finance charges, including interest
- interest on a mortgage or another type of loan to buy the property and any charges involved in taking out the loan, such as arrangement fees
- payments on an alternative finance arrangement (see page 189)
- bank charges and overdraft interest on a separate business account

Legal and professional costs
- legal fees for renewing a lease (provided it is for less than 50 years) or evicting a tenant
- fees charged by an accountant for drawing up your accounts
- management fees for the cost of letting – e.g. cost of a letting agent

Costs of services provided, including wages
- costs of services you provide such as cleaning and gardening, but only if you pay someone else to provide them; you cannot claim the cost of your own time (see 'Top tips' on page 154)

Other expenses
- advertising costs
- stationery, phone calls and other incidental expenses
- travel costs provided travel was solely for business purposes – travelling to inspect your holiday cottage and then coming straight back will count but travelling to inspect your holiday home while taking a holiday in it will not
- expenses incurred before you started letting, provided they would have been allowable if incurred once the letting had begun

Combining repairs with improvements

If you combine repair work with improvements to the property, none of the cost of the work can be claimed as an allowable expense. Similarly, if you replace fixtures and fittings, such as kitchen units, and upgrade them at the same time – you replace cheap units with designer versions, for example – the cost counts as capital expenditure and so is not allowable.

However, if an 'improvement' occurs in order to meet modern building standards, the cost is allowable. A good example is replacing single-glazed windows with double-glazed or installing insulation (see page 161). So keep good records of your maintenance work and try to keep any 'improvements' separate.

Furnishing and equipping your property

You cannot claim for capital expenditure on your property, for example buying it in the first place, doing it up and installing fixtures and fittings (although you can claim moveable items and mortgage interest as an expense, see opposite). But you can use capital expenditure to reduce any capital gains tax on the property (see page 226), and you can claim annual investment allowance or capital allowances for:

■ equipment you need to run the letting business – this includes things like ladders, lawnmowers, tools, computers, filing cabinets and other business furniture
■ furnishing and equipping a furnished holiday property, providing that this qualifies for the favourable treatment described on page 158.

See page 136 and HMRC help sheet 252 *Capital allowances and balancing charges*. You can also claim the following 100 per cent allowances:

■ business premises renovation allowance for renovating vacant business premises in disadvantaged areas
■ flat conversion allowance for the cost of converting flats over shops and business premises (although this will be abolished from 6 April 2013).

Using losses

A loss you make on letting one property is deducted from your income from other properties and so reduces the size of your taxable profit for the tax year. If you don't have any other property income to set your loss against, or your loss is greater than your income, the unused loss is carried forward to future tax years. However, losses carried forward can be set only against future profits from your rental business.

You have more options if in 2010–11 or previous tax years, you made a loss on furnished holiday property that qualifies for special treatment – see page 158. Your only option for losses made in 2011–12 or later tax years is to carry them forward and set them against future profits from furnished holiday lettings. And if you have properties overseas see page 176.

What to tell HMRC

If you don't get a tax return and your only income from property is rent below the tax-free Rent-a-Room scheme limit, you don't need to tell HMRC anything. But you must tell your tax office if:

- you have been receiving Rent-a-Room relief but want to stop claiming or no longer qualify, e.g. you have moved but are still receiving the lodger's rent, or the rent has risen above the tax-free amount or
- you receive any other income from property.

Unless you get a tax return, you must notify your tax office by 5 October after the end of the year in which you first start getting taxable property income – i.e. by 5 October 2012 for income received in the 2011–12 tax year. This is also the deadline for telling your tax office if you have sold a property and made a taxable capital gain (see Chapter 14). But if your income from property counts as trading income (see page 157), you must register as self-employed as soon as possible (see page 151).

Once you have notified your tax office, you will usually be sent a tax return, but if you are taxed under PAYE the tax may be collected by adjusting your tax code (see page 21). If so, check that your Coding Notice shows the right amount of property income. If you prefer, you can ask your tax office not to collect the tax through PAYE. This will increase your regular income, but you will have to fill in a tax return and pay the tax on your property income in one or two lump sums each year (see page 30). You will have to do this in any case if you have no income taxed under PAYE.

If you get a tax return and receive any income from property, you should put a cross in the relevant box on page TR2 of the core tax return and fill in the UK Property supplementary pages unless:

▪ the way you make money from your home counts as a trade (see page 157), in which case you should fill in the Self-employment or Partnership supplementary pages, as relevant
▪ the property is abroad – if so, fill in the Foreign supplementary pages, unless you are claiming to have it treated as furnished holiday lettings. These always go in the UK Property pages even if they are in Europe
▪ you have Property Income Dividends from a Real Estate Investment Trust or Property Authorised Investment Fund (see page 198). Enter this income under 'Any other income' in the main tax return.

Record-keeping

The records you have to keep if you have income from property are similar to those you have to keep if you run any kind of business (see page 152). You must keep them for at least five years and ten months after the end of the tax year. In addition to keeping evidence of all your income and relevant expenditure, you should keep a record of the number of days the property was offered for letting at a commercial rent, and the days when it was actually let (to see if you meet the furnished holiday lettings test and also to work out the proportion of an expense that counts as personal use – see page 161). For jointly owned property, also note the proportion in which the income and expenses were shared.

You will also need records for capital gains and inheritance tax purposes, so keep records of amounts spent on buying and doing up the property, dates you lived there, dates it was offered for rent (and let out) and how many rooms were occupied by you and how many by tenants. See pages 236 and 254.

10

Tax on foreign income

You can't forget about UK tax if you go overseas to work, or have an income from overseas property, investments or pensions. If you are resident in the UK, overseas income and capital gains are taxed in much the same way as other income or gains. This chapter explains what happens if you count as non-resident, but note that major changes to the definition of 'non-resident' are likely to apply from April 2013.

Top tips

- Don't invest offshore in the hope of saving tax if you are resident in the UK and it is your long-term home (your 'domicile'). The income is still liable to UK tax and HMRC has powers to force banks to give details of people holding offshore accounts.
- If you let out UK property while abroad, apply to have the rent paid out gross. Otherwise, it will be paid with tax deducted (see page 177).
- If you work abroad for long enough to be classed as non-resident, your foreign earnings will be free of UK tax. But this may not save UK inheritance tax or capital gains tax and may affect your right to tax credits (see pages 68, 172 and 176).
- Even if you do not have to pay UK National Insurance contributions when abroad, it may still be worth doing so to protect your rights to UK benefits.
- A special tax relief can save you UK tax if you have already paid foreign tax on overseas income or gains (see page 178).

How your residence affects your tax

For tax purposes, the Channel Islands and Isle of Man count as 'overseas'; the UK covers England, Wales, Scotland and Northern Ireland.

If you are resident in the UK, but you have overseas income, or you own property or other assets abroad, you will have to declare your foreign income and capital gains, and may have to pay tax on them. The exception is if you claim the 'remittance basis' (see page 173).

Non-residents do not have to pay UK tax on foreign income. But they may still have to pay it on UK income and (if only temporarily non-resident) UK capital gains. This is covered on page 176, and non-residence is defined on page 170. There is guidance in HMRC booklet HMRC6 *Residence, domicile and the remittance basis* (available on the HMRC website); and in the notes to the Residence, remittance basis etc. pages of the tax return.

Note that you have to be living in the UK to claim tax credits (see Chapter 5), although temporary absences of up to eight weeks (occasionally 12 weeks) are ignored.

Checking your residence status

There are currently three types of 'residence' that might affect your tax: residence, 'ordinary' residence, and 'domicile'. The effect that they have is summarised in Table 10.1 overleaf, and see Example 10.1 on page 171. Note that it is possible to be resident in two countries at once, but you can have only one domicile at a time.

If you become non-resident during the tax year

Your residence is normally fixed for the whole year. But you may be able to claim 'split-year' treatment if you can show your absence abroad is likely to meet the conditions for non-residence, or if you were not ordinarily resident before your departure. If so, you are treated as non-resident as soon as you leave. Note that the government is considering changes to these rules.

Table 10.1: Summary of how foreign income and gains are taxed in the UK

If you are	Taxable	Taxable only if remitted to UK	Not taxable in UK
Resident and			
■ ordinarily resident, domiciled	all foreign income (minus 10% of foreign pensions); foreign capital gains		
■ not ordinarily resident, domiciled	foreign capital gains	if you claim the 'remittance basis' (see page 173), all foreign income*	
■ ordinarily resident, non-domiciled	earnings from working abroad for a UK-resident employer	if you claim the 'remittance basis' (see page 173), all other foreign income and capital gains*	
■ not ordinarily resident, not domiciled			
Not resident and			
■ ordinarily resident, domiciled	foreign capital gains		all foreign income
■ ordinarily resident, non-domiciled		foreign capital gains, if you claim the remittance basis	all foreign income
■ not ordinarily resident, (domiciled or non-domiciled)			all foreign income; foreign capital gains unless only temporarily non-resident

*If you do not claim the remittance basis, the foreign income and gains are taxable in the UK.

Tax-free foreign income and gains

Table 10.1 opposite shows which types of income and gains are tax-free if you are not resident in the UK.

If you are a UK resident, the same types of income and capital gains that are tax-free in the UK are tax-free if they come from overseas. So, for example, foreign social security benefits that correspond to tax-free UK social security benefits are also tax-free. But some special tax reliefs, such as the Rent-a-Room scheme (see Chapter 9), do not apply overseas.

> ### Foreign pensions are favourably taxed
>
> 10% of the income from a foreign pension is tax-free for UK residents, and a UK pension lump sum might also be partly or fully tax-free if it came from a job that involved working overseas. Claim the relief in your tax return or contact your tax office.

How the tax is worked out on foreign income and gains

- *Step 1:* check your residence status (see overleaf).
- *Step 2:* check how much of your foreign income and gains is taxable in the UK. You may not have to pay tax on all of it (see Table 10.1).
- *Step 3:* check whether any special rules apply, if you are working abroad, or have investments or a property overseas, or if you are claiming the remittance basis (see page 173 onwards).
- *Step 4:* convert to sterling. Use the rate of exchange at the time the income arose, unless it is taxable only when you bring it in to the UK (if so, use the rate at the time it is brought in). You can use the average exchange rates on the HMRC website (see the Fact file).

Any taxable foreign income or gains are taxed at the same rate as any UK income or gains of the same type, but you can claim relief for any foreign tax already paid (see page 178).

Are you non-resident?

If you are non-resident, your foreign income is not taxable in the UK. The rules are complex and the government is planning to introduce a clearer definition from April 2013 (see page 172). But currently, you can claim to be non-resident if:

- *either* you go abroad to work full-time as an employee (or accompany a husband, wife or civil partner who is working abroad) and are away for at least one whole tax year
- *or* you have gone abroad to live permanently or indefinitely (which means at least three years). You will need to show that you are no longer resident in the UK – HMRC will look at how far you have broken your family, social and business ties with the UK, for example by buying a permanent home abroad and selling your UK home.

You can come back to the UK for visits, provided that your visits since leaving the UK have totalled less than 183 days in any tax year and averaged less than 91 days in a tax year. (The average is worked out over four tax years, or the period of your absence if less, and excludes days in the UK for exceptional reasons, such as illness.)

Counting the days

If you are in the UK at the end of the day (midnight) it counts as a day in the UK (unless you are just in transit, and not in the UK to work, see HMRC booklet HMRC6). This applies from 6 April 2008 - for tax years before then, days of arrival and departure are ignored.

Frequent flyers

Even if you spend more than 183 days abroad, and are home for less than 91 days a year, HMRC is unlikely to treat you as non-resident if you have no settled home abroad, no intention of staying abroad indefinitely, and return to a UK base and UK home at the end of each trip overseas.

Example 10.1: **Claiming non-residence**

Nigel and Ben both go abroad to work full-time for 15 months and both spend only 42 days in the UK during their absence. However, only Nigel is treated as non-resident. That's because he left in February 2011 and returned in May 2012, and so was away for the whole of the 2011–12 tax year. Ben, however, left, in May 2011 and returned in August 2012 – so he did not meet the condition of being away for a whole tax year. Because it was clear that Nigel was going to be non-resident, he could claim 'split-year' treatment for 2010–11 and all his overseas earnings were tax-free, even though he left part way through a tax year.

Are you ordinarily resident?

If you are not resident, you are usually not ordinarily resident either. But you might be classed as non-resident but ordinarily resident if, say, you usually live in the UK but have gone abroad for an extended holiday and do not set foot in the UK during a whole tax year. If so, your foreign income is not taxable in the UK but any foreign capital gains will be. Note that the government is considering restricting ordinary residence.

If you come to the UK, you may become resident but remain not ordinarily resident, for example if it is clear that you intend to stay less than three years (four years for students). If so:

■ you can claim the remittance basis (see page 173)
■ you can receive savings interest from a UK bank, building society or investment fund without having tax deducted, by completing form R105 (available from the financial organisation or HMRC)
■ interest from British Government Stock (gilts) is completely tax-free.

Are you non-domiciled in the UK?

Broadly speaking, your domicile is the country regarded as your permanent home. It is not the same as your nationality, but will normally be the country in which your father was domiciled at the time of your birth (not necessarily the country where you were born), or your mother's domicile if your parents were not married. Women married before 1974 have their husband's domicile. You can change your domicile but it is difficult. Being non-domiciled has two main implications:

- You can claim the remittance basis (see opposite)
- Your overseas assets may be free of UK inheritance tax, but if your spouse or civil partner is UK-domiciled they cannot transfer more than £55,000 in total to you without risking a tax bill (see page 243). The government is considering increasing the £55,000 limit.

Long-term planning for inheritance tax

You cannot escape UK inheritance tax on your overseas property by a last-minute move abroad. Even if you are non-domiciled, you are still liable to inheritance tax if you were domiciled in the UK in the previous three years, or if you were a UK resident in 17 of the previous 20 years. (See the *Inheritance Tax Customer Guide* on the HMRC website.)

A new definition of non-residence

The government is planning to introduce a new definition of non-residence from April 2013. This is subject to change, but under current proposals you would be:

1. *Definitely non-resident* for each tax year in which you were:
   - in the UK for under 45 days and non-resident in all of the three previous tax years *or*
   - in the UK for under 10 days and resident in the UK for one or more of the previous tax years *or*
   - working full-time abroad, provided you are in the UK for under 90 days, with no more than 20 days spent working in the UK.
2. *Definitely resident* for each tax year in which:
   - you were in the UK for 183 days or more *or*
   - all your homes are in the UK *or*
   - you worked full-time in the UK.
3. *If you fall into neither category 1 nor category 2*, HMRC will look at both

the time you spent in the UK and the factors that connect you with the UK – that is, whether your family is UK-resident, whether you work in the UK or have accommodation here, and your residence status or length of time here in previous tax years. The more factors that apply, and the longer you spend in the UK, the more likely you are to be classed as resident. It will be up to you to 'self-assess' your residence status. The government is considering developing an interactive online tool to help you do this.

Claiming the remittance basis

If you are a UK resident, all your income and gains from abroad are normally liable to UK tax from the date they become yours, even if they stay overseas. This is called the 'arising' basis. However, if you are not domiciled or not ordinarily resident in the UK, you can choose to pay UK tax only when you actually bring the money into the UK. This is called the 'remittance' basis.

You can decide each year whether to claim the remittance basis – it may not be worth claiming. It depends on whether the foreign income and gains you leave overseas come to £2,000 or more in the tax year:

- *Less than £2,000* – you get the remittance basis automatically, and there are unlikely to be any disadvantages, although you can opt for the arising basis instead. If you are sent a tax return you should fill in the Residence, remittance basis etc. supplementary pages.
- *More than £2,000* – if you claim the remittance basis you cannot usually claim UK personal allowances or the capital gains tax-free amount or (unless you elect to do so) losses on foreign assets. If you have been resident here for seven or more of the previous nine tax years, you must also pay an annual tax charge of £30,000. From 6 April 2012 the charge will be £50,000 if you have been resident for at least 12 of the previous 14 tax years, but will not apply if you are bringing money in for commercial investment in UK businesses. If you want to claim, fill in the Residence, remittance basis etc. supplementary pages. See HMRC help sheet 264 *Remittance basis*.

> ## Money stuck overseas

Whatever your residence status, if you cannot bring the money into the UK, because of exchange controls, say, you can claim that it is 'unremittable'. You pay tax on it when it does become possible to transfer it to the UK, even if you choose to leave it where it is (unless you are claiming the remittance basis anyway).

Working abroad

Provided that you go to live and work abroad on an employment contract lasting for at least a whole tax year, and you meet the conditions on page 170, you will be non-resident. All your earnings abroad will be free of UK tax.

If you are a non-resident employee, but your job involves working partly abroad and partly in the UK, your UK earnings (worked out in proportion to the number of days in the UK) are taxable unless they are 'incidental' to your work abroad. However, you may be able to claim full relief under a double taxation agreement with the other country.

If you are self-employed and non-resident, your business has to be controlled overseas for the profits to be tax-free, and the profits of any UK branch or agency are taxable here.

If you are UK-resident, your foreign earnings as an employee are taxable in the UK. However, you may be able to claim extra deductions:

- At the start or end of the job, travel costs between the UK and your workplace abroad, provided that your employer is UK-resident.
- During the course of the job, travel to and from the UK, provided that your employer pays the costs or reimburses you.
- The cost of board and lodging overseas, provided that this is paid or reimbursed by your employer, who must be UK-resident.
- If you work abroad for at least 60 days in a row, travel costs for your spouse or civil partner and children, provided that your employer pays.
- Seafarers who are out of the UK for a 'qualifying absence' of 365 days or more can claim to have their foreign earnings tax-free (see HMRC help sheet 205 *Seafarers' earnings deduction*).

■ You may qualify for tax relief on contributions to an overseas pension fund. Ask your tax office or see HMRC help sheet 211 *Employment – residence and domicile issues*.

■ If you are not domiciled in the UK (see HMRC help sheet 211).

You may get special treatment if you are working at sea, or in the gas and oil industries, or in entertainment or sport, or if you are an employee of the Crown or European Union, or a citizen of the Commonwealth, Republic of Ireland, Isle of Man or Channel Islands. Further details are given in HMRC booklet HMRC6.

National Insurance contributions while abroad

Whether you pay social security contributions in the country in which you are working or the UK depends on the country you are visiting and how long you expect to be away. See HMRC booklet HMRC6.

Not paying UK contributions means that your right to some UK state benefits, such as a state pension, may be affected. If you plan to return to the UK, it may be worth paying Class 2 or Class 3 National Insurance contributions in the UK to protect your pension. (See HMRC leaflet NI38 *Social Security Abroad* and the Department for Work and Pensions website at www.dwp.gov.uk/international.)

Investing abroad

If you are a UK resident, income from an 'offshore' investment is liable to UK tax, but dividends from most non-UK companies qualify for the same 10 per cent tax credit as UK dividends and you may also be able to claim relief for foreign tax (see page 178).

Most foreign investment income you get is added to any UK income of the same type and taxed at the same rate – so interest is taxed at 20 per cent if you are a basic-rate taxpayer, and dividends at 10 per cent (see page 193).

When you sell your overseas investments, you are liable to capital gains tax in the same way as if you sell UK investments, except for some offshore funds. With these, your gains when you sell are taxed as income, unless the fund is a 'reporting' fund. If so, any income that is 'reported' to you will be taxed as income, with any gain on disposal being liable to capital gains tax. There is a list of 'reporting' funds on the HMRC website.

Don't count on avoiding tax by investing overseas. HMRC has the power to get information from UK banks about their customers' offshore accounts, and most European countries share information about savings interest paid to non-residents. Some deduct a special 'withholding' tax instead, as well as any normal tax, unless you agree to have the interest disclosed to HMRC. If tax is deducted, make sure you claim relief for it by entering it in the Foreign pages of your tax return.

No way out of capital gains tax

You cannot escape UK capital gains tax by going abroad for a year or two. You are still liable to UK tax if you are away for less than five tax years and part with UK or overseas assets that you owned before you left. (See HMRC help sheet 278 *Temporary non-residents and capital gains tax.*) The tax is payable on your return.

A property abroad

Your profits from renting out property overseas, including furnished holiday lettings, are worked out in the same way as your profits on UK property (see Chapter 9), except that Rent-a-Room relief does not apply.

As in the UK, if you have more than one overseas property, the income and expenses for all the properties are added together. You can claim relief for interest on a loan to buy the property, reduced in line with any private use.

Although the same method for working out your profits is used as for UK property, your overseas property is treated as a separate rental business. This means that overseas expenses cannot be deducted from UK rental income (or vice versa) and, if you make a loss overseas, you cannot usually use it to reduce your UK profits. All other losses must be carried forward to set against any future profits from overseas property.

If you dispose of your property, you are liable to UK capital gains tax on any gains, unless you are non-resident and not ordinarily resident. See Chapter 14 for more on capital gains tax.

Your UK tax if you are non-resident

If you are not resident in the UK for tax purposes, you still have to pay UK tax on income arising in the UK. But:

■ *You cannot claim UK personal allowances,* unless you are a citizen of the UK or the European Economic Area, or an Isle of Man or Channel Islands resident. You *can* claim if you are a missionary, a current or former servant of the Crown (or the widow, widower or civil partner of one), abroad for health reasons, or entitled to allowances under a double taxation agreement. Countries with relevant agreements are listed in the notes to the Residence, remittance basis etc. pages of the tax return.

■ *Your tax bill is capped.* The maximum is the amount deducted at source from your investment income plus the tax due on any other income. But this is worked out without deducting any personal allowances. If you can claim allowances, you may pay less tax by working out your tax as if you were a UK resident. (See HMRC help sheets 300 *Non-residents and investment income* and 304 *Non-residents – relief under Double Taxation Agreements.*)

■ *You may still have to pay UK capital gains tax,* but you qualify for the tax-free annual amount of £10,600 in 2010–11 and 2012–13, unless you have foreign income or gains of £2,000 or more and are taxed on the remittance basis (see page 173).

■ *If you let out your UK property,* your tenant or letting agent may have to deduct basic-rate tax from the rent before paying you. You can apply to receive rent before tax. Information for non-resident landlords is on the HMRC website (see the Fact file).

Claiming relief for foreign tax

You may find yourself having to pay tax on foreign income and gains both in the UK and in the country from which they arise. You may get relief for the double tax under the terms of a double taxation agreement with the country concerned. If not, you can claim tax relief in one of two ways:

- *Tax credit relief – a special credit against your UK tax bill.* Usually, the credit is equal to the amount of UK tax on the foreign income or gain, or the amount of the foreign tax if less (so your foreign income is taxed at the higher of the two national rates – see Example 10.2 below).
- *Deducting the foreign tax from the foreign income before you work out UK tax.* If, say, you paid £50 overseas tax on £500 income, you pay UK tax on £450.

Usually, tax credit relief saves you most money because it credits you with the whole amount of the tax. Deducting the tax just saves you the UK tax payable on the foreign tax. But:

- If the UK has a double taxation agreement with the other country, the foreign tax on which you can claim tax credit relief may be restricted. Agreements are listed in the notes to the tax return Foreign pages.
- If there is no double taxation agreement, you can claim relief only if the foreign tax corresponds to UK income tax or capital gains tax.
- You can claim tax credit relief only if you are a UK resident.
- These rules do not apply to special withholding tax (see page 176). This is deducted from your tax bill in the same way as UK tax paid.

Example 10.2: **Claiming relief for foreign tax**

Hannah has interest of £860 from a foreign bank account, from which tax at 15% (£129) was deducted before she received it. However, as she is a basic-rate taxpayer, the interest is liable to 20% tax in the UK: £860 × 20% = £172. She can claim tax credit relief of either the UK tax (£172), or the foreign tax (£129), whichever is lower. So her tax credit relief is £129 and in the UK she pays tax of £172 − £129 = £43.

> ## Claiming tax back from the overseas tax authority

If more tax has been deducted from your foreign income than allowed for under any double taxation agreement, reclaim the excess from the foreign tax authorities. If you get a rebate but have already claimed relief for the excess tax in the UK, you will have to tell your tax office and repay the relief. Ask the payer if the income can be paid gross in future.

What to tell HMRC

You do not need to declare foreign income or gains that are not taxable in the UK. But if you do have any taxable foreign income or gains, and are not sent a tax return, you must tell your tax office by 5 October after the end of the tax year. You will usually be sent a tax return (see Chapter 2). But if your only foreign income is less than £2,000 of foreign interest and less than £300 of taxed overseas dividends, you can enter them on the core tax return (without having to fill in the Foreign supplementary pages). And if your only foreign income is less than £300 of taxed dividends and you would not otherwise have to fill in a full return, you may be able to use a short return – ask your tax office.

If you do get sent a full return, enter your foreign income or gains in the following parts of the return:

- *Income from working abroad* should be entered in the Employment or Self-employment pages (see Chapters 7 and 8). However, if you have foreign earnings not taxable in the UK you may need to complete the Additional Information pages of the tax return. And if you are working in the UK but not domiciled or ordinarily resident here you may not have to declare foreign employment income if it is less than £10,000, your overseas bank interest is less than £100, and all of it is subject to tax overseas (whether or not you actually had to pay tax on it). See HMRC booklet HMRC6 and HMRC help sheet 211 *Employment – residence and domicile issues.*
- *Taxable overseas capital gains* (or losses on overseas assets) go in the Capital gains pages (see Chapter 14). Again, if you want to claim tax

credit relief on your gains, you must enter it in the Foreign pages.

■ *Furnished holiday lettings in Europe* should be entered in the UK Property pages (see page 313)

■ *If your only other foreign income was interest of up to £2,000, and dividends of up to £300*, and you do not want to claim tax credit relief, this can be entered in the core tax return. If you do this you cannot claim foreign tax credit relief, but you will get the normal 10 per cent dividend tax credit.

■ *Any other foreign income* should be entered on the Foreign pages.

■ *Tax credit relief* should be claimed on the Foreign pages.

If you are leaving the UK and want to claim to be non-resident or non-domiciled in the UK, ask your tax office for form P85 or download it from the HMRC website. Your tax office will tell you if you need to complete a tax return once you have left the UK, and if you do it is up to you to 'self-certify' yourself as not resident or not domiciled by ticking the 'non-residence' box on page TR2 of the core tax return, and then completing the Residence, remittance basis etc. pages. You also need to use these pages if you want to claim the remittance basis, unless your unremitted foreign income or gains are under £2,000 and you would not otherwise have to complete a tax return, see page 173. HMRC may decide to start an 'enquiry' into your return to check your residence or domicile status – it will not issue rulings on your status in advance. Remember to notify HMRC's Tax Credit Office if you go abroad (see page 67).

Record-keeping

Keep the same records as for UK income of the same type, plus:

■ Dividend counterfoils from overseas companies.

■ Records of any overseas tax deducted.

■ Notes of exchange rates used in converting between currencies, and, if taxed on the remittance basis, the dates on which income or gains were received in the UK.

■ Records of any calculations you carried out to arrive at the figures entered in your tax return (e.g. tax credit relief working sheets).

■ Records to support any claim to be non-resident or non-domiciled in the UK, such as records of living overseas and the dates of travelling to and from the UK, and employment contracts. Keep these long-term – what happened 20 years ago could be relevant to your tax.

■ If you are claiming double taxation relief, you may need a certificate from the overseas tax authority showing that you are resident there – check the Notes to the Residence, remittance basis etc. pages of the tax return.

11

Tax on your investments

Everybody with savings and investments needs to take tax into account, particularly at current low interest rates: a 3 per cent interest rate is worth only 2.4 per cent to you if you are a basic-rate taxpayer, 1.8 per cent if you pay higher-rate tax and just 1.5 per cent if you pay tax at the additional rate of 50 per cent in 2012–13 (see page 5).

Top tips

- Invest each year through an ISA – a tax-free savings and investment account.
- Always compare the after-tax return from investments. Higher-rate taxpayers may get a better return from tax-free investments even if the headline interest rate is not the best. But do not choose an investment just to save tax.
- On a low income? The big rise in the personal allowance over the past couple of years and further rise planned for 2013–14 mean that you are more likely to be able to claim back tax deducted from your interest, or have it paid without tax.
- If you are eligible for the 10 per cent rate on savings (see opposite), make sure you claim back any extra tax deducted from your interest.
- Non-taxpayers should fill in form R85 to get savings interest paid with no tax deducted and consider investments that pay out before tax. Remember that the tax credit on dividends cannot be reclaimed.
- Watch out if you make a taxable gain on an insurance bond. Any taxable gain may affect your age-related allowance or tax credits (see page 196).

How tax is worked out on investment income

Investments may be liable to income tax and capital gains tax. This chapter covers the income tax aspects, and capital gains tax is covered in Chapter 14.

Some investments are free of income tax altogether (see page 185). The taxable investments in this chapter fall into three broad categories:

■ Savings – e.g. from a bank or building society. These produce interest which is liable to income tax (see page 188).

■ Share-based investments – these may pay dividends which are liable to income tax (see page 193). The investments themselves may also rise and fall in value. While any rise in value is liable to capital gains tax when you sell or give away your investment, any fall can be used to reduce the capital gains tax on other assets.

■ Life insurance – the insurance fund in which your money is invested is taxed; higher-rate taxpayers may have to pay income tax (but not capital gains tax) on payouts unless the policy is 'qualifying' (see page 194).

Other types of investment include property (covered in Chapter 9) and pensions (covered in Chapter 12).

If the income came from overseas, it is usually taxed in the same way as UK income of the same type – see Chapter 10. There is also a special (very complicated) regime for income from a trust, covered briefly on page 198.

How much tax?

Table 11.1 overleaf shows how much tax is payable on each category of income. The different categories are taxed in this order: first non-savings income, then interest, then dividends, then any taxable life insurance gains. So first you need to work out how much of your allowances and basic-rate tax band are used up by your non-savings income (see Chapter 1).

An added confusion is that although the government has abolished the 10 per cent starting-rate tax band for other income, it lives on for savings income. It means that if your non-savings income, after allowances, is less than £2,710 (in 2012–13), you pay tax at 10 per cent on any savings income within the £2,710 band (see page 6 and Example 11.1). Tax at the basic rate of 20 per cent applies to savings income between £2,710 and £34,370.

In most cases, the bank, building society or other organisation deducts basic-rate tax before paying you the income. But if no tax is deducted, or you are a higher-rate taxpayer, you have more tax to pay. And if you are on a low income, you might be able to claim tax back (see page 189).

Table 11.1: Rates of tax on different types of income in 2012–13

Type of income	Income within:				
	Allowances (minimum £8,105, see page 50)	Starting-rate band (next £2,710)	Basic-rate band (£2,710– £34,370)	Higher-rate band (£34,370– £150,000)	Additional- rate band (above £150,000)
Earnings/pension	0%	20%	20%	40%	50%
Interest	0%	10%	20%	40%	50%
Dividends	10%	10%	10%	32.5%	42.5%
Life insurance	None – the insurance fund is taxed			0% or 20%*	0% or 30%*

*No tax if the policy is 'qualifying' (see page 194).

Example 11.1: Are you eligible for 10 per cent tax?

Navdip, who is 66, has a pension of £10,250 in 2012–13. This is tax-free as it is within her age-related personal allowance of £10,500. She also has savings interest of £1,000. The first £250 of interest is tax-free as it is within her personal allowance. She is liable to pay 10% tax on the rest. This is £1,000 − £250 = £750 × 10% = £75. The interest has already had tax deducted at 20% (i.e. £200), so she can claim back £200 − £75 = £125 tax.

Josie has the same income as Navdip, but she 63 so gets a lower personal allowance (see page 78). In 2011–12 her pension used up all her £7,475 allowance and all her starting-rate band so she did not qualify for 10% tax on her interest. But in 2012–13 her allowance is £8,105, so her pension uses up all her allowance but only £10,250 − £8,105 = £2,145 of her £2,710 10% tax band. £2,710 − £2,145 = £565 of her interest is taxable at 10%, instead of the 20% deducted, so she can claim back tax of £56.

Tax-free income from savings and investments

You can save tax on money when you put it into a savings or investment scheme only if you invest in a pension plan (see Chapter 12), Community Investment Scheme, or Venture Capital Trust or Enterprise Investment Scheme (see page 199). However, there is no tax to pay on the interest or dividends coming out of the following investments:

■ ISAs (Individual Savings Accounts) and Junior ISAs.
■ Venture Capital Trusts.
■ Savings Certificates from National Savings & Investments (both fixed-interest and index-linked versions) and Children's Bonus Bonds.
■ Ulster Savings Certificates, if you normally live in Northern Ireland, and were living there when they were bought or repaid.
■ Child Trust Fund accounts.
■ Premium Bond prizes, lottery prizes and other gambling winnings.
■ Save As You Earn schemes (available only in conjunction with employers' share option schemes – see Chapter 7).
■ Tax-exempt friendly society life insurance policies. You do not usually have to pay tax on other life insurance policies (see page 194).
■ Part of the income from purchased life annuities (ones you buy independently, not in connection with a pension – see page 193).
■ If you are not ordinarily resident in the UK (see Chapter 10), British Government Stock.

Individual Savings Accounts (ISAs)

ISAs offer tax advantages for saving. There are two types of ISA:

■ cash, e.g. a savings account
■ stocks and shares, including unit trusts, OEICs, investment trusts, corporate bonds, British Government Stock ('gilts'), some life insurance policies and some property funds (see page 193).

Any money coming out of a cash ISA is tax-free. There is no income tax or capital gains tax to pay on payouts from a stocks and shares ISA, but they are not completely tax-free – share dividends are paid with 10 per cent tax deducted, which cannot be reclaimed even if the shares are held in an ISA.

Your ISA is run by an 'ISA manager', such as a bank, building society, credit union or National Savings & Investments, and many investment firms. You can withdraw all or part of your money at any time, although the ISA manager may impose a minimum investment period.

Are stocks and shares ISAs worthwhile?

Buying share-based investments through ISAs saves you tax only if you are a higher-rate taxpayer, or likely to pay capital gains tax. Unfortunately capital losses made on a stocks and shares ISA cannot be used to reduce your other gains (see page 227). Investing in corporate bonds or cash-based unit trusts through ISAs has tax advantages, though, as these pay interest which is tax-free.

Your ISA choices

You can take out one cash ISA and one stocks and shares ISA in each tax year. They don't have to be with the same company – you can buy your cash ISA from one company and a stocks and shares ISA from a different company.

The amount you can invest in an ISA rises in line with inflation, and in 2012–13 it is £11,280, of which up to £5,640 can be in cash (up from an overall limit of £10,680 in 2011–12, of which £5,340 could be in cash).

Your ISA choices start afresh each tax year, so you can end up with a collection of cash and stocks and shares ISAs. You can also transfer your ISA to a different ISA manager, or move your money from one investment to another offered by the same ISA manager, or switch your money from cash into stock and shares (but not from stocks and shares into cash). See Example 11.2. However, these are only the tax rules; your ISA manager may impose other restrictions.

Investments must be in cash, so if you have investments that you want to move into an ISA, you will have to sell them and reinvest – except for shares from an employer's SAYE share option scheme, approved share incentive plan or approved profit-sharing scheme (see page 94). You can transfer these shares without having to sell them.

Example 11.2: **Your ISA choices**

Last year (2011–12) James put the maximum in a cash ISA (£5,340) and the remaining £5,340 of his ISA allowance in a stocks and shares ISA. This year (2012–13) James can put as much as he wants into his stocks and shares ISA within the £11,280 limit, or up to £5,640 in a cash ISA and the rest in his stocks and shares ISA. James can switch his 2011–12 cash ISA to a new manager with better rates, or transfer it to a stocks and shares ISA. He can also move his existing stocks and shares ISA to a new manager, but he cannot move it into cash.

Junior ISAs

Following the abolition of Child Trust Funds (see page 55), the government introduced Junior ISAs in autumn 2011. However, unlike Child Trust Funds there are no government contributions to the account. Returns from the account are tax-free in the same way as for other ISAs, and cash or stocks and shares ISAs are available. Anybody can pay money into the account, up to a maximum of £3,600 a year, but you cannot transfer money in from a Child Trust Fund. Money in the account is owned by the child and locked in until the child reaches adulthood (unless the child is terminally ill). At 16, the child can make his or her own decision about the account, but cannot draw out the money until age 18, at which point it automatically becomes an adult ISA.

Withdrawing money from an ISA

Avoid withdrawing money from an ISA in the same tax year in which you invest it. If, say, you put the maximum £5,640 in a cash ISA in May 2012, and withdraw £1,000 in July 2012, you cannot put another £1,000 into a cash ISA in the 2012–13 tax year – but you can put another £5,640 into a stocks and shares ISA.

If you want to transfer your ISA

You must open your new ISA first, and then ask your existing ISA provider to transfer the money for you. (Often, the new provider will organise this for you.) Do not just take the money out and then open your new account – your money will lose its tax-free status.

PEPs and TESSAs

Personal Equity Plans (PEPs) and Tax-Exempt Special Savings Accounts (TESSAs) are no longer available. From April 2008, existing PEPs have automatically been classed as stocks and shares ISAs, and matured TESSAs reinvested in ISAs as cash ISAs. The normal ISA rules apply to them.

Savings

Savings produce interest. As well as interest from a bank or building society, interest includes:

- income from taxable National Savings & Investments products
- income from lending money to people, organisations, or governments (for example, British Government Stock and corporate bonds)
- interest distributions from a unit trust or OEIC
- the return from an alternative finance arrangement (see opposite).

Unless you have invested through an ISA or other tax-free scheme, the interest is taxable. It is paid out to you either without any tax deducted (gross) or with 20 per cent tax taken off (referred to as 'net' or 'with tax deducted at source').

If the income is paid out after tax, you have no further tax to pay provided that all your taxable income – including the interest, but after deducting your allowances – is less than £34,370 in 2012–13. Indeed, if your taxable non-savings income is less than £2,710, you are eligible for the 10 per cent tax rate on any savings income within the starting-rate band

and you will be able to claim part or all of the tax back (see page 6). On income above £34,370 in 2013–13, you will have a further 20 per cent tax to pay to bring the overall tax up to 40 per cent, plus a further 10 per cent on income above £150,000 to bring the total up to 50 per cent. The extra tax is collected through either your tax code or your tax return.

Can you claim back tax from 2011–12?

If your overall income in 2011–12 (before deducting allowances) was less than £10,035, or £12,500 if aged 65-plus, £12,650 if 75-plus (more if eligible for married couple's allowance), check to see whether tax was deducted from your bank or building society interest. If it was, it is quite likely that you have paid too much – see Example 11.1 on page 184. In 2012–13, there has been a big rise in the basic personal allowance, and you are likely to be able to claim tax back if your overall income is below £10,815, or £13,210 if aged 65-plus, £13,370 if 75-plus. To reclaim tax, contact HMRC's Repayment Claim Office on 0845 366 7850. If you think you have overpaid tax from earlier years, you can reclaim tax going back four years (see page 37).

Alternative finance

Under Islamic Shari'a law, the payment and receipt of interest is forbidden. As a result, alternative finance contracts have been developed to avoid interest, by providing the return either in the form of a profit share, or through the purchase and resale of assets. The return from these investments is taxed in the same way as interest. This means that tax is deducted unless you complete form R85 to have it paid before tax.

Bank and building society interest

This is usually paid with 20 per cent tax taken off, unless you are a non-taxpayer and have registered to receive the interest gross by completing form R85 (from the bank or building society or the HMRC website). Some banks and building societies allow you to register by phone. With a joint account, the other person must be a non-taxpayer too, unless the bank or building society agrees to pay half of the interest gross. There is a calculator that will help you work out if you can fill in a form R85 on the HMRC website at www.hmrc.gov.uk/calcs/r85/.

Saving tax as a family

See pages 52 and 80 for more on investing as a couple, and page 54 for how to save tax on children's savings.

British Government Stock, corporate bonds and other loan stocks

These are effectively interest-paying loans to various organisations. The interest you receive is taxable, but paid as follows:

- British Government Stock (or 'gilts'): the interest is normally paid gross, but you can opt to have it paid net – contact the Gilts Registrar (see the Fact file).
- Corporate bonds (loans to a company): the interest is paid gross.
- Local authority stocks: the interest is paid with tax taken off but if you are a non-taxpayer you can apply to have it paid gross.
- Permanent Interest Bearing shares (PIBs – loans to a building society): the interest is paid gross.

Once issued, all these loan stocks can be bought and sold, which means that the price goes up and down to reflect demand. In particular, if you buy stocks after they are first issued, or sell them before they mature, part of the price may reflect the right to receive the next interest payment – i.e. the 'accrued' interest. The contract note for the sale should show the amount.

If the face value of all your stocks and bonds is below £5,000, the accrued interest will not affect your tax. Otherwise, you are within the 'accrued income scheme', which is a way of deciding whether the purchaser or the seller is taxed on the accrued interest. This is how it works:

1. Find the tax year in which the first payment of interest after the transaction falls. You must apply the rules if, at any point within that tax year or the preceding tax year, you owned stocks with a total face value (not price) of more than £5,000.
2. Check whether the accrued interest was added to the price, or deducted from it (this should be on the contract note).
3. If the seller gets the accrued interest added to the proceeds of the sale (the normal practice), this counts as a 'profit' on which he or she is liable to pay tax. The purchaser has made a 'loss' which can be deducted from his or her taxable income.
4. If the purchaser gets the accrued interest by paying less for the stock, it counts as the purchaser's profit and the seller has made the loss.

Any tax is payable, or any relief is given, in the tax year of the first interest payment, not the tax year in which the sale took place. (See Example 11.3, and HMRC help sheet 343 *Accrued Income Scheme.*)

Example 11.3: **Dealing with accrued income**

On 7 January 2012, Frances sold some British Government Stock with a face (or 'nominal') value of £4,000. The next interest payment is due on 7 June 2012. She also has corporate bonds with a face value of £3,000, so she is within the accrued income scheme. Five months of accrued interest is added to the price she gets for her stock. This is a profit on which she must pay tax but, as the next interest payment is not due until June 2012, she pays tax on it in 2012–13, not the tax year in which she sold her stock.

'Strips' and 'discounted securities'

The right to receive interest can sometimes be bought and sold separately from the right to the capital repayment when a stock or security matures. The process of separating the interest from the capital is called 'stripping'. Alternatively, a security may be issued where little or no interest is paid and the return comes from the difference between the issue price and the amount payable on redemption. With such 'discounted securities' or 'strips', both the interest and any profit on the 'capital' element of the security or gilt are taxable as interest, but the exact rules depend on the type of security.

Credit union share interest

The 'dividend' from credit unions is paid gross but is taxable.

National Savings & Investments

All National Savings & Investments (NS&I) products are taxable, with the exception of Savings Certificates, Children's Bonus Bonds, Premium Bonds and NS&I ISAs. The taxable products fall into two groups:

- The Investment Account, Direct Saver Account, Easy Access Savings Account, Income Bonds, Capital Bonds, Pensioners' Guaranteed Income Bonds and Guaranteed Equity Bonds: income is paid out before tax. The income is still taxable, but any tax due is collected either by adjusting your tax code or through your tax return.
- Guaranteed Income Bonds and Guaranteed Growth Bonds: 20 per cent tax is always deducted from the income paid out by these bonds. You can reclaim overpaid tax, but non-taxpayers should consider more suitable products.

A downside of Capital Bonds

You are taxed each year on the income earned on National Savings & Investments Capital Bonds – even though it is not paid until the end of the five-year term.

Interest from a unit trust or OEIC

Unit trust or OEIC funds that are invested in gilts, loan stocks and other interest-producing investments pay out interest distributions instead of dividend distributions. The tax voucher will show the type of distribution. OEICs (Open-Ended Investment Companies) are a type of unit trust.

Unless you have invested through an ISA, 20 per cent tax will be deducted, but non-taxpayers can register to have the interest paid gross (ask your tax office for form R85). You can reclaim any tax overpaid providing that you act within four years of the end of the tax year in question (see page 37).

Purchased life annuities

A purchased life annuity is a lifetime income payable by a life insurance company, in return for a lump sum. Do not confuse it with an annuity that is bought with your pension savings – it is taxed very differently. The tax treatment of pension annuities is explained in Chapter 6.

Part of the income from a purchased life annuity – the 'capital element', which will depend on your age at purchase – is tax-free. The rest is taxable as interest, with 20 per cent taken off. Non-taxpayers can get the interest paid gross by completing form R89 (or R86 for joint annuities).

Share-based investments

These may pay out the following types of income:

■ Share dividends from UK companies and investment trusts (note that zero dividend investment trusts pay no income and therefore are not liable to income tax). See page 198 for income from property funds.
■ Stock dividends from UK companies and investment trusts. These give you extra shares in the company or trust, rather than a cash payout.
■ Dividend distributions from UK unit trusts and OEICs (but 'cash' type unit trust funds pay out 'interest' distributions, see above).

With both types, you are treated as if 10 per cent tax has been paid before you receive the dividend. This is called a tax credit. The taxable amount is the dividend you received, plus the tax credit, but you can then set the tax credit against your tax bill. So if, for example, you receive a dividend of £90, the tax credit is £90 ÷ 9 = £10: you are taxed on £90 + £10 = £100 but you can deduct the £10 tax credit from your tax bill.

If you are a starting-rate or basic-rate taxpayer, you have no further tax to pay on your dividend. But if you are a higher-rate taxpayer, you will have a further 22.5 per cent to pay, to bring the overall tax up to 32.5 per cent. So on a dividend of £90, with its £10 tax credit (a taxable amount of £100), you pay further tax of £22.50: £32.50 tax in total. And people with incomes above £150,000 in 2012–13 are liable for tax at 42.5 per cent on any dividends above the £150,000 limit.

Note that you cannot reclaim the tax credit on dividends, even if you are a non-taxpayer, and even if the shares are held in an ISA or a pension fund.

Life insurance

The life insurance fund in which your money is invested is taxed. When the money is paid out to you, you are treated as if you have already paid 'notional tax' of 20 per cent of the amount received. If you are a non-taxpayer, starting-rate taxpayer or basic-rate taxpayer, you have no further tax to pay. But you will have more to pay if:

- you have a 'non-qualifying' policy *and*
- you make a taxable gain on the policy (such a 'gain' is liable to income tax, not capital gains tax) *and*
- you are a higher-rate or additional-rate taxpayer, or a basic-rate taxpayer but the taxable gain on your policy pushes you into a higher tax band. Even so, a special 'top-slicing relief' may be due.

See HMRC help sheet 320 *Gains on UK life insurance policies*.

What is a non-qualifying policy?

This is one into which you are not expected to pay regular premiums over a period of at least ten years. So, for example, a life insurance bond into which you pay a single premium is non-qualifying. Your insurance company will be able to tell you if the policy does or doesn't qualify.

A savings-type insurance policy, e.g. an endowment policy or a 'whole life' policy, is usually qualifying and therefore no tax is payable on the proceeds. But it will become non-qualifying if you stop paying into the policy, sell it or receive benefits from it within the first ten years (or, if the policy is intended to last less than 13.4 years, within the first three-quarters of the intended term, for example 7.5 years for a ten-year policy).

Note that the government intends to cap the amount you can pay into a qualifying policy at £3,600 for policies issued from 6 April 2013.

Have you made a taxable gain?

You may make a gain during your lifetime when your non-qualifying policy matures, or if you surrender or sell it or withdraw money from it. The gain is added to your taxable income. There may also be a gain when the policy pays out on your death – though the gain is worked out using the surrender value immediately before your death, which may differ from the amount actually paid out. If you have made a loss, see page 197.

If you have made a taxable gain, the insurance company should issue a 'chargeable event' certificate which tells you the taxable amount.

At its simplest, a gain occurs when you get more out of a policy than you put in. So if you invest £10,000 in a policy that eventually produces £15,000, your gain is £5,000. But it is common to surrender only part of a non-qualifying policy – to top up income, say. If so, you can put off paying tax on these partial withdrawals until the policy finally ends.

You can put off paying tax if, in any year, you withdraw less than 5 per cent of the amount paid in to the policy plus any unused 5 per cents from previous years. Note that 'year' in this context means years you have had the policy, not tax year.

If you make no withdrawals in the first year you have the policy, you can withdraw 10 per cent in the second year, and so on. The maximum you can withdraw without triggering a taxable gain is 100 per cent (i.e. the amount you put in) after 20 years (see Example 11.4 overleaf). If you withdraw more than your accumulated 5 per cents, your taxable gain is the total amount withdrawn to date (on which you have not so far paid tax), minus the accumulated 5 per cent allowances.

When the policy comes to an end, you are taxed on your total benefits from it, minus the amount you paid in, and minus any taxable gains so far (i.e. withdrawals above your accumulated 5 per cents).

Example 11.4: Tax on a non-qualifying insurance policy

Ten years ago Patrick invested £10,000 in a single-premium insurance bond (a non-qualifying policy). From year 2 he withdrew £600 a year to top up his income, which he increased to £700 from year 7. In year 7 his total withdrawals so far came to more than his total 5% allowances so far, and he made a taxable gain of £200 in that year and the following year. He did not have to pay tax on these gains because they did not push him into the higher-rate tax bracket.

In year 9, Patrick cashed in his policy for £8,545. This, plus his regular withdrawals, made a total gain of £12,945. From this he can deduct the money he put in (£10,000) plus his taxable gains in years 7 and 8 (£400). His overall taxable gain is £12,945 – £10,000 – £400 = £2,545.

Patrick's other income in year 9 is just £400 below the top of the basic-rate band and the insurance gain would push him into the higher-rate band. But top-slicing relief (explained opposite) comes to his rescue. His average annual gain is £2,545 divided by the 8 complete years he has had the policy – £318. As none of this falls within the higher-rate tax band, he has no tax to pay.

Year	1	2	3	4	5	6	7	8	9	Totals
Paid in	10,000									10,000
Annual 5% allowance	500	500	500	500	500	500	500	500		
Previous years' unused allowance		500	400	300	200	100	0	0		
Withdrawals		600	600	600	600	600	700	700	8,545	12,945
Taxable gains during policy							200	200		400

How much tax on your taxable gain on a non-qualifying policy?

Even if you make a taxable gain, you do not have to pay tax on it unless it falls within the higher-rate band. And you do not have to pay the full top rate of tax on any gain in the higher-rate band, because almost all policies are treated as if 20 per cent tax has already been deducted. So you only pay a further 40 – 20 = 20 per cent tax; or 50 – 20 = 30 per cent if you are liable to the 50 per cent tax rate due on income above £150,000 in 2012–13.

Top-slicing relief

A problem with insurance policies is that any taxable lump sum can push your income into the higher-rate tax bracket. Top-slicing relief compensates for this. It works by first dividing the total gain by the number of complete years you have had the policy to find the average annual gain. Assuming that your total taxable income is below £150,000, if the average annual gain, when added to the rest of your income:

■ falls within the basic-rate tax band – the whole of your gain is tax-free
■ falls within the higher-rate band – top-slicing relief does not save you any tax
■ falls partly in the basic-rate band, partly in the higher-rate band – you do not pay the full top rate of tax on your insurance gain. This is achieved by charging you higher-rate tax on the amount of the average annual gain that falls within the higher-rate band, and multiplying the tax by the number of complete years you have had the policy.

Warning: over 64 or eligible for tax credits?

Even if you do not have to pay higher-rate tax on your insurance gain, it is taken into account in deciding how much tax credit you can claim (see Chapter 5) and whether you are over the limit (£25,400 in 2012–13) above which age allowance is reduced (see page 78). And top-slicing relief will not apply – so in Example 11.4 opposite, Patrick's full £2,545 gain would be included in his income for these purposes.

Tax relief for a loss on a non-qualifying policy

If you make a loss on a life insurance policy (because stock markets have fallen, say), you may qualify for a special relief called 'deficiency relief'. You can claim it only if you have previously paid tax on the policy, and you pay tax at the higher rate of 40% or the additional rate of 50% (although the relief itself is capped at 40 per cent). (See HMRC help sheet 320 *Gains on UK Life insurance policies.*)

> ## Taxable insurance policies: points to remember
>
> ■ The 5% allowance is just a way of putting off tax on an insurance gain – it is not a tax-free allowance.
> ■ It might be better to draw more than 5% during the life of the policy if you are not a higher-rate taxpayer, rather than build up a big gain at the end of the policy.
> ■ The 5% withdrawals are 5% of the premium – not the policy value.

Property funds – REITS and Property AIFs

It is possible to invest in property through various types of investment fund such as unit trusts. But there is more favourable tax treatment for two types of property fund – Real Estate Investment Trusts, known as REITs, which are constituted like investment trusts, and Property Authorised Investment Funds (AIFs), which work in a similar way to unit trusts.

Unlike other property funds, the REIT or Property AIF itself is not taxed if it pays out most of its profits as dividends. Any dividends you receive from these untaxed profits are normally treated as property income, not share dividends: they are paid out with basic-rate tax deducted, but non-taxpayers can reclaim this and higher-rate taxpayers have further tax to pay. However, the fund may also pay out other dividends, taxed like share dividends. Your investment is tax-free altogether if bought through an ISA.

Income from trusts

A trust is a legal arrangement designed to hold investments or other assets in the care of trustees for the benefit of one or more 'beneficiaries'. The person who provides the assets is called the 'settlor'. If you are a beneficiary or a settlor of a trust, some or all of the income received by the trust may be taxed as yours – and, since trusts are often set up to hold investments, the income paid is often investment income. Trusts are often set up for inheritance tax purposes, although the government has now brought this within the Disclosure of Tax Avoidance Schemes regime (see page 42).

There are various types of trust, to which different tax rules apply. See the trusts section of the HMRC website.

Part or all of a trust's income may be taxed as yours if:

■ You are a beneficiary of a 'bare' trust (one where you have an unconditional right to the trust's property and income). All the trust's income is treated as if it were yours. If the beneficiary is a child and the trust funds were provided by a parent, the income is taxed as if it were the parent's.

■ You are the settlor of any type of trust (apart from a bare trust) and you, your child, spouse, or civil partner have any right to the trust's property and income (or 'retain an interest' in tax-speak).

■ You are a beneficiary of any type of trust apart from a bare trust. The trust itself (or rather, the trustees) may pay tax and receive its own tax returns. Any income to which you are entitled is taxed as yours, but you get a credit for tax paid by the trust (see below).

The trustees should give you form R185 showing how much income is taxable as yours, and how much the tax credit is. The value of the tax credit varies, depending on the type of income and the type of trust, and the amount of income received by the trust. You can reclaim some or all of the tax deducted, if this is more than you are liable to pay, but you cannot reclaim tax if you are the settlor of the trust.

Some trusts set up for 'vulnerable' people such as disabled people or orphaned children qualify for special, more favourable tax treatment.

Tax relief on investments

Only a few investments give you tax relief on the money you pay in: private pensions (see Chapter 12), Enterprise Investment Schemes, Venture Capital Trusts and Community Investment schemes.

The Enterprise Investment Scheme (EIS) and Venture Capital Trusts (VCTs) are ways of investing in unquoted companies that give you income tax relief on the amount invested. If you sell your shares for a profit, there is no capital gains tax, but don't invest purely for the tax breaks – these are risky investments. With both schemes, you can claim your tax relief either through your tax return, or by sending the certificate provided by the company or trust to your tax office.

Reinvesting to avoid capital gains tax

If you make a taxable capital gain on any asset, you can put off paying the tax by reinvesting the proceeds in the Enterprise Investment Scheme. (See HMRC help sheet 297 *Enterprise Investment Scheme and capital gains tax.*)

Enterprise Investment Scheme (EIS)

This gives you tax relief if you buy shares in an unquoted trading company that has been approved under the scheme, or if you invest via a special investment fund. But you cannot use the scheme to invest in a company with which you are 'connected', for example as a paid director or as a major shareholder, unless, possibly, you come into the company after the shares are issued. You lose tax relief if you part with your shares within three years, and you may also lose relief if you receive some benefit, apart from normal dividends, from the company.

You get tax relief of 30 per cent of the amount you pay for shares, up to a maximum of £1 million in 2012–13 (£500,000 in 2011–12). (See HMRC help sheet 341 *Enterprise Investment Scheme – income tax relief.*) In addition, you can claim to have the whole of any investment made in 2012–13 treated as if made in 2011–12.

Any gain you make on the shares is free of capital gains tax provided you have held them for at least three years. But if the company fails and your shares become worthless, you can claim tax relief on the amount of your loss, minus the amount of tax relief received when you bought the shares. You can set the loss either against your taxable income for the year of the loss (or the preceding year), or against any taxable capital gains.

Seed Enterprise Investment Scheme (SEIS)

From April 2012, you can also get 50 per cent tax relief on investments of up to £100,000 a year in smaller new companies under the Seed Enterprise Investment Scheme (SEIS), even if you are a director of the company. As with the EIS, you can claim to have the whole of any investment made in 2012–13 treated as if made in 2011–12. Any gain you make on the shares is free of capital gains tax, and (in 2012–13 only) if you sell and reinvest existing assets in SEIS shares, those assets are also free of capital gains tax.

Venture Capital Trusts (VCTs)

With Venture Capital Trusts you invest through a company that is itself listed on the stock exchange. You get income tax relief at 30 per cent on the amount you invest in new ordinary shares, but not shares bought second-hand. The maximum investment is £200,000 per tax year. You lose tax relief if you part with your shares within five years.

You do not have to pay any tax on the dividends, but the 10 per cent tax credit on the dividend cannot be reclaimed and does not count as tax paid. Any profit on shares is free of capital gains tax, but unlike the Enterprise Investment Scheme you cannot claim relief on any losses.

Community Investment schemes

These are a way of encouraging investment in social enterprises. Investments in qualifying schemes get 5 per cent tax relief each year, for five years. See HMRC help sheet 237 *Community Investment Tax Relief – Relief for Individuals*.

What to tell HMRC

If you do not get sent a tax return, you should contact your tax office if:

■ You are a taxpayer receiving taxable investment income paid out before tax (for example, from British Government Stock), or a higher-rate taxpayer, and any tax due is not already collected through PAYE.

If so, you must tell your tax office by 5 October after the end of the tax year (that is, 5 October 2012 for income received in 2011–12).

■ Tax on your investment income is collected through your tax code but your circumstances change – e.g. you expect to receive more or less investment income in future.

■ You want to claim tax relief for an investment in an EIS or VCT.

■ You are a starting-rate taxpayer or a non-taxpayer, and think you might be able to claim tax back. In this case, contact HMRC's Repayment Claim Office on 0845 366 7850. You might be asked to fill in a form R40 to claim a tax repayment. (See Chapter 20.)

If you do get a tax return, the most common types of investment income should be entered on page TR3 of the core return. However, you will need the 'Additional Information' pages as well if you have income from British Government Stocks and other loan stock, life insurance gains or stock dividends. There are also extra pages if you receive foreign investment income (see Chapter 10) or income from a trust (except for income from bare trusts, which is entered with your other income of the same type).

Registered to receive interest before tax?

If you have filled in form R85 to have your interest paid out before tax, and you become a taxpayer, let your bank or building society know so that they can start to deduct tax.

Record-keeping

You must keep your savings income records for at least 22 months from the end of the tax year to which they relate (five years and ten months if you also have business or letting income). Remember to keep copies of any relevant emails or online statements. This is the sort of thing to keep:

■ *Shares and unit trusts*: tax vouchers sent with any dividend or distribution (you should get one even if the dividend is paid direct to your bank account).

■ *British Government Stock*: you will get an annual statement of interest if the interest is paid direct to a bank, otherwise a tax voucher is attached to the cheque. Keep any contract notes when you buy or sell.

■ *Enterprise Investment Scheme or Venture Capital Trusts*: certificates provided by the company.

■ *Interest and annuities*: you may get a 'certificate of tax deducted' at the end of each year. If you are not sent one automatically you can ask for one. Otherwise the after-tax amount of interest paid will be shown on your statements or passbook.

■ *Life insurance*: policy documents; notes of date and amount of any withdrawal; any 'chargeable event' certificates from the insurer.

■ *Trusts*: details of any income received and any vouchers or form R185 from the trustees.

12

Building up a pension

There are generous tax incentives to save for retirement through a pension. This chapter covers the various tax reliefs you can claim if you are contributing to a private pension and explains your options on retirement. See Chapter 6 for how pension income is taxed.

Top tips

- A pension is a tax-efficient way to save for the long term because most people will get full tax relief on contributions, the money grows in a fund that is largely tax-free and you can take some of your pension as a tax-free lump sum.
- Ask for a forecast of your state retirement pension, to check that your National Insurance contributions have been credited correctly. You can also contact HMRC's National Insurance Contributions Office for details of your contributions record.
- You don't have to have an income to pay into a pension. You can pay in up to £2,880 and the government will add tax relief.
- You can belong to any number of pension schemes, you don't have to stop work to draw your pension benefits, and you can take a tax-free lump sum without also having to draw your pension.
- You have various options for how you draw your pension savings (see page 211). And if your total pension savings are under £18,000, you can draw the whole lot as cash (see page 211).

Your pension choices

You build up a state pension by paying Class 1 National Insurance contributions (if you are an employee, see page 118) or Class 2 contributions (if you are self-employed, see page 148). The state pension will give you a basic amount, provided you have contributed for enough years. You still build up rights to a state pension if you are looking after children or caring for other people, and you can make voluntary contributions (see page 12).

You may also get a state second pension which depends on your earnings as an employee (but not self-employed earnings). In the past, it was common to 'contract out' of the state second pension. This meant agreeing to build up your own second pension in return for lower National Insurance contributions. Your employer's scheme could contract out all its members, promising to build up an alternative pension instead. Alternatively, you could contract out as an individual, in return for a rebate on your National Insurance contributions which was invested in an individual pension for you. From April 2012, contracting out is possible only for employers' salary-related schemes and it is no longer possible to contract out as an individual. However, whether you were contracted out in the past will still affect how much state second pension you get in future.

A state pension is unlikely to give you a comfortable retirement on its own. You can top it up with a private pension. Private pensions include:

■ *Occupational pension schemes.* Run by your employer, these may be either 'salary-related' (you earn a pension of say, one-sixtieth of your final salary for each year of membership) or 'money purchase' (the benefits depend on the investment performance of contributions).
■ *Personal pension schemes and stakeholder pensions.* These are individual pension plans taken out with a pension company, usually an insurance company. Your contributions are invested in a 'money purchase' pension fund, and how much you get out at the end depends on how well the investments in the fund perform. Stakeholder pensions are a form of personal pension with a cap on management charges.
■ *Group personal pensions.* These are just personal pension plans arranged through your employer. Both you and your employer contribute.

■ *Retirement annuity contracts*. These have not been available since 1988 but if you have one you can continue to pay in.

■ *Self-invested personal pensions* (SIPPs). A SIPP is just a personal pension, but instead of having to invest through the pension fund of an insurance company, you can choose a wide variety of investments to sit within your SIPP.

A new system of automatic enrolment into workplace pensions is being phased in from 2012, starting with the largest employers, but the same tax rules apply. Under the new system, if you earn more than the National Insurance threshold your employer must enrol you into either a workplace pension, or an account with the new National Employment Savings Trust (NEST). Both you and your employer must make contributions, but you can opt out if you wish. NEST accounts work in the same way as a personal pension, but have low charges and have been designed to meet the needs of people on modest incomes.

Tax relief on money going into a pension

Paying Class 1, Class 2 or Class 3 National Insurance contributions will entitle you to a state retirement pension, but you do not get tax relief on them. However, contributions to a private pension scheme that has been registered by HMRC qualify for tax relief at your top rate of tax, within limits. Almost all schemes are registered. Investments in a registered pension scheme grow tax-free, except for the tax credit on dividends (see page 193), which cannot be reclaimed.

There are many types of registered pension scheme, but the same general rules apply to all. The Money Advice Service, the government Pension Service and the Pensions Advisory Service all have useful leaflets.

Some schemes choose not to meet the conditions for registering. You get no tax relief on your contributions to unregistered schemes and the payouts are usually taxable. Contributions your employer pays in for you count as a tax-free benefit, but in the past they were usually taxable: if you have paid tax on employer's contributions, this will reduce the tax on any payouts.

Don't lose your pension rights

You can get a forecast of your state pension from the government Pension Service. If you have not paid in enough National Insurance contributions to get a full state pension you can pay voluntary Class 3 contributions to improve your record, but there are time limits for doing so – HMRC's National Insurance Contributions Office should write to you if you have not paid enough contributions. Make sure that they have your up-to-date address, and that you have been credited for qualifying periods of sickness, unemployment or caring for dependants.

If you cannot track down a private pension company that you have saved with, the Pension Service runs a free tracing service (see the Fact file).

How the tax relief is given

In 2012–13, contributions to a private pension get tax relief at 20 per cent if you are a basic-rate taxpayer, at 40 per cent if you are a higher-rate tax-payer and at 50 per cent if you pay the additional rate of tax (see opposite). When the additional rate of tax falls to 45 per cent in April 2013, the maximum tax relief on pension contributions will also fall. There are three ways of getting tax relief:

■ *Relief at source.* You hand over the amount that is due after 20 per cent basic-rate tax relief. The pension company claims the basic-rate tax back from HMRC (even if you are a non-taxpayer). Higher-rate or additional-rate taxpayers can claim an extra 20 per cent or 30 per cent relief through their tax return or tax code. (See Example 12.1 overleaf.)
■ *Net pay.* Your employer deducts your pension contributions from your pay and then works out the tax on what's left, giving you tax relief at your highest tax rate.
■ *Gross payment.* This applies mainly to retirement annuity contributions. You pay the full amount and get tax relief either through your tax return or through your tax code. However, the retirement annuity company can choose to move to the net pay method instead.

Example 12.1: **How much tax relief?**

Brandon, who is self-employed, decides to contribute £6,500 to his personal pension in 2012–13. But for each £1 going into his pension, Brandon pays only 80p – the remaining 20p comes in the form of tax relief that the pension company claims from HMRC. So, Brandon's £6,500 is actually worth £6,500 ÷ 0.8 = £8,125.

Brandon is a 40% taxpayer so he can also claim higher-rate tax relief. He has already had 20% relief, so he can claim the remaining 40% – 20% = 20% on his tax return. HMRC gives him the relief by increasing his basic-rate tax band (normally £34,370) by the value of his contributions. This means that an extra £8,125 is taxed at 20% rather than 40%, giving him higher-rate tax relief of £8,125 × 20% = £1,625.

Bertie is also a 40% taxpayer paying £6,500 into his pension – but he belongs to his employer's scheme. His £6,500 is deducted from his pay before his tax is worked out, so he gets tax relief of £6,500 × 40% = £2,600 through his pay packet. Only £6,500 goes into his pension, but his employer also pays in contributions for him.

How much can you contribute?

As long as you are aged under 75, you can pay in all your earnings (within limits) and get full tax relief. If you have no earnings, you can get tax relief on payments up to £2,880 a year (made up to £3,600 by basic-rate tax relief). You can belong to any number of pension schemes and there are just two limits – an annual allowance and a lifetime allowance.

If your employer contributes

- You pay no tax or National Insurance on contributions your employer makes to your pension, so a pension contribution can be worth more than a pay rise.
- If your employer contributes to your personal or stakeholder pension, its contributions are included with yours for the purposes of working out whether you have exceeded the contribution limits, but you cannot claim tax relief on them.

The annual allowance

If the money going into all your private pensions in each year is more than the annual allowance of £50,000, the excess is taxed at your top rate of tax. The following count as money going in:

- your contributions (but not National Insurance rebates contributed by the government if you contract out of the state second pension)
- if you are in a money purchase scheme (where the amount going in is fixed, but what you get out is not), contributions from your employer
- if you are in a salary-related scheme, any increase in your pension multiplied by 16, plus any increase in your right to a lump sum.

The lifetime allowance

There is a limit on the overall value of all your pension savings, which is £1.8 million for 2011–12 but has fallen to £1.5 million from 2012–13 onwards. When you take your benefits (a pension, say), you will have to pay tax on any pension savings above this allowance. The tax is 55 per cent if you draw a lump sum, 25 per cent if you draw an income (but the income will also be taxed each year).

The value of your pension savings includes:

- if you are in a money purchase scheme (where the amount going in is fixed, but not what you get out), the value of your pension fund
- if you are in a salary-related scheme, your annual pension multiplied by 20, plus any lump sum. So, if you get no lump sum, the maximum pension within the lifetime allowance from 6 April 2012 is £75,000 × 20 = £1.5 million, or £56,250 if you also take the maximum lump sum of £375,000 (see Example 12.2)
- if you draw your benefits over a number of years, the value of benefits you have already drawn.

Any dependants' pensions paid if you die before retirement will not count as part of your lifetime allowance, but any lump sum payout they receive will be taxed if it is above the lifetime allowance.

Example 12.2: **Keeping within the lifetime allowance**

Beverley is a company director. She is entitled to a deferred pension of £22,000 from her old employer. This uses up £22,000 × 20 = £440,000 of her lifetime allowance. She also belongs to her current employer's group personal pension, in which she has built up a pension fund of £250,000. She has used up £440,000 + £250,000 = £690,000 of her lifetime allowance to date, but it is the value of her pension fund when she draws her pension benefits that matters − so whether she breaches the limit will depend on how much more she contributes, and how much her pension fund grows.

Payouts from a private pension

You get tax relief on what goes into a registered private pension and on retirement you can take a tax-free lump sum of up to 25 per cent of your pension fund, up to a maximum of £450,000 in 2011–12, but £375,000 from 2012–13. However, other money coming out is generally taxable, and there are restrictions on the benefits you can draw. The main restrictions are:

- *You cannot draw money from a pension scheme before a minimum age* (with a few exceptions, this is now 55 for all types of pension scheme). You do not have to stop work to draw your benefits.
- *Limits on the amount of benefits payable.* Benefits payable by money purchase schemes are naturally limited by what your investment will buy. If you belong to a salary-related scheme you can take as much as your pension scheme allows, but any benefits above the lifetime allowance will have a one-off tax charge deducted.
- *Restrictions on how you draw your pension money when you retire.* See opposite for how this is done.

Note that even though the tax rules may permit various options, the pension scheme you are in may not. You may have to transfer your money to a different scheme that does provide the option you want.

> ## Very low pension savings?

If your total pension savings come to less than £18,000 you can draw the whole lot as cash. This is known as a 'triviality payment' or 'trivial commutation'. To do this, you must draw all your pension savings within 12 months and be aged at least 60 but under 75. A quarter of the cash is tax-free, and the rest is taxed as income – so it is best to do it in a year when you have little other income. Also check the amount of tax deducted, as many people can claim tax back. Small occupational pension funds (under £2,000) may also be paid as cash, in addition to the £18,000 limit. From 6 April 2012, personal pension funds up to £2,000 can also be taken in cash, but there is a limit of two such payments in your lifetime.

> ## Getting your money out of a pension early

You cannot get your money out of a pension before you reach the minimum age unless you are in ill-health or you have a right to draw an earlier pension from a scheme to which you belonged on 6 April 2006. You can also claim a refund of your contributions if you leave an occupational scheme within two years of joining, but tax will be deducted and you will lose your employer's contributions. The government has said it plans to remove the option of taking a refund, probably from 2014.

Providing a pension income

If you belong to a salary-related occupational scheme, the scheme will provide a pension. With any other type of scheme, the tax rules give you the option of buying an annuity (a guaranteed income for a set period, usually for life, provided by an insurance company) or withdrawing income. In both cases, the income is taxed as pension income, as described in Chapter 6.

See Figure 12.1 on page 213 for your options, but note that even though the tax rules give you options, the pension scheme you are in may not. You may have to transfer to a different scheme.

An annuity provides greater certainty than leaving your money in the fund and drawing income, but the cost of an annuity fluctuates with conditions in the financial markets. You may be stuck with a low income, and on your death your family may get nothing back. Always shop around – annuity rates vary hugely. If you have any health impairments, ask about an 'impaired life' or 'enhanced' annuity, which will pay better rates.

Income withdrawal means you can pass on any funds unused on your death to your family (minus tax in most cases), but it is risky – you could run out of money if your investments do badly or if you live longer than expected. To guard against this, the maximum you can draw each year is limited. The maximum annual withdrawal is the same amount you could have had with an annuity ('capped drawdown'), unless you are already receiving a lifetime income of at least £20,000 a year from other pensions, including your state pension, an occupational pension, or an annuity. If so, you can draw as much as you want from the rest of your pension savings ('flexible drawdown').

Reinvesting a lump sum

You can take a lump sum from some types of pension scheme without having to draw your pension – but the government does not want you to take a lump sum simply to reinvest it in your pension, thereby getting a second lot of tax relief on the contributions. So a tax charge may apply if you draw a lump sum of £18,000 or more and reinvest more than 30 per cent of it in your pension, if HMRC thinks that the reinvestment is 'pre-planned'.

What happens on death

With an occupational pension scheme, a pension paid to a partner or dependant after your death is liable to income tax like any other pension (see Chapter 6). If a lump sum is payable, it is tax-free providing the scheme trustees have discretion over who gets it (although you can say who you want to have it and they will almost always follow your wishes).

With a money purchase scheme, if you have opted for an annuity, there usually isn't anything left to pay out on your death, but there may be if you opted for income drawdown. If so, there is no tax to pay if:

■ you leave the money to charity
■ it is used to provide a drawdown pension for a dependant (the

Figure 12.1: Your options on retirement

Start here

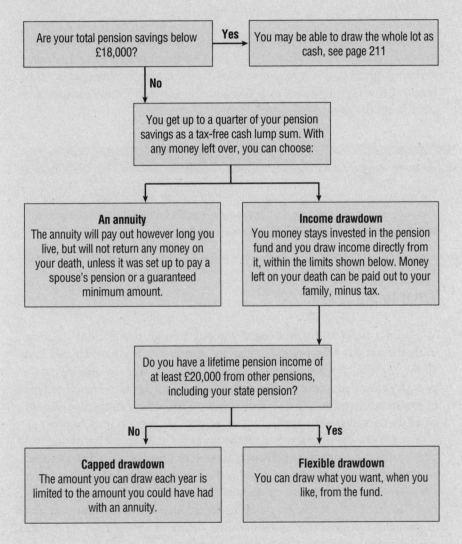

Are your total pension savings below £18,000?

Yes → You may be able to draw the whole lot as cash, see page 211

No ↓

You get up to a quarter of your pension savings as a tax-free cash lump sum. With any money left over, you can choose:

An annuity
The annuity will pay out however long you live, but will not return any money on your death, unless it was set up to pay a spouse's pension or a guaranteed minimum amount.

Income drawdown
You money stays invested in the pension fund and you draw income directly from it, within the limits shown below. Money left on your death can be paid out to your family, minus tax.

Do you have a lifetime pension income of at least £20,000 from other pensions, including your state pension?

No / **Yes**

Capped drawdown
The amount you can draw each year is limited to the amount you could have had with an annuity.

Flexible drawdown
You can draw what you want, when you like, from the fund.

dependant will pay income tax on the amount drawn down). Broadly speaking, a dependant is your spouse or civil partner, child under 23, or other person financially dependent on you

■ you die before age 75 and before drawing any benefits from your pension.

A lump sum paid out in any other circumstances will be subject to a 'recovery charge' of 55 per cent, and the charge cannot be reclaimed even if the recipient is not a taxpayer. This recovers the tax benefits already received through investing in a pension. However, no inheritance tax is payable on the money paid out.

Passing on pension savings

The easiest and most tax-effective way to pass on a pension you don't need is to draw the maximum lump sum or pension, and give away as much as you can within existing inheritance tax exemptions (such as the £3,000 annual exemption).

What to tell HMRC

You do not need to do anything if you pay into an occupational scheme using the net pay method (explained on page 207) – you have already had all the tax relief you are due because your employer worked out the tax on your pay after deducting your contributions. If you pay into any other type of registered pension scheme and you are sent a tax return, you should enter the contribution on page TR4 of the core tax return (see Chapter 17).

Even if you have already had all the tax relief you are due by paying less to the pension company, you need to make sure your tax office knows about any contributions because they will reduce your taxable income for other purposes, such as claiming tax credits or age-related personal allowances (see Chapter 6). So if you are claiming tax credits, deduct the gross amount of your contributions from your earnings before you enter them in the tax credits annual declaration form (see Chapter 5).

If you do not get a tax return write to your tax office with details of your contributions if:

■ you are a higher-rate taxpayer – you are entitled to extra tax relief *or*
■ you are 65 or over and your age-related allowance is reduced – the pension contribution may increase your allowance (see page 81).

Exceeding the pension contribution allowances

You will need to tell HMRC if, during 2011–12, your pension rights grew by more than the annual allowance or you drew any pension benefits that took you over the lifetime allowance (see page 209). You must also tell HMRC if you are liable to tax on any unauthorised payment from a UK-registered pension scheme or on some payments from overseas pension schemes. Your scheme administrator can usually give you the information you need.

You will need to fill in page Ai4 of the 'Additional Information' pages of the tax return. HMRC help sheet 345 *Pensions – tax charges on any excess over the lifetime allowance* will help you work out the taxable amount. Note, though, that if you receive a payment from an employer's pension scheme that is not registered, it should go in page Ai2 under *Share schemes and employment lump sums* (see page 291).

Record-keeping

For how long the law requires you to keep records, see page 15, but you should keep records of your pension entitlements, and pension scheme rules, indefinitely. Also keep:

■ Records of all your contributions – e.g. receipts or contribution certificates.
■ If you are paying in more than £2,880 to your pension, proof of your earnings for the tax year.
■ Any statements showing how much your pension is worth, and how much of your lifetime allowance you have used (the pension scheme administrator should tell you this when you draw benefits).
■ The pension scheme rules or contract.

13

Tax on gifts and donations

A gift you make could land you with a tax bill. Fortunately, there are ways round this, and a gift to charity could benefit you as well as the recipient. This chapter introduces you to the taxes you might have to pay on your gifts, and how to make the most of gifts to charity.

Taxes on gifts

You do not have to pay income tax on a gift you receive. But a gift you make may incur capital gains tax or inheritance tax. There's more about both taxes in Chapters 14 and 15, but this is how they affect gifts.

Capital gains tax is payable on any profit you have made when you part with an asset. So if you make your Dorset cottage over to your children, you pay tax on any increase in the value of the property since you have owned it. However, there are reliefs you can claim, and gifts of personal effects are usually tax-free. A gift of cash isn't liable to capital gains tax – but if you've had to sell some investments, say, to make the gift, there may have been capital gains tax to pay on the sale.

There is no capital gains tax on death – that's when inheritance tax takes over. The tax is payable on the total value of your estate, including gifts made in the seven years before death.

Many gifts are tax-free, and see page 221 for a tax reduction for gifts of works of art or historical objects to the state. Here are some tax-free gifts you can currently make (full lists are in Chapters 14 and 15):

- Gifts to your husband or wife or civil partner
- The first £10,600 of capital gains in 2011–12 and 2012–13
- The first £325,000 of your estate on death (more for married couples)
- Gifts of up to £3,000 a year, small gifts (up to £250) and regular gifts made out of income.

Relief for gifts to charity

Gifts to charity may reduce your tax bill. Not only are they exempt from capital gains tax and inheritance tax, they qualify for income tax relief providing you give through one of the following routes:

- payroll giving, for donations deducted regularly from your pay
- Gift Aid, for most other donations
- gifts of investments and land.

For more information, see HMRC help sheet 342 *Charitable giving* or go to the 'Charities' section of the HMRC website. There is also an HMRC Charities helpline on 0845 302 0203.

Your will can cut your inheritance tax

If you leave money to charity in your will it is deducted from the value of your estate for inheritance tax purposes (see page 243). However, from April 2012, if you leave 10% or more of your taxable estate to charity, the rate of inheritance tax on the rest of your taxable estate will be cut from 40% to 36%. This will cut the cost to your heirs of your generosity, but you need to go through the figures carefully to check that it achieves the result you want.

Payroll giving

This route is open to employees or pensioners of an employer who runs a payroll giving scheme (sometimes called Give As You Earn). You ask your employer to deduct a set amount from your pay packet, which is then passed on to one or more charities through an approved agency. Because the donation is deducted from your pay before your tax is worked out, you get tax relief at your highest rate of tax. Unlike with Gift Aid, the charity does not get part of the tax relief – you get it all – but it does get the valuable benefit of a regular stream of income.

Gift Aid

You can increase the value of your gifts to charity – whether these are one-off or regular cash donations, or donations of tax repayments – by using Gift Aid. You can also give to community amateur sports clubs this way, if they are registered with HMRC. The charity or club can reclaim basic-rate tax from HMRC. With the basic rate of tax set at 20 per cent, this is 20/80 of your gift. So, for every £10 you give, the charity gets £12.50.

If you are a higher-rate taxpayer, you benefit further – you can claim higher-rate relief either through your tax return or by asking your tax office to change your tax code. The higher-rate relief works out at 20 per cent of the value of the gift to the charity – the 40 per cent higher rate of tax, minus the 20 per cent relief the charity has reclaimed. So, for every £10 you give, you get tax relief of £12.50 × 20% = £2.50. (See Example 13.1.) People paying the 50 per cent tax rate in 2012–13 get relief of 50% − 20% = 30% (an extra £1.25). And people who donate more than £10,000 can receive a gift or other benefit from the charity worth up to 5 per cent of the donation, capped at £2,500. Free admission doesn't count as a benefit.

There are no limits on the amount of donations for which you can claim tax relief, but you must make a Gift Aid declaration for each charity you give to. Usually, the charity provides a form, but telephone, email or even text message declarations are possible. Declarations do not have to be made for each gift; they can cover a number of gifts, and they can be made after the date of the gift. From April 2013, the government also plans to introduce a scheme allowing some charities not to collect declarations for gifts of £10 or less (up to £5,000 per charity).

Example 13.1: How Gift Aid works

Ryan decides to donate to his favourite charity by monthly direct debit, and makes a Gift Aid declaration. He pays £15 a month, £180 a year, and the charity reclaims tax of the amount paid, divided by the basic rate of tax, that is £180 × 20/80 = £45. So Ryan's gift is worth £180 + £45 = £225 to the charity. If Ryan's tax bill for the year wasn't at least £45, HMRC would adjust his tax to recover the £45 the charity had already received. However, Ryan is a higher-rate taxpayer, so he pays plenty of tax to cover the gift and he can also claim higher-rate tax relief at 20% of his donation: £225 × 20% = £45.

Large donors beware

The government has said that from 2013 it intends to cap the total tax relief you can claim above £50,000 (excluding reliefs that are already subject to a limit, see page 5). The details are not yet clear, and the government has said it will explore ways to avoid affecting charities, but if you are planning a large donation it's worth getting professional advice.

Non-taxpayers beware

If you pay little or no tax do not give to charity via Gift Aid. HMRC can claw back the basic-rate tax claimed by the charity from you – unless your tax bill for the year is at least as much as the amount the charity will claim. Your tax bill for this purpose includes income tax, capital gains tax and tax credits on dividends. If you have made a Gift Aid declaration, you can cancel it by notifying the charity. If HMRC finds that a charity has claimed Gift Aid on a non-taxpayer's donation, it may ask the charity to repay the tax. But if you get a tax return, the tax will automatically be added to your tax bill.

Gifts to non-UK charities and amateur sports clubs

Until 24 March 2010, you could claim tax relief only on gifts to UK-resident charities and sports clubs. However, tax relief can now be claimed on gifts to equivalent bodies in the EU, Norway and Iceland, and you can claim on gifts going back to 27 January 2009.

Carrying back a donation

You can claim on your tax return to have a Gift Aid donation treated as if made in the previous tax year, providing that you claim by the following 31 January or when you file your tax return, if earlier. This is helpful if your top rate of tax has fallen since the previous year, and gives you tax relief more quickly (see Example 13.2).

Example 13.2: **Carrying back donations**

In June 2012 Hector made a lump sum donation of £500 to a disaster relief fund. He claims to carry this back to the 2011–12 tax year. This will reduce his tax bill for 2011–12. Because Hector is over 65, he is eligible for the higher rate of personal allowance, but his allowance for 2011–12 was reduced because his income was just above £24,000. The donation, plus the basic-rate tax relief on it, is deducted from his income when working out the allowance, taking it below £24,000 so that he gets the full allowance.

Gifts of investments and land

If you give shares and securities, unit trusts, OEICs or land and buildings (freehold or leasehold) to a charity, or sell them to a charity at a discount, you are likely to qualify for Gift Aid relief. (See the 'Charities' section of the HMRC website.) You get tax relief on the market value of the gift, plus any costs of making it (such as legal fees).

Relief for gifts to the nation

From 2012 (the date is yet to be fixed) lifetime gifts to the nation of a work of art or an object of national, scientific, historic or artistic interest will qualify for tax relief. Your proposed gift will be reviewed by a panel of experts, and if they consider it 'pre-eminent', you will get a tax reduction of 30 per cent of its value. The reduction is set against your income tax and/ or capital gains tax bill.

What to tell HMRC

If you get a tax return, you should enter any Gift Aid donations, or donations of investments and land, on page TR4 of the core tax return.

You do not need to enter any payroll giving donation on your tax return – you have already had all the tax relief due by paying less tax, and the taxable income shown on your P60 will exclude the amount donated.

If you do not get a tax return, contact your tax office to tell them how much you have paid through Gift Aid – but you need only do this if you are a higher-rate taxpayer or you are 65 and over and your personal allowance is reduced. The full amount of the donation (including the tax relief the charity gets) is deducted from your income when working out if you are eligible for the higher age-related allowances. And if you are a higher-rate taxpayer making regular donations, your tax office should adjust your tax code so that you get the higher-rate tax relief straight away.

Also contact HMRC's Tax Credit Office if you are claiming tax credits and deduct the donations (including the tax relief) from your income when completing your annual tax credits declaration.

Record-keeping

Keep the following records for the length of time shown on page 15:

- Copies of Gift Aid declarations (don't forget to keep a note of declarations you make over the phone, or by text or email) and records of amounts actually paid.
- If you give investments to charity, a copy of the stock transfer form or letter from the charity acknowledging receipt, and a note of the investments' market value at the time of the gift.
- If you give land or property to charity, you will need a certificate from the charity and records of the market value. Also keep records of any expenses (such as valuation fees) as these count as part of your donation.
- If you made gifts to individuals, make a note of all gifts of cash or assets above £250, the name of the recipient and, if you gave things rather than cash, the gift's market value at the time.

14

Tax on capital gains

You sell some shares. You retire and your children take over your business. You sell a property that you've been renting out. All these transactions, and some others, may be liable to capital gains tax. Even if you have made a loss it's worth telling HMRC as it could save you tax. This chapter explains how capital gains tax works.

> **Top tips**

- You don't have to worry about capital gains tax if you invest in British Government Stock or via an ISA (see Chapter 11).
- You can make taxable gains of up to £10,600 in 2012–13 before you have to pay tax. If you expect to make larger gains, see if you can spread your disposals over more than one year.
- Married? You each have an annual tax-free amount, so consider splitting assets between you so that you can both make full use of it.
- Made a loss last year? You can use it to reduce any taxable gains you made in the same year or, provided you notify HMRC before 6 April 2016, in future years.
- If you have more than one home, nominate which one you want as your tax-free 'main' home within two years of acquiring the second home. Choose either the home you think you will make the biggest gain on, or the one you are more likely to sell.

Will capital gains tax affect you?

Capital gains tax is simply a tax on the capital sum produced when you 'dispose' of an 'asset'. The most common disposal arises when you sell something, but you also make a taxable disposal if, for example, you give something away (or sell it at an artificially low price).

You don't need to worry about capital gains tax if your total capital gains in a tax year are less than the annual tax-free amount of £10,600 in 2012–13 (unchanged from 2011–12). Even if your total gains come to more than this, you can claim relief for losses made in earlier years, and there are various other reliefs. And some gains are tax-free – they don't count towards the £10,600 limit, and don't have to be declared.

If your total gains come to more than £10,600 you will have to pay capital gains tax on the excess, at a flat rate of 18 per cent, or 28 per cent if your gains plus your total taxable income take you above the higher-rate income tax threshold. Entrepreneurs selling a business may qualify for a 10 per cent tax rate.

Tax-free gains

Gains on the following items

- Private cars (including vintage cars).
- Foreign currency for your and your family's use and from 6 April 2012, gains on withdrawals from overseas foreign currency bank accounts arising from movements in exchange rates.
- Decorations for valour (unless you bought them).
- Personal effects and goods disposed of for £6,000 or less, such as household furniture, paintings and antiques (HMRC calls these 'chattels'). If the disposal proceeds are more than £6,000, the gain is capped at 5/3 of the amount over £6,000 (see Example 14.1 on page 226). See HMRC help sheet 293 *Chattels and Capital Gains Tax*.
- 'Wasting assets', with a predicted life of 50 years or less, providing they were not eligible for capital allowances for use in a business. Machinery is treated as a wasting asset – including antique clocks and vintage cars – if owned personally and not used in a business.

Gains on the following investments

■ Investments held in an Individual Savings Account (ISA) or Child Trust Fund.

■ National Savings Certificates.

■ SAYE schemes.

■ Shares in a Venture Capital Trust, Seed Enterprise Investment Scheme or (with some conditions) an Enterprise Investment Scheme.

■ Life insurance policies (unless you bought the policy second-hand) – but gains might be liable to income tax, see page 194.

■ Pension plans (assuming the scheme is registered with HMRC).

■ British Government Stock and most types of corporate bond.

Other tax-free gains

■ Premium Bond prizes, and betting, lottery or pools winnings.

■ Gifts to charity or for 'public benefit' (e.g. art given to the nation).

■ Gifts to amateur sports clubs open to the whole community.

■ Gains when an estate is disposed of at death (but watch out for inheritance tax instead, see Chapter 15).

■ Cashbacks received as an inducement to buy something (e.g. a new car) or take out a loan.

■ Compensation and damages, including for personal injury.

■ Compensation for loss or damage (such as insurance payouts), but you must use all of it to replace or repair the damaged property.

Special reliefs apply to gains made when selling your main home, and transfers of property between spouses and civil partners, which mean there is usually no tax to pay in these circumstances (see page 234). There are also many business reliefs (see page 234).

One downside of tax-free assets such as investments in an ISA is that if you make a loss on them, the loss cannot be set against your gains. The exception is shares in the Enterprise Investment Scheme.

Note that if you are UK-resident, or only temporarily non-resident, gains you make on assets overseas must be declared and may be taxed, unless you are claiming the 'remittance basis' (see pages 173 and 176). Any tax is worked out in the same way as for UK assets.

How capital gains tax is worked out

The basic principles are simple. They apply to all your gains that don't fall within one of the tax-free categories above.

1. Work out your gain on each asset you have disposed of in the tax year, minus any reliefs that apply to that asset (for example, entrepreneurs' relief). There is a working sheet in the tax return notes.
2. Add together the taxable gains on all the assets you have disposed of in the tax year, deduct any losses, claim any other reliefs, and deduct the annual tax-free amount.
3. Work out the tax on what's left.

Working out the gain or loss on each asset

Start with the disposal proceeds. This is the sale price, if you sold the asset. If you didn't sell it (or you sold it for less than its full price), the disposal proceeds are the market value of the asset at the time.

From the disposal proceeds you can deduct the allowable costs of the asset. The main allowable cost is usually the purchase price if you bought the asset, its probate value if you inherited it, or its market value if you acquired it in some other way. You can also deduct other allowable expenses, such as the costs of buying and selling the asset, stamp duty and anything spent on improving it (but not ordinary maintenance costs). You might also be able to claim various reliefs – see page 231 onwards.

Example 14.1: **Working out the taxable gain**

Arthur sold a family portrait for £9,000. He inherited it from his father when the probate value was only £500, and he paid auctioneer's commission of £900, so he has made a gain of £9,000 – £500 – £900 = £7,600. The painting counts as a 'chattel', so had it gone for £6,000 or less, it would have been tax-free. However, the rules provide some relief for lower-value chattels, because the gain is capped at 5/3 of the proceeds over £6,000 – which in this case works out at £3,000 × 5/3 = £5,000. He has made a taxable gain of £5,000.

Assets acquired before April 1982

Only gains made since 31 March 1982 are taken into account. This works by using the market value of the asset on that date as the allowable cost.

Working out your overall gains for the year

Once you have worked out your gains or losses on all the disposals you have made in the year, add up all your gains and deduct all your losses:

- If the overall gains for the year are less than the annual tax-free amount (£10,600 in 2011–12 and 2012–13) there is no tax to pay. But you do not get the tax-free amount if you have foreign income and gains above £2,000 taxed on the remittance basis (see page 173).
- If your losses are more than your gains, you can carry any unused losses forward to future years, but you must notify your tax office (by letter or through your tax return) within four years of the end of the tax year in which you made the loss.
- If the overall gain for the year is above £10,600, look back to see if you have any unused losses from earlier years. If so, you only need to deduct enough losses to reduce your gains to £10,600. Any losses still unused can be carried forward to future years.

As this suggests, you can deduct your losses from earlier years and your annual tax-free amount in whichever way most reduces your tax.

Example 14.2: **Deducting losses**

In 2012–13 Arthur made a taxable gain of £5,000 on a painting he sold, and a gain of £10,000 on selling some shares. His total gains are above the £10,600 annual tax-free amount. However, he can deduct some losses from a failed investment in earlier years. His losses were £18,000, so he needs £4,400 of these to reduce his 2012–13 gains to the level of the tax-free amount. He has no tax to pay this year, and the remaining £18,000 – £4,400 = £13,600 can be carried forward to set against gains in future years.

Working out the tax

Finally, deduct the annual tax-free amount (£10,600 in 2011–12 and 2012–13). What's left is your taxable capital gain for the year.

The rate of tax depends on how much taxable income you have, after deducting allowances and reliefs. If your income is above the higher-rate threshold (£34,370 in 2012–13 and £35,000 in 2011–12), all your gains are taxed at 28 per cent; if it is below, work out how far below. That amount of your gains will be taxed at 18 per cent, and anything more at 28 per cent. You can use a pension contribution or charitable donation to cut the tax (see Example 14.3).

Note that the tax is 10 per cent if you can claim entrepreneurs' relief (see page 235).

Example 14.3: **Which rate of tax?**

Hannah's total taxable income in 2012–13 is £31,370. This is £34,370 − £31,370 = £3,000 below the higher-rate threshold. If she has taxable capital gains of £5,000, she will pay 18% on the first £3,000 (£540) and 28% on the remaining £2,000 (£560). Her capital gains tax is £540 + £560 = £1,100. However, a one-off pension contribution of £2,000 would cut her taxable income to £29,370, leaving all her gains taxed at 18% and saving £200.

A charitable donation or pension payment can cut your tax

If your income is close to the higher-rate threshold, you can avoid the higher rate of capital gains tax by making a gift to charity or a pension payment. These are deducted from your taxable income and so mean you can have more capital gains taxed at the lower rate.

Which shares or unit trusts are you selling?

Imagine you bought some shares in British Utility plc when the company was privatised, and you bought more later on. Now you are selling half the holding. HMRC will assume that you have sold:

■ First: any shares acquired on the same day as the disposal in question.

■ Second: shares acquired in the 30 days following the sale. This is a way of discouraging 'bed-and-breakfasting' (selling shares and buying them back the next day, in order to realise a gain to set against your annual tax-free amount).

■ Third: all your other shares on a 'pooled' basis. This means that the allowable cost of each share is the average value of all the shares (see Example 14.4).

Similar rules apply to unit trusts and shares in investment trusts and Open Ended Investment Companies (OEICs), but you can avoid capital gains tax altogether if you invest through an ISA (see Chapter 11).

Are you 'connected'?

Beware of giving taxable assets to 'connected persons' such as family members or business associates. You will still be liable to pay capital gains tax on the full market value and you cannot use any losses to reduce other gains.

Example 14.4: How pooling works

Ernie bought 2,000 shares in British Bottles plc in July 1995 for £2,000 and another 2,000 shares in July 2000 for £3,000. These are pooled, so the allowable cost of each share is £5,000 ÷ 4,000 = £1.25.

Stock dividends

These are extra shares issued instead of a cash dividend. The dividend voucher will tell you the amount of the dividend on which income tax is payable (see page 193). For capital gains tax purposes, you are treated as if you paid that amount in cash for the new shares.

Mergers, takeovers, rights issues and other reorganisations

If a company in which you have shares has issued extra shares, or has been taken over, merged or otherwise reorganised, the company will usually tell you how the reorganisation is treated for tax purposes in the circular or prospectus sent to shareholders. Also see HMRC help sheet 285 *Share reorganisations, company take-overs and Capital Gains Tax.*

If you receive extra shares through a bonus or rights issue, this is not treated as a new purchase. Instead, your new shares are pooled with the shares you already have of the same class. With a bonus issue, you pay nothing for the shares so your acquisition cost remains the same; with a rights issue, you add the cost of the new shares to the cost of the old ones. Examples are in HMRC help sheet 285.

Unit trusts and Open Ended Investment Companies (OEICs)

These are treated like shares, but there is some special treatment:

- You might see a figure for 'equalisation' on the tax voucher that accompanies distributions. This is an adjustment of the cost of the units and should be deducted from the allowable cost.
- With 'accumulation' units, any income is reinvested automatically by increasing the value of your existing units. The increase in value is treated as extra expenditure on your original holding.
- If you make regular investments, each counts as a new purchase, but the allowable cost will usually be the average cost of all the units you own (as for shares, see page 228).

A failed investment?

If you have assets that become worthless, you can claim a loss even if you still own them, and if the assets are shares in an unlisted trading company or an Enterprise Investment Scheme, you can set the loss against either capital gains or income. See HMRC help sheets 286 *Negligible value claims* and 297 *Enterprise Investment Scheme and Capital Gains Tax.*

Tax reliefs you can claim to reduce your capital gains

Your only or main home

If you sell your only or main home, 'private residence relief' makes any gain tax-free. See HMRC help sheet 283 *Private residence relief*. However, you may lose part of your relief if:

■ you have tenants (you may be able to claim lettings relief instead, see page 233). You do not lose relief if you have a single lodger or if you are a 'shared lives' carer (see page 51)
■ part of your home is used exclusively for business
■ you sell off part of your property
■ the garden is larger than necessary 'for your reasonable enjoyment' (HMRC uses half a hectare as a guide to what is reasonable)
■ HMRC thinks you are in the business of property development. If so, you get no relief and profits are taxed as income, not capital gains.

If only part of your home qualifies, the gain will be split between parts of the home which qualify and parts which do not. There are no set rules for how the gain is split, but it is usual to take into account the number of rooms in each part.

You may also lose part of your relief if the home was classed as your only or main home for just part of the time. The gain is split depending on how long it was your only or main home – so if you owned the house for 120 months, say, and lost relief for 40 of those months, 40/120 of the gain is potentially taxable. See Examples 14.5 and 14.6 on pages 232 and 233. If you bought the property before April 1982, use the value at the end of March 1982 to work out the allowable cost.

You do not lose the relief for:

■ the first year of ownership (exceptionally two years) if you have not been able to live in the home because you are doing it up or have still to sell your old home
■ absences if you are living in job-related accommodation
■ the final three years of your ownership.

Example 14.5: **Is your home tax-free?**

Martin and Fiona bought a Cotswolds cottage in May 2002 and sold it in May 2012 for a gain of £200,000. As they owned the cottage jointly, the gain is split between them and is £100,000 each, see page 234. It was their main home for the first two years, but then they moved, letting out the cottage until they sold it. The first two years qualify for private residence relief and the final three years always do – five years in total. They each qualify for private residence relief on $^5/_{10}$ of their gain, i.e. £100,000 $\times$ $^5/_{10}$ = £50,000.

The following absences also count as periods of residence, providing you lived in the property before and after the absence and had no other main home:

- absences because you are employed outside the UK
- absences of up to four years, if you have to be away for work
- other absences which add up to less than three years altogether.

More than one home

You can choose which home is your main one, but you must do so within two years of the date you had a particular combination of homes. A new two-year period begins on any further change in your combination of homes. You can save most tax by choosing the property that is most likely to increase in value, but also take into account how long you are likely to want to keep each one.

If you do not make an election, which property counts as your main home will depend on the facts. You will need to take a view in order to fill in your tax return, but HMRC can challenge your interpretation so it's best to plan ahead and make an election. See HMRC help sheet 283 *Private residence relief*.

Note that property rented on a tenancy agreement can still be your 'residence' – so if you have a property you own as well as one rented on this basis, nominate the home you own as your main residence.

Property you let

When you sell a property that you let, the whole of any gain is potentially liable to tax. It will not qualify for entrepreneurs' relief unless it is taxed as a trade, or unless it met the conditions to be treated as furnished holiday lettings (see page 158). You can reduce the tax if you genuinely live in the property as your main residence at some point. That way you qualify for private residence relief for at least the final three years of ownership (see Example 14.6). You may also qualify for lettings relief.

Lettings relief

This relief is available only if you let out residential accommodation in what is or has been your only or main home, or part of it. It is part of your home if you have made no structural alterations, even if the let part has its own kitchen and bathroom, but you cannot claim it for a self-contained flat.

Lettings relief is worth the same as private residence relief, up to a ceiling of £40,000. So if your private residence relief is:

- £40,000 or less, just double the private residence relief
- over £40,000, you add £40,000 to your private residence relief.

Property abroad?

Gains on a property abroad may be liable to UK capital gains tax (see page 176). However, you can claim private residence relief and lettings relief if it has been your only or main home at some time, or entrepreneurs' relief if it is classed as furnished holiday lettings.

Example 14.6: **Tax on a home that you let**

Martin and Fiona made a gain of £100,000 each on their cottage, £50,000 of which qualifies for private residence relief (see Example 14.5 opposite). The remaining gain is £50,000 each, on which they can claim lettings relief. This is the same amount as their private residence relief, or £40,000 each if less. So their taxable gain is reduced to £50,000 – £40,000 = £10,000 each. They made no other gains in 2012–13. They each have a gain below their annual exemption (£10,600 in 2012–13) so they have no tax to pay.

Tax on your home if you have a partner

If you are married or a civil partner, your main home (for private residence relief) must be the same for both of you, unless you are permanently separated. But whether or not you are married, if you make a taxable capital gain on a property you own with someone else, the gain will be split between you. And both partners and spouses can claim lettings relief on their share of a gain – so lettings relief of up to £80,000 on one property may be available. (See Example 14.6 on page 233.)

Reliefs for spouses and civil partners

Husbands and wives each get their own annual tax-free amount. If you give (or even sell) something to your husband or wife, there is no tax to pay at the time, provided that you are living together, or in the year of separation. Any tax is payable only when your spouse disposes of the asset – but at that stage, the gain is worked out as if your spouse had owned the asset from the moment you acquired it. The same rules apply to civil partners, but other couples do not qualify for this special treatment.

Reliefs for your business

If you dispose of part or all of your business you may qualify for the following reliefs:

- Entrepreneurs' relief (see below and HMRC help sheet 275 *Entrepreneurs' relief*)
- Roll-over relief – this allows you to put off paying tax on disposing of business assets if you reinvest the gains in new business assets. (See HMRC help sheet 290 *Business asset roll-over relief*.)
- Incorporation relief – this allows you to put off paying tax if you transfer your business to a company in exchange for shares. (See HMRC help sheet 276 *Incorporation relief*.)

Note that if you have unused trading losses from self-employment or a partnership, you can choose to set them against your capital gains rather than carry them forward to future years (see page 145). If you made a loss on furnished holidays before 6 April 2011 you can also do this, providing you claim by 31 January 2013 (see page 147). The Capital gains summary pages of the tax return call these 'income losses'.

Entrepreneurs' relief

This relief reduces the rate of tax to 10 per cent if you sell all or part of:

- a trading business that you have had for at least a year *or*
- business assets you sell after ceasing to trade *or*
- shares in a trading company, provided that you were a director or employee and had at least a 5 per cent shareholding *or*
- assets used in a trading company or partnership *or*
- shares acquired as a result of exercising an option received under the Enterprise Management Incentives scheme (see page 94). This proposal has yet to be implemented, but the plan is to backdate it to 6 April 2012.

This rules out a property business with the exception of qualifying furnished holiday lettings in the circumstances shown above.

The reduced tax rate applies to the first £10 million of your gain. However, this is a lifetime limit, so if you set up several businesses, you have to deduct any entrepreneurs' relief previously claimed. Any gains over the eligible amount are taxed at normal rates. See HMRC help sheet 275 *Entrepreneurs' relief*.

What to tell HMRC

If you aren't sent a tax return, you should tell your tax office by 5 October after the end of the tax year in which you make the gain if you have a taxable capital gain above the annual tax-free amount. You will probably be sent a tax return (although it may be the short version). If you get a 2011–12 return (including the short version), you will need to complete the capital gains tax supplementary pages if any of the following apply:

- you disposed of taxable assets worth more than £42,400 in total
- your taxable gains (before deducting any losses) come to more than £10,600
- you want to make a claim or election, for example you want to claim a loss or entrepreneurs' relief
- you are claiming the remittance basis on any overseas gains (see page 173).

Chapter 18 gives more information about how to complete the Capital gains summary pages.

If you incurred losses in 2011–12 that you want to set against gains made in past or future years, notify your tax office before 6 April 2016. There is no time limit for losses made before 6 April 1996. Once losses have been notified, you can carry them forward indefinitely.

Record-keeping

You should keep the following for at least 22 months or, if you have a business or rental income, for five years and ten months from the end of the tax year to which they relate. But it's best to keep the records for as long as you own the asset, or until you use any loss arising from it.

- Contract notes, correspondence or other documentation when you buy, sell, lease or exchange assets such as investments.
- Stock dividend vouchers.
- Invoices or other evidence of payment records (e.g. bank statements) for costs you claim for the purchase, improvement or sale of assets.
- Documents relating to assets you acquired but did not buy yourself, such as gifts or an inheritance.
- Details of assets you have given away or put into a trust.
- Copies of valuations taken into account in your calculation of gains and losses (e.g. probate values for inherited assets).
- If you acquired or disposed of an asset other than on the open market (e.g. if you gave shares away), a note of the market value.
- If you use an asset partly for business, partly privately, records to show

what proportion of the use is for each purpose.

■ If you start using an asset for a purpose that might change its tax treatment (e.g. you start letting out part of your home or using an asset in your business), notes of dates on which the use changes.

■ If you have more than one property, records of dates when you lived in them, evidence that you actually lived there and copies of any elections to choose one as your 'main' home (see page 232).

■ A record of claims for entrepreneurs' relief or other business reliefs. Keep evidence to show you met the conditions for claiming.

15

Tax on inheritances

Inheritance tax may have to be paid on whatever you leave when you die (your 'estate'), if it is above a tax-free band of £325,000. It may also be payable on some lifetime gifts. This chapter explains the rules about how much you can give away tax-free, how the tax is worked out on gifts above the tax-free band, and simple ways of saving tax.

Top tips

- For married couples and civil partners, the unused tax-free band of the first partner to die can be used to reduce the tax on the death of the second partner.
- It's important to keep good records, so that it is clear how much of someone's tax-free band is unused.
- Make a will and review it regularly. If you want to leave money to charity, new rules from 6 April 2012 have cut the cost of giving large amounts (see page 248).
- You can make significant inroads into a potential tax bill by using tax-free gifts. Share your wealth with your partner so that he or she can do so too.
- Make sure that the cash is there to pay any tax on your death, and that your partner has enough ready money to live on until your estate can be distributed.
- Your beneficiaries can alter your will within two years after your death, with a deed of variation. This allows your money to be passed on as best suits your heirs at the time.

Do you need to worry about inheritance tax?

Inheritance tax is payable when the taxable value of your estate, including any home you own and gifts you made in the seven years before death, is above a tax-free band. This was £325,000 for deaths in 2011–12 and has been frozen at that level until 2014–15. The tax is 40 per cent of everything above this, with reductions for lifetime gifts, but from 6 April 2012 the tax is 36 per cent if you leave at least 10 per cent of your estate to charity (see page 248).

Husbands and wives

Both husband and wife (and civil partners) have their own tax-free band, but the first partner to die often does not use it – because many people leave everything to their husband or wife and such gifts are tax-free.

  If the first partner to die does not use all their tax-free band, the unused proportion can be transferred to the surviving partner. This reduces the tax when the second partner dies. So if, for example, you leave everything to your wife (a tax-free gift), when she dies her estate can claim double the tax-free band at the time. And it's not the unused amount that's transferred, but the unused proportion – so her estate will benefit if the tax-free band increases (see Example 15.1 overleaf). You can claim the unused amount however long ago the first partner died (but see below for deaths before March 1972). There is a list of tax-free bands from previous years in the Fact file.

  This effectively doubles the tax-free amount to £650,000 for married couples and civil partners, but there are a few things to watch out for:

■ The claim to transfer unused tax-free band has to be made after the second death, using either form IHT217 or form IHT402. Form IHT402 asks not only what the first partner left, but also about gifts they made in the seven years before they died. So you both need to keep good records of gifts.
■ If you are married more than once (or your partner was), the total tax-free band you can inherit from all previous spouses is limited to the amount applying on your death – so you can never have more than two tax-free bands.

■ If the first death was before March 1972, it is unlikely that there will be any unused tax-free band, because at that time there was no exemption for transfers between spouses.

Non-married couples

You cannot transfer unused tax-free band unless you are married or in a civil partnership. So other couples still need to plan very carefully, make a will and follow the tips given opposite.

Example 15.1: Transferring unused tax-free band

Ethel died in August 2012, leaving an estate of £500,000, which is more than the £325,000 tax-free band. However, when Ethel's husband George died in 2007, he did not use all his tax-free band (which was £300,000 at that point). He left his share in the house to Ethel (a tax-free gift) but £100,000 investments to the children. He used only 100/300 = 1/3 of his tax-free band, which means that 2/3 is available to transfer to Ethel. As the tax-free band is £325,000 in the year Ethel dies, her executors can claim to transfer a further 2/3 × £325,000 = £216,667. Her total tax-free band is £216,667 + £325,000 = £541,667 – so there is no tax for her family to pay.

Review wills that used trusts

Before married couples were allowed to transfer unused tax-free bands, many tax advisers recommended setting up various types of trust in your will – the legacy to the trust would make use of your tax-free band but the trustees could use the assets in the trust to benefit your widow or widower. If your will does this, you should ask your solicitor whether you should rewrite it. That's because under the current rules you can wait until both deaths, and use the combined tax-free bands then, rather than using one tax-free band earlier on (see Example 15.1). If a relative with this type of will has died recently, it may not be too late to rewrite their will – you can use a 'deed of variation' providing you act within two years of their death (see page 251).

> ## Saving tax through life insurance

Ask the insurance company about getting your policy 'written in trust' for your beneficiaries – the proceeds are not part of your estate and can be paid out before probate is granted. The premiums are a gift to your beneficiaries, but regular premiums are usually tax-free as a gift out of your normal expenditure. Transferring an existing policy also counts as a gift, and under the rules for trusts tax may be due if it is worth more than the tax-free threshold. Alternatively, your beneficiaries may be able to take out a policy on your life.

Planning to pass on your money

The ability to transfer unused tax-free band means that for married couples with combined estates below £650,000, the best advice may be to do nothing. The same applies to widows and widowers who can transfer the full tax-free band from their spouse. Other people with estates above £325,000 may need to take action, particularly if they are living with someone without being married. If a lot of money is at stake, or a business or farm is involved, or one partner is 'domiciled' abroad (see page 171), get professional advice. Tax planning schemes are available, often involving insurance policies or trusts, but the Disclosure of Tax Avoidance Schemes rules apply to inheritance tax (see page 42). Simple things to do include:

- Make, or review, your will. For what happens if you die without a will, search under 'intestacy' on www.direct.gov.uk.
- Use your exemptions. See the list of tax-free gifts overleaf.
- Make gifts early – they will be tax-free if you survive for seven years – but don't jeopardise your own financial security. You should also get advice first if you want to leave a large gift to charity to benefit from the new reduced tax rate (see page 248), as a large lifetime gift may make this more difficult. Remember too that capital gains tax may be due on a lifetime gift (see Chapter 14).
- Check whether any reliefs apply – see page 251.
- If you are married or a civil partner, you each have your own tax-free band and set of tax-free gifts, and transfers between you are tax-free.

This means that if one of you has most of the money, you can give some to your partner, so that he or she can make use of the exemptions. (But the gift must be outright, without strings.)

What not to do

Do not make a gift in name only – such as giving away a house you continue to live in. This is a 'gift with reservation' and will still count as part of your estate unless you pay a market rent for it.

Even if the gift is not caught by this rule, if it benefits you in any way it may be classed as a 'pre-owned asset' and you may be charged income tax. This applies to gifts, and possibly sales, going back to 18 March 1986. You are also affected if you gave cash or a loan to someone to buy something from which you now benefit (such as a house you now live in). Other cash gifts are usually exempt, except some gifts to trusts.

The pre-owned asset rules do not apply if you pay a full market rent for the asset, or if you sell your home to an equity release company. Nor do they apply to gifts to a spouse or civil partner, or to maintain a dependent relative, or small gifts (within the £250 and £3,000 exemptions, see opposite), or if you were left something which you gave away under a 'deed of variation' (see page 251).

If you are affected, you may have to pay income tax each year on a percentage of the asset's value (4 per cent), or on the rental value of land – but only if the benefit amounts to £5,000 or more. Alternatively, you can elect to have a pre-owned asset treated as part of your estate, and liable to inheritance tax rather than income tax. You must make the election by 31 January after the end of the tax year for which the income tax charge would first be payable, but if you miss that date HMRC has discretion to accept late elections. There is more information on the 'pre-owned assets' area of the HMRC website at www.hmrc.gov.uk/poa/.

Tax-free gifts

Although inheritance tax is payable on death, it may be charged on some lifetime gifts. But some lifetime gifts are tax-free and almost all others are

'Potentially Exempt Transfers' (PETs). A PET is taxable only if you die within seven years of making the gift and your total taxable lifetime gifts come to more than the tax-free band. The tax is reduced if you die after three years but within seven years of making the PET. Gifts to trusts are not PETs and may be taxable immediately – see page 248.

Tax-free lifetime gifts

■ Gifts to someone getting married or registering a civil partnership – up to £1,000 or £5,000 if you are a parent of one of the couple, £2,500 if you are a grandparent.
■ Payments to maintain your family or dependent relatives. This includes ex-wives, ex-husbands and ex-civil partners.
■ Gifts that are normal expenditure out of your income and leave you with enough to maintain your normal standard of living – e.g. regular payments into an insurance policy to benefit your children.
■ Small gifts – up to a maximum of £250 per recipient in any tax year.
■ An annual exemption of £3,000 in each tax year, plus any unused balance of £3,000 from the previous tax year. If you give more than £3,000, the amount above £3,000 counts as a PET.

You can combine tax-free gifts, with the exception of the small gifts exemption – e.g. you could give a grandchild a £2,500 wedding gift plus £3,000 under your annual exemption, but not a 'small gift' of £250 as well.

Always tax-free

■ Gifts to spouses or civil partners. If they are 'domiciled' abroad, only £55,000 in total is tax-free (currently under review, see page 171).
■ Gifts to good causes – i.e. UK charities, community amateur sports clubs or housing associations.
■ Gifts to some institutions, such as universities and the National Trust.
■ Gifts to qualifying political parties.
■ Gifts of decorations for valour or gallant conduct, provided that these have never been sold.
■ The estate of someone who dies on active service.

> ## If you received a Potentially Exempt Transfer (PET)

After the donor's death, all PETs must be declared to HMRC's Inheritance Tax office by the executors, and any tax must be paid by the recipient. If this applies to you, HMRC will contact you, so make sure you keep records of PETs received, and that your records match the donor's (see page 254).

How inheritance tax is worked out on death

Tax is payable after a death if the value of the estate (as defined on page 247), plus any PETs made in the previous seven years, but minus debts and tax-free legacies, comes to more than the inheritance tax threshold.

- Step 1: calculate the tax-free band due, including any amount transferred from a deceased spouse (see page 239).
- Step 2: set the tax-free band against PETs made in the seven years before death, starting with the earliest gift (see Example 15.2).
- Step 3: work out tax at 40 per cent on any PETs above the tax-free band. The tax is reduced by taper relief if death occurs three or more years after the gift (see Table 15.1 opposite).
- Step 4: work out how much tax-free band is left, after deducting any PETs. So if a single person dies in 2012–13 with PETs of £175,000, say, the remaining tax-free band is £325,000 – £175,000 = £150,000.
- Step 5: calculate the taxable value of the estate (see page 247).
- Step 6: if the taxable value of the estate is below the remaining tax-free band (from step 4), there is no tax to pay on it. If it is above, deduct the tax-free band. So if someone dies with an estate of £300,000, and has a tax-free band after PETs of £150,000, tax is payable on £300,000 – £150,000 = £150,000.
- Step 7: work out tax at 40 per cent on everything above the tax-free band, i.e. £150,000 × 40% = £60,000.
- Step 8: if necessary, adjust the amount each beneficiary receives from the estate (see page 250).

See the inheritance tax section of the HMRC website. Note that:

■ if you made taxable lifetime gifts things get very complicated and you will need professional advice
■ the rate of tax is reduced from 40 per cent to 36 per cent for deaths after 5 April 2012 where 10 per cent or more of the taxable estate is left to charity. See page 248.

Example 15.2: **Tax on PETs**

Mr Kumar, who was single, gave £120,000 to each of his nephews when they reached 21. The first nephew reached 21 in 2006, the second in 2008 and the third in 2010. He died in May 2012. All the gifts were made in the seven years before he died, but the first £3,000 of each gift falls within the annual exemption for each year, and a further £3,000 within the exemption for the previous year, so the taxable amount of each gift is £114,000.

The first two gifts fall within the £325,000 tax-free band, leaving only £325,000 − £114,000 − £114,000 = £97,000 of the band available. So his third nephew must pay tax on £114,000 − £97,000 = £17,000. This amounts to £17,000 × 40% = £6,800, and no taper relief is available because the gift was made less than three years before Mr Kumar died. Because the tax-free threshold has been used up by his PETs, the whole of Mr Kumar's estate on death is taxable, apart from any tax-free legacies.

Table 15.1 Taper relief on lifetime gifts

Years between date of gift and death	Percentage of full tax payable	Equivalent to tax rate of
Less than 3 years	100%	40%
More than 3 but less than 4	80%	32%
More than 4 but less than 5	60%	24%
More than 5 but less than 6	40%	16%
More than 6 but less than 7	20%	8%
7 or more years	No tax	No tax

Example 15.3: **How taper relief works**

If you have to pay tax on a lifetime gift that was made at least three years before death, a reduced rate of tax is payable (see Table 15.1). So in Example 15.2 on page 245, Mr Kumar's youngest nephew received a PET of £17,000 within three years of his uncle's death, on which £6,800 tax was payable. If Mr Kumar had made the gift in the fourth year before his death, only 80% of the full tax bill would have been payable: £6,800 $\times$ 80% = £5,440.

Large lifetime gifts can increase the tax

The tax-free threshold (£325,000 in 2011–12 and 2012–13) is set first against your lifetime gifts, with anything left over set against your estate on death. So tax is not payable on a PET, even if this was made within seven years of death, unless your total taxable lifetime gifts made in the last seven years come to more than the tax-free threshold. But even if your gifts in the seven years before death are not themselves taxable, they can still push your estate on death above the inheritance tax threshold. And do not pin too much hope on taper relief. It reduces the tax payable, not the taxable value of the gift, so it applies only if your total PETs are above the tax-free band. Lifetime gifts can also make it harder to benefit from the reduction in the tax rate if you leave 10% or more of your estate to charity. See page 248.

Saving tax on the family home

The chances of having to pay tax on the family home are much reduced now that unused tax-free band can be transferred to the surviving spouse (see page 239). If your house does push you above your total tax-free band, there are tax-saving schemes involving trusts or giving your house away and then paying a market rent to live in it, but tax changes over the years have made many such schemes ineffective. A simpler way to save tax is to move to a smaller home and give away the cash released. You can take out a mortgage to do this instead, but the mortgage may cost more than the tax saved.

The taxable value of an estate

When you die, your taxable 'estate' consists of:

■ everything owned in your own name (see page 172 for overseas property)

■ your share of any jointly owned property (see below)

■ a payout on your death from a life insurance policy that you took out, unless it has been 'written in trust' for someone else (see page 241)

■ a gift from which you or your spouse continue to benefit – either a 'gift with reservation' or a 'pre-owned asset' which you have opted to have treated as part of your estate (see page 242)

■ assets in certain trusts from which you have a right to some personal benefit, such as an income (see overleaf)

■ *minus* tax-free legacies (see page 242), such as to a spouse or charity

■ *minus* reasonable funeral expenses (including a headstone)

■ *minus* any money or property owed by you

■ *minus* some forms of compensation, e.g. to holocaust survivors or British prisoners of war in Japanese camps.

ISAs become taxable on death

Any investments in an Individual Savings Account (ISA) form part of your estate and lose their tax-free status when you die.

Jointly owned property

The law assumes that joint property is shared equally, in the absence of any documents that say otherwise – e.g. the deeds to a house. But with a joint money account, your share (for inheritance tax purposes) is in line with the money you each contributed to it.

Often, jointly owned assets such as houses and bank accounts are set up so that they pass automatically to the survivor (although the deceased person's share still counts as part of his or her estate). Under English law, this is called a 'joint tenancy'; in Scotland, it is called passing 'by survivorship' (although with a joint bank account, the survivor may operate the account but not necessarily be entitled to the money in it).

Automatic transfer has the advantage of giving the survivor immediate access to the money. However, the advantage of owning joint assets as 'tenants in common' (in England) or with no special destination (in Scotland) is that you can leave your share to whomever you wish.

Assets in a trust

Trusts – legal arrangements that hold investments or other assets in the care of trustees for the benefit of one or more 'beneficiaries' – have often been used in inheritance tax planning. Once assets have been given to the trust, they are usually no longer part of the donor's estate, and any growth in value belongs to the trust, not the donor. However, changes to the tax treatment have removed many of the advantages.

A gift to most trusts is now liable to an immediate tax charge if, within a seven-year period, your total gifts to trusts come to more than the inheritance tax threshold. The tax rate is 20 per cent, but on death the tax is recalculated and more may be payable. However, there is an exception for gifts to trusts set up to protect the assets of some disabled people, trusts set up to benefit employees, trusts set up to compensate asbestos victims, and some trusts set up in a will (for bereaved children, say).

With some types of trust, tax is also charged every ten years on trust assets if the current value of these is above the tax-free band.

Trusts do still have a role in tax-planning (for example, trusts can be set up in a will to give the executors more flexibility after the death), but you will need professional advice. And if you are involved in a trust, it is worth checking what effect any recent changes have had on its tax treatment.

Tax reductions for large charitable legacies

Gifts to charity are not part of your taxable estate, but for deaths after 5 April 2012 they can reduce the rate of tax on the rest of your estate from 40 per cent to 36 per cent. To qualify, you must leave 10 per cent or more of your taxable estate, minus the tax-free band, to charity. See Example

15.4. Property classed as a 'gift with reservation' (see page 242) does not qualify.

In addition, if you own a property or investment jointly with somebody else that passes to them automatically on your death, or assets in a trust, these are treated separately when deciding if you have met the 10 per cent threshold. So if half of Mr Smith's estate (see Example 15.4) came from a property owned jointly with his daughter, and half from investments, the taxable part of each is £350,000 ÷ 2 = £175,000. He would qualify for a 36% rate on his investments (but not his property) if he gave £175,000 × 10% = £17,500 to charity.

Example 15.4: **Tax reductions for charitable legacies**

Mr Smith, a widower, dies leaving an estate of £1 million. His tax-free band (including amounts unused by his wife) is £650,000, so his taxable estate is £1 million − £650,000 = £350,000. With no gift to charity, he will pay £350,000 × 40% = £140,000, leaving £860,000 for his family.

Mr Smith will qualify for the 36% tax rate if he leaves £350,000 × 10% = £35,000 to charity. The gift itself reduces his taxable estate, so tax is due on £350,000 − £35,000 = £315,000. The tax is £315,000 × 36% = £113,400, leaving £1 million − £35,000 − £113,400 = £851,600. The £35,000 gift costs his family £860,000 − £851,600 = £8,400.

Should you give 10% to charity?

Once you have reached the 10% threshold, each £100 you give costs your estate only £24. Below the 10% threshold, each £100 costs £60 (£100 minus £40 inheritance tax saved). But the gift will always reduce the amount left for your beneficiaries, so consider it only if you want to give to charity. And even if you do, see Chapter 13 and consider taking professional advice because it's not straightforward. A lifetime gift to family or friends in the last seven years of your life reduces the tax-free band available on your estate and means that the 10% threshold is higher. If you do not want to decide now, your family can use a deed of variation after your death to give to charity (see page 251).

Who pays the tax?

Any inheritance tax due is paid out of the 'residue' of the estate (what is left after all specific legacies have been paid), unless:

- The will says a legacy is before tax ('subject to the payment of taxes' or must 'bear its own tax'). If it does, the recipient pays the tax (see Example 15.5).
- There would not be enough money left to pay the tax after all legacies have been paid. If so, specific bequests may have to be reduced.
- A PET was made in the seven years before the donor's death. If so, the recipient is liable to pay any inheritance tax on it – though the money may be provided by a further gift from the estate.

Tax is payable on the loss to the giver, not the benefit to the recipient. So if a gift is intended to be tax-free in the hands of the recipient, it must be 'grossed-up' to find the amount that, after 40 per cent tax, leaves the intended gift. An after-tax legacy of £12,000, say, would actually count as a gift of £20,000 minus tax of £20,000 × 40% = £8,000, i.e. £20,000 – £8,000 = £12,000.

Example 15.5: **Tax on an estate**

Mr Smith-Jones made no PETs in his lifetime. When he died in May 2012, he left:

- a house worth £300,000 to his wife – this was tax-free as a bequest to his wife
- £250,000 to his son – tax-free as it fell within the tax-free band
- the residue of his estate (£250,000), split between his son and his wife. His wife's share is tax-free; his son's share is taxable, but there is still £325,000 – £250,000 = £75,000 of the tax-free band to set against it.

If the will says the residue should be divided before tax, his son and his wife will both get £250,000 ÷ 2 = £125,000, and his son will have to pay tax at 40% on £125,000 – £75,000 = £50,000. If it is after tax, the gift has to be 'grossed-up' to include the tax, and the calculations can be very complex.

Take care when making a will

Think about how any tax will be paid and don't give so much in specific bequests free-of-tax that whoever inherits the residue (e.g. your spouse) has less to live on than you intended. If the recipient can afford it, it is simpler for gifts in a will to bear their own tax.

Deeds of variation

However carefully you do your tax planning, you never know when you will die or what the inheritance tax position will be. Your heirs should bear in mind that they can alter an inheritance after a death, by using a 'deed of variation' (sometimes called an 'instrument of variation'). It can also be used if someone dies without leaving a will ('intestate'). A variation allows beneficiaries to disclaim gifts and legacies in favour of their children, say. It must be made in writing within two years of death, but all the original beneficiaries must agree, and if a beneficiary is a child, court approval may be needed, so consult a solicitor.

Tax reliefs you can claim

For details of all the following reliefs, see the inheritance tax section of the HMRC website at www.hmrc.gov.uk/inheritancetax or contact HMRC's probate and inheritance tax helpline (see the Fact file).

Agricultural property relief

Tax relief may be available if you give away agricultural land and property during your lifetime or on your death, provided that you or your spouse or civil partner used it for agricultural purposes for at least two years. If you did not use it yourself, you must have owned it for at least seven years and it must have been tenanted for agricultural purposes throughout.

If the property is let on a tenancy that started after 31 August 1995, 100 per cent relief applies. If not, 100 per cent relief still applies if you have the right to vacant possession within 12 months. Otherwise, the rate of relief is normally 50 per cent.

Business property relief

If you give away a business or a share in a business, or unquoted shares in a business, 100 per cent relief is available provided that you or your spouse owned it for at least two years. However, if you give away business land, buildings, plant or machinery, or a controlling shareholding in a quoted company, only 50 per cent relief is available.

Relief is not available for pure investment companies, nor is it available for plant or machinery used partly for the business, partly privately. You can claim relief for just part of land or buildings, provided that that part is used exclusively for the business.

Double taxation relief

If you have property or assets abroad, UK inheritance tax is still likely to be payable (see page 172) and the overseas tax authorities may charge the equivalent of inheritance tax on any gift or bequest. If so, you can claim some relief for it against UK inheritance tax.

Quick succession relief

This relief (also known as 'successive charges' relief) applies where someone dies having inherited assets from someone who died in the previous five years. If inheritance tax was paid when the first person died, the tax payable on the second death is reduced.

What to tell HMRC

You do not have to tell HMRC about tax-free gifts or PETs made during your lifetime. However, you must tell HMRC if you are liable to income tax on a 'pre-owned' asset, under 'Other UK income' in the main tax return (see page 279).

When someone dies, whoever is handling their affairs has to send an 'account' of all the taxable assets of the deceased person to HMRC's Inheritance Tax office, and pay any inheritance tax due (or, for land and property and some business assets, arrange to pay it in instalments), before they can distribute the assets of the estate. The account also covers lifetime gifts, so that HMRC can check whether tax is due on those. The main form used is

IHT400 *Inheritance Tax account,* but this is not required for estates worth less than the inheritance tax threshold or less than £1 million with everything left to a spouse or to charity, or estates where the deceased person lived and died abroad and had assets worth less than £150,000 in the UK. All the forms are available on the HMRC website, and IHT400 has a working sheet which tells you how to calculate the tax. If you need help, HMRC has a probate and inheritance tax helpline on 0845 302 0900.

If the person who died was predeceased by a husband or wife, or civil partner, either form IHT217 or form IHT402 should be completed in order to claim any unused tax-free band (see page 239).

Inheritance tax must be paid within six months of the death. If the deceased person had money in most bank or building society accounts, or in National Savings & Investments or British Government Stock, this can be used to pay the tax, through what is called the direct payment scheme. And you can opt to pay the tax on some types of asset, such as land and property and a stake in a business, by instalments. Otherwise, the executor or personal representative may have to take out a loan. You might want to consider taking out an insurance policy so that cash is available to pay the tax (see page 241). As with other taxes, there are penalties for sending in forms late or paying late, as well as interest on tax overdue.

Income from estates

Before the paperwork is completed, the estate may receive income, such as interest on a bank account or dividends from investments. If the income tax and capital gains due on the estate during the period of administration come to more than £10,000, whoever is administering it may have to complete a special Trust and Estate tax return. If smaller amounts of tax are owed – for example, a bit of tax on savings interest received before tax – they can just contact the deceased person's tax office.

If you are a beneficiary of the estate, some or all of the estate's income may be taxed as yours. If so, it is taxed in the same way as any other income within the same category – e.g. dividends or interest. Whoever is administering the estate should give you a form R185 stating how much income you have received in each category, and how much tax has been paid on your behalf.

Record-keeping

Keep track of the value of your assets in the same way as for capital gains tax (see Chapter 14), and make sure there is documentation to prove the value of any assets at the date you give them away. With jointly owned assets, record how much each of you contributed to the purchase price.

You should also keep records of any gifts you have made or received for at least seven years (14 years in the case of gifts to trusts). A dated copy of a letter, saying that it is a gift, is all that is needed. Even if gifts are not taxable, good records are helpful for winding up your estate on your death. And if you are relying on a gift being tax-free as 'normal expenditure out of income' (see page 242), whoever deals with your estate will need to show your income and expenditure. Also keep records of any debts you have – they reduce the value of your estate.

Finally, make sure that your will is kept in a secure place (a solicitor can advise you) – and most importantly, tell somebody where to find it. Do not keep it in a safe deposit box. Your heirs will need probate to open it – and probate cannot be granted without the will.

If you have been responsible for winding up the affairs of someone who has died (as executor of their will, say), you should keep the following:

- A copy of the will and all signed inheritance tax forms (plus records you used to complete the forms).
- Records of any unused tax-free band on the death of a first spouse or civil partner to reduce tax on the second partner's death.
- Any paperwork that shows how you arrived at the value of items such as property, investments and personal possessions ('probate value').
- The letter that HMRC sends confirming that inheritance tax has been paid – or use form IHT30 to apply for a 'clearance certificate'.
- Receipts from any creditors and beneficiaries.
- Details of income and capital gains received by the estate before it is distributed (for example, savings interest).
- Receipts for any expenses you incurred in your role as executor (you can claim these from the estate).

HMRC may request a copy of the paperwork to check the return. You should also send a copy of any relevant documents to each of the beneficiaries – for example, the 'probate value' of any assets they receive may be needed for their capital gains tax.

Although it is not legally required, it is a good idea to keep all documents for at least 12 years – and indefinitely if the deceased person did not use all their tax-free band and left a spouse or civil partner on whose death it could be used.

Part 3
Filling in the forms

16

If you get a tax return

If you are sent a tax return, you are within the 'self-assessment' system of paying tax. This has its own set of forms and deadlines, but you still have a number of choices to make about how to file your return and whether to file on paper or online. This chapter explains what you have to do and when, and how to make the process as simple as possible.

Top tips

- Don't put off doing your return. The deadline for filing a paper tax return is 31 October.
- If you can, file online. It gives you more time (the filing deadline is 31 January, or 31 December if you want tax collected through PAYE) and the calculation is done automatically – but allow ten days to register and activate the service first.
- HMRC rarely accepts excuses for being late with your tax or your return. Keep a copy and print off the online filing receipt, or get proof of posting if you are sending in a paper return (tax offices do not give receipts).
- If your tax office issues a formal decision or a penalty you disagree with, act fast – you usually have only 30 days in which to appeal.
- Even if you ask HMRC to work out your tax for you, check any calculation or self-assessment statement it sends you. There is a rough calculator on the back page of the HMRC Tax Return Guide. If you send in a paper return, also check that all your information has been carried across correctly to HMRC's computer.

Which tax return?

Once HMRC decides that you need to fill in a tax return (see page 28), you are within the self-assessment system. HMRC will send you the forms it thinks you need, with explanatory notes. The full tax return includes:

- A six-page core tax return that everybody needs to complete.
- A four-page Additional Information document for less common items.
- Supplementary pages to cover capital gains, employment, self-employment, partnerships, property, trusts, foreign income and claims to be classed as non-resident or use the remittance basis.

As well as your income tax, the full tax return covers capital gains tax, Class 4 National Insurance contributions (payable by the self-employed) and student loan repayments.

As explained on page 28, you might get sent a short tax return instead of the full return if your affairs are straightforward. This consists of four pages, plus an extra page if you have capital gains to declare (or capital losses to claim). Chapter 19 shows you how to fill in a short tax return.

You cannot opt to use the short return, and even if you are sent one, you cannot use it if you have income or reliefs not covered by the form. You may also choose to fill in the full return instead, either on paper or online. You will have to do this if you want to file online as the short return can only be filed on paper.

Which filing method?

The government is encouraging people to use online services, and there is an added incentive to do so as the deadline for sending in a paper return (short or full versions) is three months earlier than an online return. Filing online has several advantages – see page 262 – but there is no obligation to file online. If you want to stick with paper but are having difficulty and do not have a professional adviser, you should contact HMRC's helpline, or make an appointment at your local Tax Enquiry Office or, if your income is low, contact one of the charities that might be able to help (see Chapter 4).

There is a very small number of people – such as MPs – for whom HMRC does not provide online facilities and they can continue to file a paper return up to 31 January.

Once you have filed online once, or your tax adviser has done so on your behalf, you will not be sent a paper return the following year. Instead you will get a one-page *Notice to Complete a Tax Return* (SA316), which is a formal notification that you need to fill in a return. If you decide you want to go back to paper, contact the HMRC Orderline for the forms.

Filing a paper return

These are the steps to take if you are submitting a paper return:

■ Check that the form you have been sent covers all the types of taxable income and gains you have, and all the deductions you can claim. If it does not, contact the HMRC Orderline on 0845 9000 404. You can download pages for the full return, but not the short return, from the HMRC website (see the Fact file). You must enter your Unique Taxpayer Reference on the downloaded form – the ten-digit number shown on any letters you get about self-assessment (see page 45).

■ Enter the necessary information on the return itself. Chapters 17 to 19 will take you through the forms. Work on a copy first.

■ Work out the amount of tax due, if you want, but you can ask HMRC to do this for you. If you want to do the calculation yourself, you should ask the HMRC Orderline for a *Tax Calculation Summary*.

■ Post or hand-deliver the form by 31 October, making sure you keep a copy. It's best to get proof of posting, particularly if the 31 October deadline is approaching.

HMRC does not acknowledge receipt of a paper return, although it will let you know when it has been processed. However, if you have made a very basic mistake, such as failing to sign it, your return may be rejected. You will have to correct and resubmit it within 14 days (or by 31 October if later).

Once your tax return has been logged the information on it is transferred to the HMRC computer and an initial check is run for obvious mistakes, such as inconsistencies, faulty arithmetic and so on. HMRC has nine months to correct any such mistakes and inform you. If you disagree with a correction, you have the right to reject it.

HMRC will send you a tax calculation (on form SA302) if you have asked it to work out your tax, or if you have calculated your own tax but it disagrees with it. If you cannot reconcile the calculation with your tax return, contact your tax office without delay. If your query is not resolved by 31 January, when the tax is due (see page 264), pay the tax anyway – you will get a refund if you have paid too much, whereas if you don't pay you could find yourself faced with interest and possibly a penalty.

If you miss the deadline for filing a paper return

If you send in a paper return after the 31 October deadline HMRC will still process it, but you will be charged a £100 late filing penalty unless you have a reasonable excuse. You also have to pay any tax due by 31 January or risk a penalty, and there is no guarantee that HMRC will tell you how much you owe by then. So if you miss the deadline, it's best to file online. Once you have filed a paper return for the year you cannot file online.

Filing online

Most people can complete their returns using HMRC's free internet service. Filing online doesn't save you any tax, but your return – and any tax repayment – should be processed more quickly and accurately, your tax will be worked out automatically, and if you have made an obvious mistake your return will be rejected immediately. There is a helpline if you get stuck. You can also view your self-assessment statements online.

These are the steps to take if you want to file online:

■ Register for HMRC's online self-assessment service – to do this, go to www.hmrc.gov.uk and look in the panel on the left headed 'Do it online'. You will need your Unique Taxpayer Reference (UTR – the ten-digit number printed on the front of your tax return) and other references such as your National Insurance number. If you do not have a UTR, you will need to complete form SA1 or form CWF1 if self-employed (see pages 29 and 151).

■ Decide whether to use HMRC or commercial software to complete your return. HMRC's own online tax return should be adequate for most people, but more comprehensive software is available from companies approved by HMRC, listed on the HMRC website at www.hmrc.gov.uk/efiling/sa_efiling/soft_dev.htm, and the prices start at around £20.

■ Enter your data. The software will guide you through the process, work out the tax due automatically, and alert you to any obvious errors. You can save your data and then file it when you are ready.

■ Log in and file your return by 31 January or within three months of issue if later. But the deadline is 31 December if you want tax collected through PAYE.

The HMRC computer will reject your return immediately if there is some basic error, such as figures that do not add up (you will get an error message to help you diagnose the problem). If it files successfully, the HMRC computer will email you an acknowledgement and a reference number, called an 'IRMark'. Print this out and keep it as your receipt.

Allow time to register online

When you register you will be issued with a User ID, and asked to choose a password, but you will not be able to use the service until you have received an Activation Code in the post and logged online to use it. You should allow 7 working days. If you do not activate your account within 28 days the Code will expire and you will have to ask for a new one.

Penalties and interest

Penalties are charged if you pay your tax late, get your return in late or your return is inaccurate (unless you take reasonable care to get it right). You can appeal against a penalty within 30 days if you think it is wrong, or you have a reasonable excuse (see page 265), but interest is charged on any amount paid late, including penalties, so you may prefer to pay the amount demanded even if you are appealing. Penalties for inaccuracy are covered on page 41, and see page 265 for late returns and late payment of tax.

Table 16.1: Self-assessment timetable for 2011–12 tax year

31 January 2012	If you are liable to make payments on account, your first instalment of tax for 2011–12 is due. If you don't pay, interest starts to clock up on the outstanding amount.
April 2012	Tax returns for the 2011–12 tax year are issued.
31 May 2012	Your employer must give you your end-of-year statement (P60) by now. You need this to complete your return.
6 July 2012	Your employer must give you your statement of taxable expenses and benefits (P11D or P9D) by now.
31 July 2012	Second instalment of tax for 2011–12 due. If you don't pay, interest is charged on the outstanding amount.
5 October 2012	If you do not get a tax return you must tell HMRC by this date if you had taxable income in 2011–12 on which tax was not collected at source, or taxable capital gains.
31 October 2012	Filing a paper return? You must get your 2011–12 return in by this date or pay a £100 penalty. If the return is still not in by 31 January 2013, HMRC can charge £10 a day, plus further penalties if it is six months or twelve months late (see opposite).
31 December 2012	Latest date for filing your return if you are filing online and you want tax of under £3,000 collected through PAYE.
31 January 2013	Filing online? You must file your 2011–12 tax return by this date, or pay a £100 penalty. If the return is still outstanding on 30 April 2013, HMRC can charge £10 a day, plus further penalties if it is six months or twelve months late (see opposite). You must also pay any tax still outstanding for 2011–12 by this date, or pay a penalty of 5% of the tax outstanding on 2 March 2013, and a further 5% of tax still owed on 31 July 2013 (plus interest).
31 January 2014	Latest date for amending your 2011–12 return, if necessary. If you still owe tax for 2011–12, you can be charged a third 5% penalty. Your tax office should have told you within 12 months of receiving your return if it intends to run a check on it (it has longer to do so if you sent your return in late or amended it, if further information comes to light, or if you have been negligent or fraudulent).

Late tax returns

If you do not get your 2011–12 return in by 31 January 2013 (31 October 2012 for a paper return) you pay a flat penalty of £100 (even if you owe tax of under £100). However, if your return was issued after 31 July 2012, the filing deadlines are extended to three months after the date of delivery (usually taken to be seven days after the date on either the return itself or the SA316 *Notice to Complete a Tax Return*). In addition, if your return is:

■ over three months late – a penalty of £10 a day
■ over six months late – an additional £300 or 5 per cent of the tax due if this is higher
■ over twelve months late – a further £300 or a further 5 per cent of the tax due if higher or, if HMRC thinks you are deliberately withholding information, up to 100 per cent (as shown in Table 3.2 on page 41).

Note that 2010–11 was the first year of this system of penalties – a different system applies to returns for 2009–10 and earlier tax years.

Late payment of tax

If you have not paid your tax more than 30 days after the 31 January when it was due, you must pay a penalty of 5 per cent of the tax outstanding, plus a further 5 per cent of any tax still outstanding on 31 July (plus interest). A third 5 per cent penalty applies for any tax that is a year late. See page 39 if you are struggling to pay tax.

Acceptable and unacceptable excuses

HMRC will not accept the following as an excuse for late returns or late payment of tax: pressure of work, a failure by your tax adviser, lack of information (you can send provisional figures if necessary), difficulty with the tax return or inability to pay (ask about 'time to pay' arrangements, see page 39). An acceptable excuse might be losing records in a flood, by fire, theft or an unforeseen postal strike; a bereavement or serious illness; or trying to file online but failing because of an HMRC system error (keep a record of the error message).

After your tax office gets your return

You may not hear anything apart from the email acknowledgement if you file online. However, you can view your account online, and you will receive a statement in the post when tax is due (January and July if you make payments on account) and at other times if something changes or a return or payment is late.

You will also hear from HMRC if your return is selected for further checking, in addition to the initial check made when your return is submitted. A 'compliance check', as these are called, may be instigated because something looks odd, or entirely at random.

You need to keep all the documentation backing up the information in your return in case your return is checked (and you have a legal duty to do so in any case, see page 15). HMRC has a range of factsheets explaining how compliance checks are run – see factsheet CC/FSI *Compliance checks – general information* and you may also find leaflet HMRC *HM Revenue & Customs decisions – what to do if you disagree* helpful. However, you should consider getting professional help in responding to the check (see Chapter 3). You can claim reasonable professional costs as a business expense, unless the check uncovers fraudulent or negligent behaviour on your part.

Avoiding a compliance check

HMRC assesses your return against a number of factors when deciding whether or not to select it for checking. You can reduce your risk of problems by:

- getting it in on time, and paying your tax on time
- explaining anything that might look odd (such as a big change in expenses, turnover or gross profit) in the 'Additional information' boxes on the return
- double checking your entries to make sure you've got any sums right and everything is in the right box
- ensuring your records are in good shape and back up the figures in your return.

Chapter 3 gives more information on what to do if you have problems.

You may find a mistake on your return. If so, you can correct it online or by contacting your tax office, but you must act within 12 months of 31 January after the end of the tax year (i.e. by 31 January 2014 for 2011–12). But this won't protect you from HMRC action if it thinks you have been fraudulent or negligent. If you have overpaid tax as a result of a mistake, contact your tax office – you may be able to claim relief up to four years after the end of the tax year (see page 37).

Understanding your self-assessment statement

The statement you receive in January and July shows how much tax is due, or how much you are owed (and statements can also be viewed online). The statement works a bit like a credit card bill, showing the transactions on your account over the period of the statement, and the balance at the beginning and end of the period. However, you can ask your tax office for a more detailed statement if you wish. Below we explain what some of the common entries on the statement mean, and see Example 16.1 on page 269.

As explained on page 29, you might not have tax to pay if you are opting to have it collected through PAYE on your job or pension and have sent your return in by 31 October (if filing a paper return) or 31 December (if filing online).

Payment on account

You are liable to make a 'payment on account' in January and July if both of the following apply:

■ less than 20 per cent of your tax bill for the previous tax year was met from tax paid at source *and*
■ the tax *not* deducted at source was £1,000 or more.

Each payment on account is half of your income tax bill for the previous tax year (excluding tax deducted at source). The full amount of each payment is shown on the statement, even if it is being collected through PAYE, and even if you have made a claim to reduce your payments (see page 31). If so, the amount to be collected through PAYE, or the amount of the reduction, will appear as a credit adjustment.

Balancing payment/overpayment

A balancing payment will be shown in your January 2013 statement if you still owe tax for the previous tax year (after deducting any tax you have already paid as a payment on account). However, if this is being collected through PAYE you will also see a credit adjustment called 'Balancing payment for 11–12 included in PAYE code'.

If you paid too much for 2011–12, it will appear as an overpayment.

Interest/repayment supplement

If you have been late paying your tax, the amount of interest incurred will appear. If you have overpaid, you might see a 'repayment supplement' instead – HMRC-speak for the interest you get if you have overpaid tax. The repayment supplement was 0.5 per cent when this book went to press.

If you receive a self-assessment statement and you know your payment is overdue, you might want to pay a bit extra to cover any interest clocked up from the date of the statement to the date you pay. Your tax office should be able to give you an idea of how much.

Amount to pay/You have overpaid

A payslip will be attached to the statement, showing the amount due, or zero if you have no tax to pay. If you have paid too much, the money usually stays in your account, to be set against any future tax, unless you ask for it to be paid to you. To claim a repayment, complete page TR5 in your tax return or contact your tax office.

Don't count your chickens

HMRC has 12 months from the date you file your return to notify you if it plans to run a compliance check of your return – longer if you file late or amend your return, or if fraud or negligence is suspected. So even if your return passed through the initial check without problems, don't assume that everything has been settled, and don't throw away any supporting paperwork.

> Example 16.1: **Understanding your self-assessment statement**

In December 2011 Steven received the statement below, showing that he owed HMRC £5,524.91 (7). This is how the amount was calculated.

The amount brought forward (1) is Steven's second payment of account for 2010–11. This was due at the end of July, but Steven paid it late, in August (2) and as a result he is charged interest for the period between 31 July and 27 August (3).

Steven's payments on account for 2010–11 came to less than the tax owed, and as a result he has a balancing payment to make in January 2012 of £1,478.54 (4). At the same time he must make his first payment on account for the 2011–12 tax year, which is £4,544.18 (5). However, because he expects his income to fall slightly in 2011–12, in his tax return he made a claim to reduce his payment on account by £500 (6). So in total he is liable to pay the balancing payment and payment on account, plus late payment interest, but minus the reduction in his payment on account – £5,524.91 in total (7).

HM Revenue & Customs   **Self Assessment Statement**

Date	Description	Tax Due	Credits	Balance
	Brought forward from previous statement ❶			3,804.91
26 Aug 11	Payment – thank you ❷		3,804.91	0.00
26 Aug 11	Interest ❸	2.19		
31 Jan 12	Balancing payment due for year 10/11	1,478.54 ❹		
31 Jan 12	1st payment on account due for year 11/12 ❺	4,544.18		
		6,024.91		6,024.91
31 Jan 12	Claim to reduce 1st payment on account for 2011-12 ❻		500.00	5,524.91
	Amount to pay			5,524.91
	Amount due by 31 Jan 12			5,524.91 ❼

(SA300 (Shipley) HMRC 06/06)

Please make sure that your payment reaches us by the date it becomes due. You will be charged interest if you pay late.

▼ Please detach payslip here when making payment direct to the Accounts Office or by Girobank ▼

17

The full tax return

The full tax return – the one you get unless your affairs are simple – is made up of several different forms, and some items are dealt with on separate pages. So it is important to ensure you don't miss the bits that are relevant to you. This chapter guides you through your 2011–12 tax return. It focuses on the the six 'core' pages and the Additional Information pages, while Chapter 18 covers some of the supplementary pages you might get. If you get the short four-page tax return, see Chapter 19.

Top tips

- The hard part of completing your tax return is collecting the necessary information. It helps to gather it together as it comes in, in a separate file for each tax year.
- Forget the pennies – you are allowed to round to the nearest £ in your favour. This means rounding income down and deductions up.
- Use HMRC's help sheets. Many include work sheets to help with calculations.
- If you are filing a paper return, make sure you write clearly in the boxes in black ink. When filling in the 'amount' boxes you can start on the left by the £ sign or on the right before the decimal point – it does not matter which.
- Use the 'Any other information' boxes to explain anything that might look odd or any major changes from last year.
- When calculating tax, take into account tax paid through your tax code. See page 285.

Getting started

If you are filing your tax return online, either on the HMRC website or using commercial software, the programme will guide you through the return. The rest of this chapter illustrates the paper return, but what you need to enter in each section is the same however you file.

First, collect the documents you need, such as your accounts, P60 or statements of interest received. The 'Record-keeping' sections at the end of each chapter in Parts 1 and 2 of this book will help.

Next, check that the contact details HMRC holds about you are correct and put a cross in box 2 at the bottom of page TR1 if they are not. Give your date of birth, so that HMRC can give you the right amount of personal allowance once you are 65. Give your National Insurance number in box 4 unless it is already printed at the top of the page.

What makes up your tax return – page TR2

The paper tax return pack consists of a core six-page return, together with 'Additional Information' pages for unusual items, and the HMRC Tax Return Guide, *How to fill in your tax return*. But you may also need supplementary pages, covering matters such as employment income, business income, foreign income and capital gains, and if you want to work out your own tax you can ask for a Tax Calculation Summary. Each form has notes to help you, but there is also a self-assessment helpline on 0845 9000 444.

Page TR2 is a checklist of the supplementary pages you need. Put a cross in the relevant box and make sure that you have the right pages. If HMRC knows that you need one of the supplementary pages, it will have sent it to you in the tax return pack (they are colour-coded so that you can spot them easily). If you need a form it hasn't sent, it's up to you to get it, either by phoning the HMRC Orderline on 0845 9000 404, or by printing off copies from www.hmrc.gov.uk/sa/forms/content.htm.

Go to:

- page 289 for how to fill in the Additional Information pages
- Chapter 18 for how to fill in the most common supplementary pages.

Student loan repayments – page TR2

Box 2 applies only if your employer is deducting student loan repayments from your pay (see pages 13 and 121). If so, the amount to enter should be shown on your P60. But watch out if you have nearly paid off your loan: HMRC collects your student loan repayment, but the Student Loans Company won't tell HMRC if you have paid off your loan until after the end of the tax year. So tell your tax office separately if you paid off your loan after you sent in your return, but before 1 January 2013. And, if you think you are getting to the end of your loan term, but have not heard whether your loan has been fully repaid, contact the Student Loans Company.

Income – page TR3

Interest and dividends

In this section you should enter any taxable income from a bank or building society account, a taxable National Savings & Investments Account, dividends and distributions from UK shares, unit trusts and OEICs. See Figure 17.1 on page 275. Remember, you do not have to enter tax-free income, listed on page 185. But less common types of income that you should enter here include:

- Income from a purchased life annuity – only part of this income is taxable, but it is usually paid with tax deducted. Enter it in box 1 (or box 2, if no tax has been deducted).
- 'Alternative finance receipts' – for example, income from Islamic finance accounts that do not pay interest. Enter these in box 1 or 2 depending on whether tax has been deducted.
- Income from accounts in your child's name if the money in the account was a gift from you, but only if the total income per child, per year comes to more than £100 before tax (see page 54). The amount goes in the relevant box for the type of income received.
- Small amounts of foreign interest and dividends – see opposite.
- Interest from a loan you have made to an individual or organisation – this goes in box 2.

Note that income from British Government stocks, stock dividends and non-qualifying dividends goes in the Additional Information pages (see page 289), not here. Taxable payouts from a life insurance policy also go in the Additional Information pages.

You only need to enter the total income you have in each category. You should be able to get the details you need from the tax vouchers sent with dividends, from your regular account statements, or from the certificates of interest paid that are supplied at the end of each tax year by some banks and building societies (or available on request).

Box 1. Taxed UK interest etc.

Include any interest paid with tax deducted from bank and building society accounts or savings bonds, purchased life annuities, National Savings & Investments (NS&I), Guaranteed Income Bonds and Guaranteed Growth Bonds. Other NS&I accounts pay interest before tax and should go in box 2. Also include 'interest distributions' paid out by a unit trust, OEIC or investment trust that invests in interest-bearing accounts. These are usually paid with tax deducted – the amount should be shown on the tax voucher.

Small amounts of foreign income?

If your only overseas income was untaxed foreign interest (up to £2,000) and/or taxed foreign dividends (up to £300) you can enter it in this section of the tax return, rather than completing the Foreign supplementary pages. However, if you have any other overseas income you will have to enter all your foreign income in the Foreign pages instead. You should convert the income to sterling (see page 169 for how to do this) before entering it.

You can share the income from a joint account

If you have a joint account, only enter your share of the income (usually half, but see page 52). Otherwise, you'll pay too much tax.

Box 2. Untaxed UK interest etc.

Enter in this section any interest from a bank, building society or unit trust/ OEIC where you have filled in form R85 to have the interest paid gross. You can include overseas interest of up to £2,000 (converted to sterling), but note that if you do this there is nowhere to claim tax relief for any foreign tax deducted (see page 178), so only enter untaxed interest. Also include income from NS&I Investment Account, Direct Saver Account, Easy Access Savings Account, Income Bonds, Capital Bonds, Pensioners' Guaranteed Income Bonds and Guaranteed Equity Bonds.

Box 3. Dividends from UK companies

When the dividend is paid, a tax voucher is issued which shows all the information you need. Enter the total of all the dividends actually received: do not include the tax credit. Include any dividends received through an employee share scheme, unless the dividends were reinvested in an approved share incentive plan.

However, do not include stock dividends or non-qualifying distributions, which go in the Additional Information pages (see page 289), or any Property Income Dividends from Real Estate Investment Trusts (REITs) or Property Authorised Investment Funds (PAIFs), which go under 'Other UK income' (see page 279). Compensation for not taking up your shares under a rights issue counts as a capital gain, not a dividend. And if you are affected by the IR35 rules as an employee of your own service company (see page 98), you *may* be able to claim that dividends received from your company are tax-free – contact your tax office.

Box 4. Other dividends

This box is for dividend distributions from a unit trust, OEIC or investment trust. Enter only the total dividends received, as for share dividends above. Don't include any 'interest distributions' – these go in box 1 or 2. But do include any distributions from 'accumulation' units – these are retained in the trust, rather than paid out to you, but they count as taxable income and you should get a tax voucher. You do not have to enter any figures shown as 'equalisation' – these only affect capital gains tax (see page 230).

Boxes 5 and 6. Foreign dividends (up to £300) and tax taken off

Enter the sterling equivalent of the dividends in box 5 and the foreign tax deducted in box 6. You will get a 10 per cent tax credit for this in the same way as for UK dividends, rather than the normal tax treatment for foreign tax (see page 178). You can opt for the normal tax treatment to apply, which may save a bit more tax, but if so you will have to enter the dividends in the Foreign pages, not here. For most people, it's not worth it.

Example 17.1: **Declaring interest and savings**

Page TR3 of Jermaine's tax return is shown in Figure 17.1. He received £245.34 after tax from his Bedfordshire Building Society account. He also has a joint account with his wife that paid out £130.58 after tax, but only half of this (£65.29) is taxed as his. He enters £245.34 + £65.29 = £310.63, rounded down to £310, in box 1. He also had a NS&I Income Bond in his name which paid out £488 before tax: this goes in box 2. He has a few shares in UK companies which paid out total dividends of £63. He also received £25 dividends from an offshore investment fund, which counts as foreign income. He paid 20% foreign tax on these (£5), which he enters in box 6, but he will only get a 10% tax credit for them.

Figure 17.1: Interest and dividends

	1	Taxed UK interest etc. - *the net amount after tax has been taken off (see notes)*	£ 3 1 0 . 0 0		4	Other dividends - *do not include the tax credit (see notes)*	£ . 0 0

1 Taxed UK interest etc. - *the net amount after tax has been taken off (see notes)*
£ **3 1 0** . 0 0

2 Untaxed UK interest etc. - *amounts which have not been taxed (see notes)*
£ **4 8 8** . 0 0

3 Dividends from UK companies - *do not include the tax credit (see notes)*
£ **6 3** . 0 0

4 Other dividends - *do not include the tax credit (see notes)*
£ . 0 0

5 Foreign dividends (up to £300) - *the amount in sterling after foreign tax was taken off. Do not include this amount in the Foreign pages*
£ **2 5** . 0 0

6 Tax taken off foreign dividends - *the sterling equivalent*
£ **5** . 0 0

UK pensions, annuities and other state benefits

Box 7. State pension

Enter the total of your state retirement pension, state second pension, graduated pension, addition for a dependent adult and the other taxable state pensions listed on page 73. But you can ignore tax-free amounts, such as the winter fuel allowance and the Christmas bonus. Your weekly entitlement will be shown on the letter you get from the Pension Service before the start of each year, but you will have to convert this to an annual amount – for how to do this, see page TRG12 of the HMRC notes. If your pension was reduced, perhaps because you were in hospital, remember not to include the amount you lost. Contact the Pension Service helpline on 0845 606 0265 and ask for form BR735 for the 2011–12 tax year if you are not sure what to enter.

Box 8. State pension lump sum

You may have put off receiving your state pension, in return for a higher pension later on or a lump sum (see page 73). The higher pension is taxed like the normal state pension and should be entered with your other state pension in box 7. If you chose a lump sum, this will normally be paid with tax deducted. Enter the amount before tax in box 8, and the tax in box 9 (this will be shown in the letter you receive from the Pension Service).

Box 10. Pensions (other than state pension)

This is where you should enter the before-tax amount of any private pension, such as a pension from a UK occupational pension, personal or stakeholder pension, free-standing additional voluntary contributions (FSAVC) plan, or retirement annuity plan. If instead of buying an annuity with your pension fund you took an income withdrawal, include the amount of income withdrawn. And if you drew the whole of a small pension as a lump sum (a 'triviality' payment, see page 211), enter the lump sum. If you have more than one pension, enter the total amounts in boxes 10 and 11.

Do not include:

- any tax-free cash lump sum from your pension
- a taxable lump sum from a pension scheme that is not registered – this is taxed as income from employment (see page 206)

■ any tax-free amount paid because of a work-related accident or illness
■ a foreign pension – these go in the Foreign pages, except for a UK pension for service to an overseas government, which goes in box 10 (but enter only 90 per cent of the amount received as 10 per cent is tax-free)
■ a purchased life annuity (see page 193). This goes in box 1 or 2.

In most cases, tax will be deducted from your pension before you get it. Enter the tax in box 11 – whoever pays the pension should give you a P60 or other statement each year showing the amount. Occasionally, the pension provider may *refund* tax already paid. If so, enter the amount as a minus figure, writing a minus sign in the box after the £ sign.

For each pension or annuity, also enter the name of the payer, the PAYE reference, your reference, the payment before tax and the tax deducted under 'Any other information' on page TR6.

Mistakes to avoid when entering state pensions and benefits

■ Entering tax-free amounts, such as attendance allowance and additions to state benefits for children. You can ignore tax-free amounts.
■ If you received pension credit in addition to your state pension, only the pension itself is taxable. Pension credit is tax-free.
■ If you received Jobseeker's Allowance or Employment and Support Allowance for more than one period in the tax year, remember to add together the taxable amounts given on each of the P45 forms you received, plus that shown on the P60 you get if still claiming on 5 April 2012.
■ Don't confuse bereavement allowance with the lump sum bereavement payment. The allowance is taxable – the payment is not.
■ Don't include statutory maternity, paternity, adoption or sick pay in this section unless they have been paid to you directly by HMRC. If paid by your employer, enter them on the Employment supplementary pages.

Boxes 12 and 13. Taxable Incapacity Benefit and Employment and Support Allowance

Incapacity Benefit is only taxable after the first 28 weeks (and not at all if you first received it before 13 April 1995). Your Jobcentre Plus will give you a P60(IB) after the end of the tax year showing the taxable amount, or a P45(IB) if you stopped claiming before the end of the tax year. Enter this amount – before tax – in box 12 and the tax taken off in box 13.

Only contribution-based Employment and Support Allowance is taxable. You will get a P60(U) showing the taxable amount after the end of the tax year, or a P45(U) if you stopped claiming earlier, but no tax is deducted so enter the whole amount in box 12 and nothing in box 13.

Box 14. Jobseeker's Allowance

Jobseeker's Allowance is taxable, but the taxable amount is capped (see page 56). Only enter the taxable amount, which you can find on the P60(U) or P45(U) that your Jobcentre Plus should give you.

Box 15. Total of other taxable state pensions and benefits

Other taxable state benefits are widow's pension or bereavement allowance, widow's benefit or widowed parent's allowance, industrial death benefit pension and Carer's Allowance. Your benefits office can tell you how much is taxable. Enter the total amount in box 15.

Example 17.2: **Declaring pension income**

Josephine received a state retirement pension of £105.24 a week in 2011–12. In box 7 (see Figure 17.2) she entered £105.24 × 52 = £5,472.48, rounded down to £5,472. She also received a pension from her job of £2,800, and a widow's pension of £3,790 from her husband's employer. She enters her total private pension – £2,800 + £3,790 = £6,590 in box 10. All the pensions are taxable, but the state pension was paid out with no tax deducted, and all the tax was taken off her private pensions. The P60s she received from the pension companies in May told her that in total £570 was deducted, which she enters in box 11. She also writes the names of the companies that paid her the private pensions, any reference numbers, the amount paid, and the tax deducted under 'Any other information' on page TR6.

Figure 17.2: UK pensions, annuities and other state benefits received

7	State Pension - *the amount due for the year (see notes)*	11	Tax taken off box 10
	£ **5 4 7 2** · 0 0		£ — **5 7 0** · 0 0

8	State Pension lump sum	12	Taxable Incapacity Benefit and contribution-based Employment and Support Allowance - *see notes*
	£ · 0 0		£ · 0 0

9	Tax taken off box 8	13	Tax taken off Incapacity Benefit in box 12
	£ · 0 0		£ · 0 0

10	Pensions (other than State Pension), retirement annuities and taxable triviality payments - *give details of the payers, amounts paid and tax deducted in the 'Any other information' box, box 19, on page TR 6*	14	Jobseeker's Allowance
	£ **6 5 9 0** · 0 0		£ · 0 0

		15	Total of any other taxable State Pensions and benefits
			£ · 0 0

Other UK income

This is a catch-all section of the return for income that doesn't fit anywhere else, or on any of the supplementary pages. If you're not sure where something goes, contact the self-assessment helpline.

Income that does belong here includes Property Income Dividends from a REIT or PAIF (see page 198), bits of freelance income that do not amount to a trade, income received after a business has ceased, and taxable sick pay from an employer you no longer work for.

You may be able to deduct allowable expenses and losses from the income, but first read HMRC help sheet 325 *Other taxable income* as it depends on the type of income. Allowable expenses can be claimed in box 17, but any unused losses should be claimed under 'income losses' on page Ai3 of the Additional Information pages (see page 297).

You may also have to enter something in box 19 if you are caught by the 'pre-owned assets' rules. These stop people avoiding inheritance tax by giving something away but continuing to benefit from it (see page 242).

Reliefs – page TR4

Paying into a pension scheme

This is the section to use if you want to claim tax relief on payments you make to a private pension (see Chapter 12). Don't enter payments into an employer's scheme where full tax relief was given by deducting the contributions from your pay before it was taxed. Do enter payments made to any other UK-registered pension scheme, whether it was run by your employer or was a personal or stakeholder pension, free-standing voluntary contribution (FSAVC) scheme or retirement annuity contract. But remember that if you go over the annual or lifetime allowances for pension saving, you should enter here only the amount that qualifies for tax relief, and you may also have to complete the Additional Information pages of the tax return (see Chapter 12 and page 298).

Include any payments made between 6 April 2011 and 5 April 2012. The most that qualifies for tax relief is £3,600 (before tax relief) or your taxable UK earnings if higher. Also include any contributions to a 'pension term insurance' policy applied for before 14 December 2006. These qualify for tax relief, although later policies do not. See HMRC help sheet 347 *Personal term assurance contributions to a registered pension scheme*. Don't include contributions your employer paid into your plan – you don't get tax relief on these.

Which box?

Most pension payments these days are made with basic-rate tax relief given at source and go in box 1. Remember, though, that it is the gross amount that you should enter – that is, the amount you handed over, plus the basic-rate tax relief the pension company claims from HMRC. To work this out, divide the amount you paid by 0.8.

However, if you pay into a retirement annuity contract and the pension company does not allow you to make payments with tax relief deducted, enter the amount paid in box 2. And if, unusually, you made a payment to your employer's pension before tax (for example, you paid in more than you earned from that job), enter it in box 3.

Finally, use box 4 if you paid into a pension scheme based overseas that qualifies for UK tax relief under an agreement with the country concerned.

Example 17.3: **Entering your pension contributions**

Oscar is a member of a group personal pension scheme to which he contributes £160 a month. The pension company reclaims basic-rate tax relief on Oscar's contributions, so the total regular payment into his plan in 2011–12 was £160 ÷ 0.8 = £200 a month, or £2,400. Oscar also paid in his annual bonus as a lump sum – £2,000 (£2,500 gross) in December 2011. On his tax return, Oscar enters in box 1 on page TR4 his total contribution for the 2011–12 tax year: £2,400 + £2,500 = £4,900.

Figure 17.3: Paying into registered pension schemes

Do not include payments you make to your employer's pension scheme which are deducted from your pay before tax or payments made by your employer.

1	Payments to registered pension schemes where basic rate tax relief will be claimed by your pension provider (called 'relief at source'). Enter the payments and basic rate tax

£   4 9 0 0 . 0 0

2	Payments to a retirement annuity contract where basic rate tax relief will not be claimed by your provider

£   . 0 0

3	Payments to your employer's scheme which were not deducted from your pay before tax

£   . 0 0

4	Payments to an overseas pension scheme which is not UK-registered which are eligible for tax relief and were not deducted from your pay before tax

£   . 0 0

Mistakes to avoid when entering pension contributions

■ Entering the amount you actually paid into a personal or stakeholder pension or FSAVC plan (the net amount) in box 1, rather than the gross payment.

■ Entering payments made with no tax relief deducted in box 1 rather than in box 2. If in doubt, check with the pension company.

Charitable giving

Use this section to claim tax relief on gifts to charity, or gifts to Community Amateur Sports Clubs (the club can tell you if it qualifies, or look online at www.hmrc.gov.uk/casc/clubs.htm). See Chapter 13 for more information. But don't include payments to charity deducted from your pay under the payroll giving scheme (see page 218): you have already had all the tax relief due on these.

First, enter in box 5 the total amounts you actually handed over to charities or sports clubs in the UK during 2011–12 under the Gift Aid scheme. Gifts to equivalent European bodies go in box 15. The figure to enter is the amount you actually paid – do not add on the basic-rate tax. See Example 17.4.

Then, work out how much of the payments already entered in box 5 were one-off gifts rather than regular donations, and enter the amount of one-off gifts in box 6. Your tax office will adjust your tax code if necessary, to give you any higher-rate tax relief due on the regular donations.

You can claim to have donations treated as if made in a previous tax year. If you claimed, in last year's return, to have donations made in 2011–12 treated as if paid in 2010–11, enter the amount in box 7. If you want any amounts paid after 5 April 2012 but before you sent in your return treated as if paid in 2011–12, enter them in box 8.

Gifts of investments, land and buildings to charity

You can also claim tax relief on gifts to charity of shares or securities, unit trusts or OEICs, land or buildings. If so, enter the value of the gift in box 9, 10 or 11, as relevant. If you are giving land or buildings, you will need a certificate from the charity. (For more information, see the 'Charities' section of the HMRC website and HMRC help sheet 342 *Charitable giving*.)

Example 17.4: **Charitable donations**

Hector makes regular Gift Aid donations of £15 a month, but in 2011–12 he also made a lump sum donation of £150. He enters in box 5 the total paid in 2011–12 (£330), not including the basic-rate tax relief, with the one-off donation in box 6. In June 2012 Hector made another donation of £500. He claims to carry this back to the 2011–12 tax year by entering it in box 8 (making a note to enter it in box 7 in next year's return as well). This will increase the amount of personal allowance Hector gets in 2011–12 (see Example 13.2 on page 220).

Figure 17.4: Charitable giving

5 Gift Aid payments made in the year to 5 April 2012	£ _ _ _ _ _ 3 3 0 . 0 0	**9** Value of qualifying shares or securities gifted to charity	£ _ _ _ _ _ _ _ _ . 0 0
6 Total of any 'one-off' payments in box 5	£ _ _ _ _ _ 1 5 0 . 0 0	**10** Value of qualifying land and buildings gifted to charity	£ _ _ _ _ _ _ _ _ . 0 0
7 Gift Aid payments made in the year to 5 April 2012 but treated as if made in the year to 5 April 2011	£ _ _ _ _ _ _ _ . 0 0	**11** Value of qualifying investments gifted to non-UK charities in boxes 9 and 10	£ _ _ _ _ _ _ _ _ . 0 0
8 Gift Aid payments made after 5 April 2012 but to be treated as if made in the year to 5 April 2012	£ _ _ _ _ _ 5 0 0 . 0 0	**12** Gift Aid payments to non-UK charities in box 5	£ _ _ _ _ _ _ _ . 0 0

Giving a tax repayment to charity

In 2010–11 and previous tax years you could ask HMRC to give a tax repayment direct to charity. This is no longer possible, but if you gave any tax repayment to charity in last year's return, it counts as a Gift Aid payment for this year – so include it in box 5.

Don't forget your gifts to charity

A gift through the Gift Aid scheme will allow the charity to reclaim basic-rate tax relief on the donation – but you also benefit. If you are a higher-rate taxpayer, you get extra tax relief, and if you are over 65 the gift could reduce your tax bill (see page 81).

Warning for non-taxpayers

Don't claim tax relief on gifts to charity if you pay less tax than the amount of basic-rate tax relief the charity can claim. HMRC will ask you to pay the difference.

Blind person's allowance

If you were eligible for blind person's allowance of £1,980 in 2011–12 (see page 50), put a cross in box 13, and enter the name of the authority with which you are registered as blind in box 14, or 'Scotland' or 'Northern Ireland' as appropriate. See Example 17.5.

You can transfer blind person's allowance to your spouse or civil partner if your income is too low to use it all. To transfer allowances, put a cross in box 15 or 16 as relevant (and ask your partner to complete the appropriate boxes on their form). You cannot lose out by completing these boxes – your tax office will transfer allowances only if it is in your interests.

If your spouse or civil partner is transferring allowances to you, and you are working out your own tax, remember to include their unused amount with your allowances.

Just registered as blind?

Even if you were only registered as blind after 5 April 2012, you can still claim blind person's allowance for 2011–12 if you have evidence that your sight condition existed then.

Example 17.5: **Claiming blind person's allowance**

In 2011–12 Andrew, aged 72, can claim blind person's allowance as well as married couple's allowance. He puts a cross in box 13 and completes box 14. However, his £11,155 income is too low to use all of his allowances. He has £765 of his blind person's allowance left to transfer to his wife Anna, and the whole of the married couple's allowance.

Andrew puts a cross in box 16 on his tax return to transfer his blind person's allowances – he doesn't have to enter any figures. Anna puts a cross in box 15 on her tax return. To transfer the married couple's allowance, he will need the Additional Information pages (see page 289).

Figure 17.5: Blind person's allowance

13 If you are registered blind on a local authority or other register, put 'X' in the box	**15** If you want your spouse's, or civil partner's, surplus allowance, put 'X' in the box
X	
14 Enter the name of the local authority or other register	**16** If you want your spouse, or civil partner, to have your surplus allowance, put 'X' in the box
SCOTLAND	**X**

Service companies – page TR4

This box applies only if you work for yourself through a company which is caught by the IR35 rules. If so, you might have extra income to declare here (see page 98).

Finishing your tax return – pages TR5 and TR6

Tax refunded or set off

You may have received a tax refund part way through the tax year, for example if you are a non-taxpayer and reclaimed tax deducted from a savings account, or if you became unemployed. Enter any such refunds here, including amounts that have not actually been paid to you but set against tax you owe. Only include tax which has been refunded directly by HMRC or by Jobcentre Plus – refunds from your employer will be taken into account in your P60 or P45.

If you have not paid enough tax

Boxes 2 and 3 apply only if you have a job or pension taxed under PAYE. Otherwise, you can ignore them – you will have to pay your tax in a lump sum and will get a statement from HMRC saying how much you owe.

Box 2. If you owe tax for 2011–12
If you owe less than £3,000, HMRC will usually collect it by adjusting your

tax code for 2013–14, if you have a job or pension taxed under PAYE, and providing you get a paper tax return in by 31 October 2012, or file online by 31 December 2012. Only put a cross in this box if you would prefer HMRC not to collect the tax this way. But if you do, you will have to pay the tax in a lump sum by 31 January 2013. See page 30.

Box 3. If you are likely to owe tax for 2012–13

If your return includes income that was paid out without tax deducted (such as untaxed interest or rental income), HMRC will assume that it will continue in 2012–13 and adjust your 2012–13 tax code accordingly. But if you don't want HMRC to do this (for example, because you think the income might fall), and would prefer to pay tax in a lump sum instead, put a cross in box 3. HMRC will not include untaxed income of more than £10,000 in your code, unless you have agreed to this.

If you have paid too much tax

Use this section to say whether you want a repayment to be credited to your bank or building society account, or a payment to be sent to your nominee (such as a tax adviser). HMRC does not send repayments of less than £10, unless requested. And if you have a payment coming up soon, it will usually set the repayment against that bill instead.

Signing your form and sending it back

Sign and date the return at box 22, or it will be rejected. If you are signing someone else's return – because they have died and you are their executor, or they are incapable of signing and you have been legally appointed to act for them – enter the capacity in which you are signing in box 23. If this is the first time you are signing a form for someone else, you will have to send the tax office evidence of your right to do so with the return.

Box 20. Provisional or estimated figures

A provisional figure is one where you will need to supply a final amount, for example because your accounts are not yet finalised; an estimate is your best attempt at a figure and is unlikely to be changed in future. In spite of the wording of box 20 you need to put a cross in it only if you have used *provisional* figures – although you are asked to identify estimates at particular points in the return (such as the Capital gains summary pages). If you show an estimate, make sure you explain the basis of your estimate under 'Any other information'.

HMRC accepts provisional figures only if you have taken 'all reasonable steps' to get the final figures. You should put a cross in box 20 and explain under 'Any other information' on page TR6 why the figures are provisional and the page and box numbers for the figures affected. If HMRC does not accept your reasons and you do not supply the figures as soon as you can, the return is incomplete and will attract a late filing penalty. HMRC may start a compliance check of your return and you may be penalised if it believes you have been negligent or fraudulent.

You haven't finished yet

As well as completing any relevant supplementary pages, don't forget to check through the Additional Information pages. They cover some important items, including married couple's allowance for people born before 6 April 1935. If you are sending in a paper return, you may also choose to complete the Tax Calculation Summary.

The Tax Calculation Summary

This applies only if you are filing a paper return and want to work out the tax you owe yourself (see page 261). You will need to ask the HMRC Orderline (0845 9000 404) for a copy of a separate form (SA110) called the Tax Calculation Summary, or download it from the HMRC website. The accompanying notes take you through the calculations and you then carry the final figures across to the Summary. You do not have to send this in with your return unless you are claiming to reduce your payments on account, as HMRC will work out what you owe. The following figures in the Summary also affect the tax owed:

■ *Boxes 7 and 8 – Underpaid tax.* If you are taxed under PAYE, any tax outstanding from one year may be collected by adjusting your tax code for a future year. Amounts to go in box 7 will be shown as 'Underpaid tax' on your most recent coding notice for 2011–12 (remember to enter the unpaid tax, not the reduction in your code – see page 21). Box 8 applies only if your tax code for 2011–12 was reduced during the year, for example because you got a new taxable employment benefit. This may result in an underpayment for the part of the year before your code was changed, but it will normally be collected by adjusting your final tax bill. You need to make an entry here only if you asked to have the underpayment collected through your 2012–13 tax code instead (see HMRC help sheet 208 *Payslips and coding notices*).

■ *Boxes 9 and 10 – Payments on account.* Put a cross in box 9 if you are claiming to reduce your payments on account due in January and July 2013. Write the reduced amount of your first payment in box 10 and the reasons for your claim under 'Any other information' (e.g. your income has fallen, see page 31).

■ *Boxes 11 and 12 – Surplus allowances.* These apply if your husband, wife or civil partner was eligible for either blind person's allowance or married couple's allowance and their income was too low to use it all (see pages 50 and 83). If you do not know the unused amount, ask your partner to contact their tax office.

■ *Boxes 13 to 15 – Adjustments to tax due.* These apply if you want to have income or expenditure treated as if earned or incurred in an earlier year – most likely if you are carrying back business losses or capital losses (see pages 145 and 234) or you are a farmer, writer or artist claiming to average your income over several years (see HMRC help sheets 224 and 234). Enter the difference that the amount carried back has made to your tax bill for the earlier year, in box 13 if you owe extra tax, box 14 if it is a tax saving for 2011–12 and box 15 if you are claiming to carry back to 2011–12 losses made in 2012–13.

The Additional Information pages

Interest from gilt-edged and other UK securities

Enter here income from British Government Stock, corporate bonds and other loan stocks (see page 190 onwards). This may be paid before tax, or with tax deducted: if tax has been deducted, fill in all three boxes, but if no tax has been deducted just fill in box 3. You should get a voucher or statement from the payer saying how much tax has been deducted.

If you bought or sold stocks and the first interest payment after the transaction falls in the 2011–12 tax year, your tax may be affected by accrued interest (see page 190). If it is affected:

■ add together any accrued interest profits
■ deduct any accrued interest losses.

There is a working sheet in HMRC help sheet 343 *Accrued Income Scheme*. If the result is a positive number (i.e. you have more profits than losses), add it to the figure you enter in box 3. If the result is negative, deduct it from the figure in box 3. If this would give a minus amount in box 3, enter zero and make a note of the unused amount. Do not change the figure in boxes 1 or 2. You can set the unused amount against any profits in future.

Life insurance gains

Complete this section only if you have made a taxable gain on a non-qualifying life insurance policy. The insurance company or friendly society should send you a 'chargeable event' certificate showing the taxable amount. See HMRC help sheet 320 *Gains on UK life insurance policies* if it does not. The certificate will say whether the policy is treated as having had tax paid on it. This will almost certainly be the case. If so, enter the taxable amount in box 4. If it is a joint policy, only enter your share (see HMRC help sheet 320 *Gains on UK life insurance policies*).

Note that if you have made a taxable gain on the partial surrender of a policy, you should report it in the tax return for the tax year in which the *next* anniversary of taking out your policy falls. A surrender in January

2012, say, should go in your 2012–13 return if you bought the policy in May. This applies only to partial surrenders – other gains are taxable in the tax year they occur.

More than one policy?

You should enter the total gains from all your policies, and the total tax treated as paid. However, if you have more than one policy, do not complete the 'Number of years' boxes (5 or 7). Instead, give details of the gain, tax paid and number of years for each policy in the 'Additional information' box on page Ai4.

Sometimes, insurance policies are sold in 'clusters' – your money is invested in several identical policies to give flexibility when cashing them in. If you have identical gains from any such policies you can add all the gains together and enter them as one policy, but enter the details in the 'Additional information' box on page Ai4.

Box 8. Gains on life insurance policies in voided ISAs

This will apply only if you have invested in the insurance component of an ISA which is invalid because of a breach of the ISA rules. Your ISA manager should tell you what to enter.

Box 11. Deficiency relief

This will apply only if you paid tax on a partial withdrawal from a policy in the past, the policy has now ended and the tax you paid earlier proves to have been too high. You can claim tax relief only if you pay tax at the higher or additional rates. (See HMRC help sheet 320 *Gains on UK life insurance policies.*)

Stock dividends, non-qualifying distributions, loans written off

The items in this section are all non-cash payouts to shareholders:

■ Stock dividends are extra shares issued instead of a cash dividend. The dividend voucher will tell you the amount on which income tax is payable – look for 'the appropriate amount in cash' or 'the cash equivalent of the share capital'.

■ Bonus redeemable shares or bonus securities. These are potentially taxable both when they are issued (as 'non-qualifying distributions') and when they are redeemed (as a 'qualifying distribution'). See the HMRC notes for what to enter.

■ Loans written off, if the loans were made by a close company to a shareholder or other associate. See the HMRC notes for what to enter.

You are treated as having paid 'notional tax' at 10 per cent on these payouts. This is effectively the same as a dividend tax credit: non-taxpayers cannot reclaim the tax and higher-rate or additional-rate taxpayers will have more to pay.

Business receipts taxed as income of an earlier year

This applies only if you received income from a business that has closed down.

Share schemes and employment lump sums, compensation and deductions

Share schemes

Many employers issue free or cheap shares, or options to buy shares, to employees. In some cases, these count as a tax-free perk – see the list on page 94. Otherwise they are taxable (see page 108), but you need to fill in this section only if the full amount of tax has not already been deducted by your employer. If so, enter in box 1 on page Ai2 the taxable value of your shares or options, and in box 2 the amount of any tax taken off. There are working sheets in HMRC's notes on how to fill in this section, and a wealth of information on the HMRC website at www.hmrc.gov.uk/shareschemes.

Lump sums and redundancy pay

If you received a redundancy payment in 2011–12, the first £30,000 is tax-free. Put the tax-free amount in box 9 and the taxable amount (anything above £30,000) in box 5.

However, it is not always clear whether a payment counts as 'redundancy', and amounts such as pay in lieu of notice are often taxable (see page

111). If you are unsure, or receive any payments within the 'always taxable' category on page 111, or are claiming deductions other than the £30,000 exemption, check with your ex-employer and read the HMRC notes. These contain working sheets to help you work out the taxable amount. To sum up:

- Box 3 is for payments received under the terms of your employment – the 'always taxable' category on page 111.
- Box 4 is for lump sums from non-registered retirement schemes, minus any tax-free amounts (which should be entered in box 8).
- Box 5 is for other payments in the 'sometimes taxable' category on page 112, including redundancy, minus deductions for foreign service or disability (which should go in box 10) and minus the £30,000 exemption (box 9).

Note, though, that the £30,000 exemption is per job, so if you received payments relating to one job in more than one tax year you may already have used part of the exemption. If so, you should use the working sheets in the HMRC notes.

Your employer may deduct tax on your lump sum. If the tax is included in your P60 or P45 (you may need to check this with your employer), you will have entered it with the other tax on your pay in the Employment supplementary pages. If so, make sure you leave box 6 empty and put a cross in box 7. Only enter in box 6 tax deducted by your employer that you have not already entered in the Employment supplementary pages.

Seafarers, foreign earnings and foreign tax

If you have been working outside the UK, not all your income may be taxable (see Chapter 10). You may be able to claim deductions:

- in box 11 if you were a seafarer working outside the UK (see HMRC help sheet 205 *Seafarers' earnings deduction*). Also enter the names of the ships you worked in under 'Additional information' on page Ai4.
- in box 12, depending on whether or not you are a UK resident for tax purposes, where the job was done and whether you are claiming the 'remittance basis' (see page 173 and HMRC help sheet 211 *Employment – residence and domicile issues*).

▪ in box 13 to account for any foreign tax you have paid. Note, though, that 'tax credit relief' may be a better option – if so, you will need to complete the Foreign supplementary pages (see page 179).

▪ In box 14, if your employer has made contributions to an overseas pension scheme for you and they are tax-free. See HMRC help sheet 344 *Exempt employers' contributions to an overseas pension scheme*.

Other tax reliefs

Venture Capital Trust shares, the Enterprise Investment Scheme and Community Investment Tax relief

These are all investments that qualify for tax relief (see page 199).

Enter in box 1 on page Ai2 the amount you invested in Venture Capital Trust shares in 2011–12, up to a maximum of £200,000.

Enter in box 2 the amount of any Enterprise Investment Scheme (EIS) investment in 2011–12, up to a maximum of £500,000. Quite a bit of 'Additional information' needs to be given on page Ai4 (see the HMRC notes). You also need to complete and return the claim form included in the form EIS3 or EIS5 that you should have received from the scheme.

You can claim to have your investment in EIS shares carried back to get tax relief in the previous tax year. Remember to adjust the figure you enter in box 2:

▪ by deducting any amounts you claimed to 'carry back' to 2010–11
▪ by adding any amounts you are carrying back from 2012–13.

If you have put money into a Community Investment Scheme and received the necessary certificate, enter the amount invested in 2011–12 in box 3.

UK royalties and annual payments, qualifying loan interest, post-cessation expenses

These boxes cover tax relief related to a business or job which is set against your income as a whole. Check the HMRC notes for what to enter.

▪ Payments made under some legal obligations for business purposes (e.g. to buy out a retiring partner) can be claimed in box 4, as well as royalties for the use of a UK patent.

- Interest on a loan to buy into a business or partnership, or to buy plant or machinery, can be claimed in box 5, unless you are claiming it as a business expense in the Self-employment or Partnership supplementary pages.

- If you were an employee, you may be able to claim in box 6 costs and liabilities arising from problems with your work.

- You can claim post-cessation expenses for up to seven years after you stop trading, for example the costs of collecting debts of your former business. And if you are transferring your business to a limited company, you may be able to claim some pre-incorporation losses. Enter the total in box 6, but do not enter other business losses – they are claimed on the Self-employment or Partnership pages.

Box 7. Maintenance payments

This applies only if you, your former spouse or former civil partner were born before 6 April 1935, and the payments are made under a legally binding order or agreement. If so, enter the total maintenance paid in 2011–12 up to a maximum of £2,800. If your ex-partner has remarried, enter only payments up to the date of marriage. See Example 17.6.

Box 8. Payments to a trade union or friendly society for death benefits

This applies if your trade union subscription entitles you to benefits, but the most you can claim is half the subscription or £100 if less.

Box 9. Relief for employer's compulsory widow's, widower's or orphan's benefit scheme

Only enter here any payments where (unusually) tax relief has not been given through PAYE. You can get relief at 20 per cent on up to £100. Note that in 2012–13 will be the last year for which you can claim this relief.

Box 10. Relief claimed on a qualifying distribution

This applies only if you included with your dividend income on page TR3 of the main return an amount received when you redeemed bonus shares and securities, and you pay higher-rate or additional-rate tax. If so, see the HMRC notes.

Example 17.6: **Claiming reliefs**

Geoff pays maintenance to his ex-wife under a court order, and as he is 80 he can claim tax relief. He pays her £4,000 a year, but he enters £2,800, as this is the most he can claim in 2011–12.

Figure 17.6: Other tax reliefs

1. Subscriptions for Venture Capital Trust shares - *the amount on which relief is claimed*
   £ [   ] · 0 0

2. Subscriptions for shares under the Enterprise Investment Scheme - *the amount on which relief is claimed (and provide more information on page Ai 4)*
   £ [   ] · 0 0

3. Community Investment Tax Relief - *the amount on which relief is claimed*
   £ [   ] · 0 0

4. UK royalties and annual payments made
   £ [   ] · 0 0

5. Qualifying loan interest payable in the year
   £ [   ] · 0 0

6. Post-cessation expenses and certain other losses
   £ [   ] · 0 0

7. Maintenance payments (max £2,800) - *only if you or your former spouse or civil partner were born before 6 April 1935*
   £ **2 8 0 0** · 0 0

8. Payments to a trade union etc. for death benefits - *half the amount paid (max £100)*
   £ [   ] · 0 0

9. Relief claimed for employer's compulsory widow's, widower's or orphan's benefit scheme - *(max £20)*
   £ [   ] · 0 0

10. Relief claimed on a qualifying distribution on the redemption of bonus shares or securities
    £ [   ] · 0 0

Age-related married couple's allowance

This applies only if you, your spouse or your civil partner were born before 6 April 1935 (see page 80 and Table 6.2 on page 82 for the amounts you can claim). Make sure you have completed box 1 on the front page of the tax return.

Boxes 1 to 5 – for husbands/higher-income partners

Fill in these boxes only if you are a husband or a higher-income partner, or if you married or registered as a civil partner after 4 December 2005. Enter your partner's name in box 1, and if your partner is older than you enter his or her date of birth in box 2. See Example 17.7 overleaf.

However, if you were living with a previous spouse or partner during

2011–12, enter their date of birth in box 5. If you were already entitled to married couple's allowance on the basis of that relationship, it is usually better to carry on with this, as you will get only one-twelfth of the allowance for each month of the new marriage (see page 83). HMRC will use whichever date of birth saves you most tax.

You may have allocated the whole of your allowance to your spouse or partner before the start of the tax year. If so, put a cross in box 3 or 4 as relevant. It's not too late to transfer unused allowance (see page 83), but boxes 3 or 4 apply only if you made a formal allocation before 6 April 2011.

Boxes 6 to 8 – for wives/lower-income partners

Fill in these boxes only if you are a wife or, if you married or registered as a civil partner after 4 December 2005, you are the lower-income partner *and* all or half the minimum allowance was allocated to you. This had to be agreed before 6 April 2011 (or before 6 April 2012 if married or registered as a civil partner during the year). If so, put a cross in box 6 or 7 as relevant, and enter your spouse or partner's name in box 8.

Box 9. Date of marriage

If you married or registered as a civil partner between 6 April 2011 and 5 April 2012, enter the date of marriage or registration in box 9 so that your tax office can work out how much of the full allowance to give you (one-twelfth for each month of marriage).

Example 17.7: **Claiming allowances**

Andrew, from Example 17.5 on page 284, can claim blind person's allowance as well as married couple's allowance. However, his income is too low to use all of his allowances. Andrew puts a cross in box 11 on his tax return to transfer his allowance to his wife Anna (see Figure 17.7). Anna needs to put a cross in box 10 on her tax return, and, because she is calculating her own tax, she includes the unused allowances in her calculation.

Figure 17.7: Age related married couple's allowance

If you, or your spouse or civil partner were born before 6 April 1935, complete the relevant boxes

| 1 | Your spouse's or civil partner's full name |
| | ANNA CONDON |

| 2 | Their date of birth if older than you (and at least one of you was born before 6 April 1935) *DD MM YYYY* |
| | 0 4 0 4 1 9 3 2 |

| 3 | If you have already agreed that half the minimum allowance is to go to your spouse or civil partner, put 'X' in the box |

| 4 | If you have already agreed that all of the minimum allowance is to go to your spouse or civil partner, put 'X' in the box |

| 5 | If, in the year to 5 April 2012, you lived with any previous spouse or civil partner, enter their date of birth |

| 6 | If you have already agreed that half of the minimum allowance is to be given to you, put 'X' in the box |

| 7 | If you have already agreed that all of the minimum allowance is to be given to you, put 'X' in the box |

| 8 | Your spouse's or civil partner's full name |

| 9 | If you were married or formed a civil partnership after 5 April 2011, enter the date of marriage or civil partnership *DD MM YYYY* |

| 10 | If you want to have your spouse's or civil partner's surplus allowance, put 'X' in the box |

| 11 | If you want your spouse or civil partner to have your surplus allowance, put 'X' in the box |
| | X |

Transfer of surplus allowances

You can transfer married couple's allowance to your spouse or civil partner if your income is too low to use it all. To do this, tick boxes 10 or 11 as relevant (and ask your partner to tick the equivalent boxes on his or her form). You cannot lose out by ticking these boxes – your tax office will transfer allowances only if it is in your interests.

Income tax losses

This section applies only if you are claiming a loss to set against some of the types of income which go under 'Other UK income' on page TR3 of the core tax return. This is unusual – see page 279 and HMRC help sheet 325 *Other taxable income*.

Pensions savings tax charges

You need to worry about this section only if, during 2011–12:

- you started to receive pension benefits that took you over your lifetime allowance (£1.8 million for 2011–12), or
- you paid pension contributions during the year that came to more than £50,000 plus unused allowance from the previous three tax years, or
- you received any unauthorised payments from a UK pension scheme (the scheme should tell you if this is the case), or
- you received taxable lump sums from an overseas pension.

See Chapter 12 and HMRC help sheet 345 *Pensions – tax charges on any excess over the Lifetime Allowance and Annual Allowance, and on unauthorised payments* and help sheet 346 *Pensions savings tax charges – guidance for members of overseas pension schemes.*

Tax avoidance schemes

Professional advisers who devise or market particular types of tax avoidance schemes are required to notify HMRC. Ordinary taxpayers who have not used such schemes are unlikely to be affected, but if you are, your adviser will normally give you a reference number to enter in box 18. If in doubt, see the anti-avoidance pages on the HMRC website at www.hmrc.gov.uk/avoidance/ or contact HMRC's Anti Avoidance Group on 020 7438 6733.

Now you've finished....

Before you file your return, have you:
- Remembered to sign and date your tax return on page TR6, if you are sending in a paper return?
- Filled in all the supplementary pages that you've said you need on page TR2 of the core return?
- Remembered to say where you want any repayment to be sent on page TR5?
- Kept a copy for your records?

18

Filling in the supplementary pages

If you are sent the full tax return, you will usually have 'supplementary' pages to complete. This chapter tells you how to fill in the more common supplementary pages – employment, self-employment, UK property and capital gains tax.

Top tips

- You won't necessarily be sent the pages you need. It's your responsibility to check that you have the right ones – see HMRC's Tax Return Guide for a list.
- If you are an employee, you can get most of the information you need for your supplementary page from the P60 and P11D your employer gives you.
- Unusual entries may trigger a check of your return, such as any 'blips' in expenses compared with the year before. Use the 'Any other information' boxes to explain anything that might look odd and make sure that your records support your explanations.
- Be particularly careful to enter all the tax you have already paid.
- If you made a business loss, or a capital loss on selling an asset, use the Self-employment or Capital gains summary to notify HMRC – otherwise you will not be able to use the loss to reduce your tax in future.
- You may need to submit supporting documentation, such as capital gains tax calculations – check HMRC's notes. You can send attachments with your return (online or paper), or follow up an online return with paper copies.

The Employment page

Fill in this page if you were an employee (even if you owned the company), a casual or part-time worker, or an agency worker. You also need to complete it if you received any income or benefit from a directorship or other post such as chairperson, secretary or treasurer. If you had more than one job during the tax year, you will need to fill in one page for each employer.

Usually, you can just carry information across from the P60 your employer gives you after the tax year (or P45 if you left a job), and from your P11D *Expenses and benefits* form, or the equivalent form P9D if you are 'lower-paid'. However, if you had two jobs, or are unemployed at the end of the tax year, your P60 may include figures for both jobs and any taxable Jobseeker's Allowance. If so, you will need to separate the figures to put them on separate pages, using your payslips, P45 or other records.

Note that some items related to employment should be entered on other parts of the return:

- Jobseeker's Allowance goes in the main tax return.
- If you received a lump sum, such as redundancy pay, or a taxable benefit from a share scheme, complete the Additional Information pages of the tax return.
- If you worked abroad, your foreign income should usually also go in the Employment page, but if you are claiming to be non-resident you will also need the Residence, remittance basis etc. supplementary pages, and if you are claiming tax credit relief on any foreign tax you will need the Foreign pages as well. See Chapter 10 and HMRC help sheet 211 *Employment – Residence and domicile issues*.

Box 1. Pay

You should enter in box 1 any of the following received in 2011–12:

- all the taxable income listed on page 97. But don't include expenses payments (these go in box 16) or pension contributions and payroll-giving donations (your P60 will already have excluded these)
- any extra taxable pay, if you are a director or partner affected by the IR35 rules (see page 98)

■ any taxable income from share schemes that has already been taxed under PAYE (this should be included in the figure on your P60).

It is not always clear what your employer has included in the P60 figure – if you have received a taxed lump sum on leaving a job, say – so you may need to ask your employer.

Box 2. UK tax taken off

This box is for any tax deductions shown on your P60 (or P45). Do not include non-UK tax – either enter this in the Additional Information pages of the tax return or claim a separate relief for it in the Foreign supplementary pages (see Chapter 10). And if tax has been deducted from a lump sum, and you entered it under Additional Information, do not enter it here as well.

Box 3. Tips and other payments not on your P60

Tips are taxable, however they are paid. Employers must notify HMRC if they know that a tip-sharing scheme (tronc) is in existence. (See HMRC leaflet E24 *Tips, gratuities, service charges and troncs.*)

Boxes 4 to 7. Details of employer

Your employer's PAYE reference will be on your P60 or P45. If (exceptionally) they do not have one, enter 'none' in box 4. Special rules often apply to directors, so tick box 6 if you are a director, and box 7 if a director of a 'close' company (one controlled either by its directors or by fewer than six shareholders or other key 'participators').

Boxes 9 to 16. Benefits

Enter here any taxable benefits and expenses payments you have received. You should be able to take all the figures straight from your P11D or P9D. See page 99 onwards for how these figures are arrived at. Note that the 'balancing charges' referred to in box 16 apply only if you have disposed of (e.g. sold) something on which you previously claimed capital allowances.

Boxes 17 to 20. Expenses

Enter here work expenses for which you are claiming tax relief – there is a list of expenses you might be able to claim in Table 7.3 on page 115.

Figure 18.1: The Employment page (see Example 18.1)

HM Revenue & Customs

Employment
Tax year 6 April 2011 to 5 April 2012

Your name

ELIZABETH GEORGE

Your Unique Taxpayer Reference (UTR)

9 6 9 6 9 1 2 1 2 1

Complete an *Employment* page for each employment or directorship

1 Pay from this employment – the total from your P45 or P60 – *before tax was taken off*

£ 3 8 5 0 0 . 0 0

2 UK tax taken off pay in box 1

£ 9 1 4 5 . 0 0

3 Tips and other payments not on your P60
- *read page EN 3 of the notes*

£ . 0 0

4 PAYE tax reference of your employer (on your P45/P60)

1 2 3 / X 4 5 6

5 Your employer's name

DUSTY MILLER'S BAKERY

6 If you were a company director, put 'X' in the box

7 And, if the company was a close company, put 'X' in the box

8 If you are a part-time teacher in England or Wales and are on the Repayment of Teachers' Loans Scheme for this employment, put 'X' in the box

Benefits from your employment – use your form P11D (or equivalent information)

9 Company cars and vans – the total 'cash equivalent' amount

£ 5 4 0 0 . 0 0

10 Fuel for company cars and vans
- *the total 'cash equivalent' amount*

£ 2 8 5 0 . 0 0

11 Private medical and dental insurance
- *the total 'cash equivalent' amount*

£ 1 2 0 0 . 0 0

12 Vouchers, credit cards and excess mileage allowance

£ . 0 0

13 Goods and other assets provided by your employer
- *the total value or amount*

£ . 0 0

14 Accommodation provided by your employer
- *the total value or amount*

£ . 0 0

15 Other benefits (including interest-free and low interest loans) – *the total 'cash equivalent' amount*

£ 1 0 2 4 . 0 0

16 Expenses payments received and balancing charges

£ . 0 0

Employment expenses

17 Business travel and subsistence expenses

£ 8 4 0 . 0 0

18 Fixed deductions for expenses

£ . 0 0

19 Professional fees and subscriptions

£ 9 6 . 0 0

20 Other expenses and capital allowances

£ . 0 0

ℹ **Shares schemes, employment lump sums, compensation, deductions and Seafarers' Earnings Deduction** are on the *Additional information* pages enclosed in the tax return pack

Common mistakes on the Employment page

■ Failing to complete a separate supplementary page for each job.
■ Entering your pay in box 1 but not entering any tax deducted in box 2.
■ Entering your gross pay in box 1, before deducting pension contributions and payroll giving.
■ If you have a cheap or free loan, entering in box 15 the amount borrowed instead of the taxable amount.

Example 18.1: **Filling in the Employment page**

Liz is a personnel manager. In her Employment page (shown in Figure 18.1), she enters the 'Pay' figure (£38,500) from her P60 in box 1, and the 'Tax' figure (£9,145) in box 2. (She contributes to the company pension scheme but the 'Pay' figure in her P60 has taken account of this.)

Liz takes the figures for her benefits and expenses from her P11D. These add £10,474 to her pay, but in boxes 17 and 19 she can claim tax relief for some expenses – £840 for travel expenses and £96 for her subscription to her professional institute. Her taxable pay is £38,500 + £10,474 – £936 = £48,038.

The Self-employment pages

You normally enter figures for your accounting period ending between 6 April 2011 and 5 April 2012, but see page 139 if you have recently started or closed your business. The information you need should be in your business records, but if any figures are provisional remember to put a cross on page TR6 of the core tax return, and give an explanation under 'Any other information' (see page 287). If you have more than one trade you will need to complete a separate form for each. See HMRC help sheet 220 *More than one business*.

There is a shorter version of the pages for people with a turnover below £73,000 for a full year. This means that if the accounting period you are reporting is shorter or longer than 12 months, you must adjust the £73,000 proportionately. So if your accounting period is nine months, the threshold is £73,000 × $^9/_{12}$ = £54,750. However, even if you meet this condition, you will still need to use the longer version if:

- Your accounting period is not the same as your 'basis period' (the period for which tax is payable). This will be the case in the first or second tax years you are in business, unless your year end is between 31 March and 5 April (see page 143). See HMRC help sheet 222 *How to calculate your taxable profits.*
- Your business ceased during the tax year and your accounting period did not start on 6 April 2011.
- You wish to claim 'overlap relief' (see page 143).
- You can adjust your profits for Class 4 National Insurance.
- You are making other accounting changes or adjustments, e.g. if you are changing your accounting date, or claiming to spread income from agriculture, writing or art over several years.
- Yours is a service business, and you have made an entry to adjust your income on earlier returns. See HMRC help sheet 238 *Revenue recognition in service contracts.*
- You entered the figures from your most recent set of accounts in last year's tax return (possible if you are just starting up).
- You want to claim any capital allowances apart from annual investment allowance or other allowances for plant and machinery.
- Your business was carried on abroad.
- You are a practising barrister (advocate in Scotland).
- You are on HMRC's Managing Deliberate Defaulters programme (see page 41).

This chapter covers the shorter version of the Self-employment pages.

Boxes 1 to 7. Business details

Enter the business or partnership's name and postcode, and the date the business started up or ceased (if this was after 5 April 2011 and before 6 April 2012) and the date of your year end. These dates will give your tax office the information it needs to check your basis period.

You are asked to tick box 4 if you are in business as a foster carer or shared lives carer, but note that most income of this type is tax-free – see

HMRC help sheet 236 *Qualifying care relief: Foster carers, adult placement carers, kinship carers and staying put carers.*

Boxes 8 to 9. Business income

Your business turnover – all the income from your business, including sales, commissions and payments 'in kind' – goes in box 8. Service businesses should also include work in progress (see page 130 and Example 18.2 below). The 'Other business income' to go in box 9 includes VAT savings if you are in the Flat Rate VAT scheme (see box overleaf), rental income from your business property (unless you are required to complete the Property supplementary pages) and payments under the 'New Deal' scheme. But do not include:

■ Non-trading income relating to your business that you have entered elsewhere in your tax return (e.g. interest from a business bank account).
■ Business Start-up Allowance – this goes in box 29.

Example 18.2: **Work in progress for service businesses**

Mark runs a research consultancy with a year end of 31 March. On 31 March 2012 he was two-thirds through a contract worth £18,000, so his work in progress was £18,000 × $^2/_3$ = £12,000. Under the rules for work in progress, he added £12,000 to his turnover and included it in box 8 of his tax return. See HMRC help sheet 238 *Revenue recognition in service contracts.*

Boxes 10 to 19. Allowable business expenses

You can only claim expenses that qualify for tax relief – see Table 8.2 on page 132, and also the list in the notes to the full Self-employment pages. If your annual turnover is less than £73,000 (or would be if you were trading for a full year), you do not need to break down your expenses – you can simply enter them all in box 19, 'Total allowable expenses'. Otherwise you will need to enter them under the categories shown.

Remember that if only part of the expense was for business purposes, you will have to reduce the amount you claim in line with the proportion of business use (see page 131).

Dealing with VAT

If you are VAT-registered, you can show your turnover and expenses either including VAT, or with VAT taken off, as long as you are consistent. However, if you are not VAT-registered, be sure to include any VAT paid in your expenses, so that you can get tax relief on it.

If you are in the Flat Rate Scheme (see page 128), and your figures are VAT-inclusive, enter your payments to HMRC under 'Other expenses' in box 18. But if your figures exclude VAT, any VAT saved counts as taxable income. You will need to work out the VAT saved and enter it in box 9; any extra VAT incurred can be claimed as an expense in box 18.

If you registered or deregistered for VAT during this period, enter the date of the change under 'Any other information' on page TR6 of the main tax return, and say whether your figures while you were registered include VAT.

Tax allowances for vehicles and equipment

If you bought equipment or cars, or did so in previous years, you will be able to claim either annual investment allowance or capital allowances to deduct from your profits. The notes to the Self-employment pages include working sheets and see HMRC help sheets 222 *How to calculate your taxable profits* and 252 *Capital allowances and balancing charges*.

If you bought equipment, you can claim the total cost (up to an annual limit of £100,000 in 2011–12) as an annual investment allowance. But this does not apply to cars – for these, and any purchases above the annual limit, you have to claim capital allowances instead. Capital allowances do not normally allow you to claim the whole cost in one year. Instead, the cost of your purchase is added to a 'pool' of expenditure and you claim a percentage of the pool each year.

Before you enter the allowances in your return, you must adjust the amount you are claiming if:

■ You use an item partly for business, partly privately. The allowance is restricted in line with the business use.

■ Your accounting period is not 12 months (e.g. when starting up in business). If your accounting period is eight months long, say, you get eight-twelfths of the full allowance (see page 137).

Box 22. Annual investment allowance

Enter in box 22 the total cost of any purchases made in your accounting period (excluding cars) that qualify for annual investment allowance, up to a total of £100,000, adjusted if there was any private use or if your accounting period is not 12 months. See help sheet 252 *Capital allowances and balancing charges*.

Boxes 23 and 24. Other capital allowances, allowance for small balance

If you bought any equipment in your accounting period that does not qualify for annual investment allowance, claim the following capital allowances in box 24:

■ For the items listed on page 137, and new cars with CO_2 emissions of less than 110g/km, claim the whole cost.
■ For cars bought before 6 April 2009 claim 20 per cent (capped at £3,000 for cars costing more than £12,000).
■ For cars bought after 5 April 2009, claim 20 per cent of the cost if the CO_2 emissions are 160g/km or less, and 10 per cent if they are higher.
■ For other equipment bought during this accounting period, claim 20 per cent of the cost.

You can also claim a 'writing-down' allowance for expenditure on equipment in earlier accounting periods. This expenditure is 'pooled' at the end of the year of purchase. Each following year, you deduct from your pool the proceeds from selling any equipment in it (or the market value of any equipment you gave away or started using for non-business purposes). The writing-down allowance, for the 2011–12 tax year, is 20 per cent of the remaining pool. See Example 18.3 overleaf.

Once the value of the pool is £1,000 or less, you can claim the whole lot in one year – if you want to do this (you do not have to), enter the amount claimed in box 23. Any other capital allowances you are claiming go in box 24, adjusted if there was any private use or if your accounting period is not 12 months. Note that this is a simplified explanation and the records you have to keep are complex, so see HMRC help sheet 252 *Capital allowances and balancing charges*.

Box 25. Total balancing charges

If you sell an item in your pool for more than the value of the pool so far, the difference is a 'balancing charge' and it is added to your profits. Enter any balancing charge in box 25 (adjusted if you use the item for private as well as business purposes, or if your accounting period is not 12 months).

Example 18.3: Working out capital allowances

Noah opened his shop in 2000. The written-down value of his business assets on 5 April 2011 (his year end) was £3,650. In May 2011, he sold his old chiller cabinets for £2,450 and bought new ones for £6,198. The new cabinets qualify for 100% annual investment allowance so he enters £6,198 in box 22. But in box 24 he can claim a writing-down allowance for his existing business assets, worked out as shown below.

Because the written-down value of his pool at the end of 2011–12 is under £1,000, in his 2012–13 return Noah can claim the whole £960 as a 'small balance' in box 23.

	Allowances £	Pool £
Pool at start of period		3,650
Sales		−2,450
		1,200
Writing-down allowance £1,200 × 20%	240	−240
		960

You don't have to claim your allowances

You don't have to claim annual investment allowance or capital allowances if you would not have to pay tax anyway. If you do not claim, you can claim writing-down allowance on the expenditure in future years.

Figure 18.2: Tax allowances for vehicles and equipment

22 Annual Investment Allowance	24 Other capital allowances
£ **6 1 9 8** · 0 0	£ **2 4 0** · 0 0
23 Allowance for small balance of unrelieved expenditure	25 Total balancing charges – where you have disposed of items for more than their value
£ · 0 0	£ · 0 0

Boxes 26 to 31. Calculating your taxable profits

First, in this section, you should *add* to your profits any goods taken out of your business for private use (which count as a sale for tax purposes) and any balancing charges. Next you can *deduct* your capital allowances and any losses carried forward from previous years – but you only need to deduct enough to reduce your taxable profits to zero. Finally, you have to add in any other business income not already entered, such as Business Start-up Allowance. There is a working sheet in the notes.

Boxes 32 to 34. Losses

These boxes tell your tax office what you want to do with any losses you made in 2011–12. (See Figure 8.1 on page 146 and HMRC help sheet 227 *Losses* for the choices you have.) If you want to use your loss:

■ to reduce your tax on other taxable income that doesn't come from your business, enter the relevant amount in box 32; if the loss is more than your other income, you can claim the unused loss against any capital gains by entering it in box 14 on the Capital gains summary pages
■ to claim a rebate on tax paid in previous years, enter it in box 33.

Any unused losses go in box 34. To work these out, see the working sheets in the notes and in HMRC help sheet 227 *Losses*.

Figure 18.3: Self-employment (see Example 18.4 on page 312)

HM Revenue & Customs

Self-employment (short)
Tax year 6 April 2011 to 5 April 2012

Your name
ALEX BRODSKI

Your Unique Taxpayer Reference (UTR)
1 2 3 4 5 6 7 8 9

Read page SESN 1 of the *notes* to check if you should use this page or the *Self-employment (full)* page.

Business details

1 Description of business
LANDSCAPING

2 Postcode of your business address
XY23 1BZ

3 If your business name, description, address or postcode have changed in the last 12 months, put 'X' in the box and give details in the 'Any other information' box of your tax return

4 If you are a foster carer or shared lives carer, put 'X' in the box - *read page SESN 2 of the notes*

5 If your business started after 5 April 2011, enter the start date *DD MM YYYY*
0 1 1 0 2 0 1 1

6 If your business ceased before 6 April 2012, enter the final date of trading

7 Date your books or accounts are made up to - *read page SESN 3 of the notes*
3 1 0 3 2 0 1 2

Business income - if your annual business turnover was below £73,000

8 Your turnover - *the takings, fees, sales or money earned by your business*
£ *2 8 3 0 2* . 0 0

9 Any other business income not included in box 8 - *excluding Business Start-up Allowance*
£ . 0 0

Allowable business expenses

If your annual turnover was below £73,000 you may just put your total expenses in box 19, rather than filling in the whole section.

10 Costs of goods bought for resale or goods used
£ . 0 0

11 Car, van and travel expenses - *after private use proportion*
£ . 0 0

12 Wages, salaries and other staff costs
£ . 0 0

13 Rent, rates, power and insurance costs
£ . 0 0

14 Repairs and renewals of property and equipment
£ . 0 0

15 Accountancy, legal and other professional fees
£ . 0 0

16 Interest and bank and credit card etc. financial charges
£ . 0 0

17 Phone, fax, stationery and other office costs
£ . 0 0

18 Other allowable business expenses - *client entertaining costs are not an allowable expense*
£ . 0 0

19 Total allowable expenses - *total of boxes 10 to 18*
£ *2 5 1 1 5* . 0 0

Net profit or loss

20	**Net profit** – *if your business income is more than your expenses (if box 8 + box 9 minus box 19 is positive)*	21	**Or, net loss** – *if your expenses exceed your business income (if box 19 minus (box 8 + box 9) is positive)*
	£ 3 1 8 7 · 0 0		£ · 0 0

Tax allowances for vehicles and equipment (capital allowances)

There are 'capital' tax allowances for vehicles and equipment used in your business (you should not have included the cost of these in your business expenses). Read pages SESN 4 to SESN 8 of the *notes* and use the example and Working Sheets to work out your capital allowances.

22	**Annual Investment Allowance**	24	**Other capital allowances**
	£ 2 4 5 0 · 0 0		£ · 0 0

23	**Allowance for small balance of unrelieved expenditure**	25	**Total balancing charges – where you have disposed of items for more than their value**
	£ · 0 0		£ · 0 0

Calculating your taxable profits

Your taxable profit may not be the same as your net profit. Read page SESN 9 of the *notes* to see if you need to make any adjustments and fill in the boxes which apply to arrive at your taxable profit for the year.

26	**Goods and/or services for your own use** *– read page SESN 8 of the notes*	28	**Loss brought forward from earlier years set off against this year's profits** *– up to the amount in box 27*
	£ · 0 0		£ · 0 0

27	**Net business profit for tax purposes (if box 20 + box 25 + box 26 minus (boxes 21 to 24) is positive)**	29	**Any other business income not included in box 8 or box 9** *– for example, Business Start-up Allowance*
	£ 7 3 7 · 0 0		£ · 0 0

Total taxable profits or net business loss

30	**Total taxable profits from this business (if box 27 + box 29 minus box 28 is positive)**	31	**Net business loss for tax purposes (if boxes 21 to 24 minus (box 20 + box 25 + box 26) is positive)**
	£ 7 3 7 · 0 0		£ · 0 0

Losses, Class 4 NICs and CIS deductions

If you have made a loss for tax purposes (box 31), read page SESN 9 of the *notes* and fill in boxes 32 to 34 as appropriate.

32	**Loss from this tax year set off against other income for 2011–12**	35	**If you are exempt from paying Class 4 NICs, put 'X' in the box** – *read page SESN 10 of the notes*
	£ · 0 0		☐

33	**Loss to be carried back to previous year(s) and set off against income (or capital gains)**	36	**If you have been given a 2011–12 Class 4 NICs deferment certificate, put 'X' in the box** *– read page SESN 10 of the notes*
	£ · 0 0		☐

34	**Total loss to carry forward after all other set-offs** *– including unused losses brought forward*	37	**Deductions on payment and deduction statements from contractors** – *construction industry subcontractors only*
	£ · 0 0		£ · 0 0

Example 18.4: **Filling in the Self-employment pages**

Alex started up his landscaping business in October 2011, ending his accounting year on 31 March 2012. (See Figure 18.3 on pages 310–11.) His turnover over the six months was £28,302 (£56,604 over the full year), so he is below the £70,000 limit for using the short Self-employment pages, and because his year end is treated as the end of the tax year, there are no complexities which would require him to use the full pages. Nor does he need to break down his expenses into separate categories; the total (£25,115) goes in box 19.

Alex has made a profit of £3,187 at box 20. However, he had to buy business equipment, so his annual investment allowance of £2,450 at box 22 cuts his profit in box 30 to £737.

Boxes 35 and 36. Class 4 National Insurance contributions

Class 4 National Insurance contributions are payable on your 2011–12 business profits, at the rate of 9 per cent on any profits between £7,225 and £42,475, and 2 per cent on profits above £42,475. See page 148 for how these contributions are calculated, and HMRC help sheet 220 *More than one business* if relevant. However, you do not need to pay contributions at all if you were over state pension age on 6 April 2011, so make sure you enter your age on the first page of the core tax return. And professional divers or trustees may be exempt – contact your tax office.

Box 36 applies only if you have a job as well as your business, and have a certificate from HMRC's National Insurance Contributions and Employer Office entitling you to defer your contributions (see page 121).

Box 37. Deductions (construction industry)

This applies only if you are a subcontractor in the building trade, and you have received payment with tax already deducted (as shown on your CIS vouchers). You do not need to send in the vouchers with your return.

Using losses to reduce National Insurance

As shown in Example 8.10 on page 149, you can use unused business losses from earlier years to reduce your National Insurance contributions – and these losses may be different from those that apply for income tax. If this applies to you, you will need to fill in the longer version of the Self-employment pages, and enter the losses you want to use in box 101.

Common mistakes on the Self-employment pages

- Including in expenses the amount spent on plant and machinery, instead of claiming annual investment allowance or capital allowances, or entering the full expense in box 24, not just the allowance.
- Not reducing your allowances or expenses to reflect any private use (of a car, say). Explain the basis on which you split expenses between private and business use under 'Any other information' on the core tax return.
- If you are working out your own tax, forgetting to enter in boxes 13 to 15 of the Tax Calculation summary any adjustment from carrying back business losses, or from averaging your income if you are a farmer, writer or artist.

The UK property pages

These pages cover income from property in the UK that does not count as income from a trade (see page 157), but you can also use them if you have property in the European Economic Area (EEA) that you are claiming to have treated as furnished holiday lettings. Trading income goes in the Self-employment or Partnership pages instead. However, if the only property income you receive is money from a lodger who shares your home and this amounts to less than £4,250 (£2,125 if you let jointly), you only need to put a cross in box 4 and boxes 2 and 3 if relevant. And if this is the last tax year in which you expect to receive taxable income from property, put a cross in box 2 so that your tax office can adjust your tax code if necessary.

Jointly owned property

If you receive income from jointly owned property, put a cross in box 3 and enter only your share of the income, expenses and any allowances or reliefs claimed. You do not need to give details of expenses and so on if someone else deals with that side of things and just tells you your overall profit, but if so, you should give the name and address of that person under 'Any other information' on page TR6 of the main tax return.

Furnished holiday lettings

Complete the rest of the first page only if you let out holiday property that passes the 'furnished holiday lettings' test (see page 158 and HMRC help sheet 253 *Furnished holiday lettings*). If it does, favourable rules apply. The test became tougher in April 2012, but provided you passed the test in 2010–11, you can claim a period of grace for 2011–12 and be treated as passing it even if you do not. To claim, put a cross in box 19.

You can enter your income from non-UK lettings on page UKP1, but remember to put a cross in box 18. You need to keep separate records for your UK and non-UK lettings and fill out a separate page UKP1 for them, but you can put all your non-UK lettings on one page. If you paid foreign tax on the income, don't forget to claim tax credit relief for it on page F6 of the Foreign supplementary pages.

Boxes 5 to 9. Income and expenses

Enter in box 5 the total amount of income you received from furnished holiday lettings, then check page 160 for what expenses you can claim. If your total income from all properties (furnished holiday lettings or not) is £73,000 or more over a whole year, you must break down your expenses according to HMRC's headings in boxes 6 to 9. However, if your income is under £73,000, you can simply enter the total figure for all your expenses in box 9 without giving any details.

Example 18.5: Splitting expenses between tax years

Lucy's buildings insurance on her rental property runs from 5 October 2011 to 5 October 2012 and she pays a lump-sum premium of £500: half of the premium belongs to the 2011–12 tax year (which ends on 5 April 2012), and half to the 2012–13 tax year.

Relating income and expenses to a tax year

Unless you are using the 'cash basis' for working out your profits (see page 160), you must give details of business or property income due to you in a tax year and expenses which relate to a particular tax year even if you paid the bill at an earlier or later date. For example, if you had your business premises repainted in March 2012 but didn't pay the bill until the end of April, the expense still belongs to the 2011–12 tax year. In addition, if you have an expense that straddles two years, you need to divide the payment between the two tax years, in line with the number of days between the date you incurred the expense and the end of the tax year (see Example 18.5).

Boxes 10 to 17. Tax adjustments and taxable profit

There is a useful working sheet to help you calculate your profit or loss in the notes. Before you arrive at the figure for your taxable profit from letting holiday property, you may need to:

■ add back the proportion of your expenses which relate to private use in box 10, unless you have already taken this into account in the expenses figures entered in boxes 5 to 9

■ add any 'balancing charges' in box 11, if you have made a profit from selling something on which you previously claimed capital allowances (see HMRC help sheet 252 *Capital allowances and balancing charges*)

■ subtract any annual investment allowance or capital allowances you can claim in box 12. See page 163.

■ subtract any losses made on furnished holiday lettings in earlier years and not set against earlier years' profits. You can also subtract any losses made on other types of property in earlier years. The unused losses you want to deduct go in box 14, but only enter the amount you need to reduce your profits to zero (or the total losses if they are less than your profits). See HMRC help sheet 227 *Losses*.

If you have any profits left after these deductions, enter them in box 15. If you made a loss for the year, enter it in box 16; you can carry it forward to set against profits in later tax years, as well as any unused losses from earlier years. The total losses you made on furnished holiday lettings to carry forward go in box 17.

Other property income

The second page of the UK property supplementary pages deals with property that doesn't pass the 'furnished holiday lettings' test. You must give details of not only rents you receive but also all other property income (see page 159).

Boxes 20 to 23. Property income

- In box 20 enter the total figure for all your income from UK property which hasn't already been accounted for. The form has changed this year – do not include any profits from letting furnished holiday property.
- Box 21 applies only to landlords who are resident abroad – their tenants may be required to deduct basic-rate tax from the rent and pay the tax to HMRC (see page 177).
- The premiums in box 22 apply only if you received a lump-sum payment from your tenant when granting a lease of less than 50 years. If this applies, fill in the working sheet on page UKPN 8 of the notes to get the correct figure to enter.
- Ignore box 23 unless you sublet a leased property and received a lump-sum payment (a 'reverse premium') to encourage you to take on the lease. Check with your tax office if you think that this applies.

Boxes 24 to 29. Property expenses

You don't need to fill in this part of the form if your income from property is made up solely of income from a lodger who lives with you and you are claiming relief under the Rent-a-Room scheme (see page 156).

Otherwise see page 160 for the expenses you can claim and:

■ If your property income is less than £73,000 over a full year, enter a total figure for all your expenses in boxes 29.
■ If your property income is £73,000 or more, enter separate figures split according to the headings given in boxes 24 to 29.

Boxes 30 to 40. Calculating your taxable profit

Before you arrive at the figure for your taxable profit from UK property, you may need to:

■ add back the proportion of your expenses which relates to private use in box 30, unless you have already taken this into account in the expenses figures entered in boxes 24 to 29 (see page 161)
■ add any 'balancing charges' referred to in box 31 if you have made a profit from selling something on which you previously claimed capital allowances (see page 308)
■ enter any capital allowances or annual investment allowance you can claim (see page 163 and HMRC help sheet 252 *Capital allowances and balancing charges* for how to calculate them) in boxes 32 to 34
■ if you have made energy-saving improvements, enter in box 35 any Landlord's Energy Saving Allowance you qualify for, up to £1,500 per property (see page 161)
■ enter your 'wear and tear' allowance (see page 162) in box 36 if you let furnished property and you have chosen not to claim the actual cost of repairing and replacing furniture and so on
■ if you get rent which is tax-free under the Rent-a-Room scheme, enter in box 37 the amount of relief you are claiming – i.e. £4,250 (£2,125 if you let the property jointly) or the amount of rent to which the relief applies if less.

Boxes 36 to 41. Adjustments and losses

Now you have to work out the effect that any adjustments have on your profits or loss. There is a working sheet on page UKPN 16 of the UK Property Notes, but to sum up:

- add up all the income in boxes 20 to 23
- add any private use adjustment and balancing charges (boxes 30 and 31)
- deduct all your expenses in boxes 24 to 29
- deduct the allowances claimed in boxes 32 to 37.

This will give you your adjusted profit (which goes in box 38) or loss for the year (which goes in box 41). However, this is not the end of the story:

- If you have made a profit enter in box 39 any losses made in an earlier tax year and so far unused (from box 41 on last year's return), deduct them from your profits and enter the result in box 40. If the brought-forward loss is bigger than your adjusted profit, only enter the amount you need to reduce your profit to zero; you can set the rest against any profits on furnished holiday lettings by entering them in box 14, or carry them forward to future years by entering them in box 43.
- Box 42 applies only if you have made a loss – either partly or wholly – as a result of claiming capital allowances and you want to set this loss against other income rather than carrying it forward to set against future income from property. This will be unusual, and you cannot claim to do it for any other loss.
- You will have losses to carry forward to a future year either if you made a loss in this year or if you made a profit but it was less than your loss brought forward from previous years. Enter in box 43 any losses brought forward and not used this year, plus any loss made this year, minus any loss which you are claiming to use against other income in box 42.

> ## Example 18.6: **Filling in the UK property pages**

Edgar has rent of £5,250 from a buy-to-let property and £3,000 from letting a garret in his home to a lodger (see Figure 18.4 on pages 320–1). He enters the total – £8,250 – in box 20. As he is claiming Rent-a-Room relief on his lodger's rent, he can claim expenses only on his buy-to-let property, which come to £3,500. His total property income is less than £73,000 over a full year, so he doesn't need to break down his expenses and he enters the total in box 29. He claims the tax-free amount of rent from his lodger in box 37, and 10% wear and tear for his buy-to-let property in box 36. This gives him a total profit at box 38 of only £1,225. However, his buy-to-let property was empty for part of 2010–11 and he made a £1,845 loss for that year, which he enters in box 39. This wipes out his profit and leaves £1,845 – £1,225 = £620 of unused loss to carry forward to 2011–12.

The Capital gains summary pages

You will need to complete these pages if you have made a taxable capital gain of £10,600 or more in 2011–12, but also if you have disposed of assets worth more than £42,400 overall, or if you want to claim a capital loss or other relief or exemption. See Chapter 14 for a general explanation of capital gains tax.

The pages consist of just a summary of your taxable gains or losses, but you have to send in your computations as well – the accompanying HMRC notes include a working sheet you can use, and there is a long list of help sheets on the last page of the notes.

Below, we explain how to get the figures to enter in each of the boxes on the first page of the Capital gains summary. Also see Figure 18.5 on page 327. But before you can start, you need to work out the gain or loss on each individual asset you disposed of in the 2011–12 tax year.

Work out your gain or loss on each asset

You can ignore assets that are tax-free – see the list on page 327. You can use the working sheet on page CGN 21 of the notes, but to sum up:

Figure 18.4: The UK property pages (see Example 18.6 on page 319)

HM Revenue & Customs

UK property
Tax year 6 April 2011 to 5 April 2012

Your name

EDGAR DEGAS

Your Unique Taxpayer Reference (UTR)

9 8 7 6 5 4 3 2 1 0

UK property details

1 Number of properties rented out

2

2 If all property income ceased in 2011–12 and you do not expect to receive such income in 2012–13, put 'X' in the box

3 If you have any income from property let jointly, put 'X' in the box

4 If you are claiming Rent a Room relief and your rents are £4,250 or less (or £2,125 if let jointly), put 'X' in the box

X

Furnished holiday lettings in the UK or European Economic Area (EEA)

Fill in one page for UK businesses and a separate page for EEA businesses. Please read pages UKPN X to UKPN X before filling in boxes 5 to 19 if you have furnished holiday lettings.

5 Income – *the amount of rent and any income for services provided to tenants*

£ · 0 0

6 Rent paid, repairs, insurance and costs of services provided – *the total amount*

£ · 0 0

7 Loan interest and other financial costs

£ · 0 0

8 Legal, management and other professional fees

£ · 0 0

9 Other allowable property expenses

£ · 0 0

10 Private use adjustment – *if expenses include any amounts for non-business purposes*

£ · 0 0

11 Balancing charges – *read page UKPN X of the notes*

£ · 0 0

12 Capital allowances – *read page UKPN X of the notes*

£ · 0 0

13 Adjusted profit for the year (if the amount in box 5 + box 10 + box 11 minus (boxes 6 to 9 + box 12) is positive)

£ · 0 0

14 Loss brought forward used against this year's profits

£ · 0 0

15 Taxable profit for the year (box 13 minus box 14)

£ · 0 0

16 Loss for the year (if the amount in boxes 6 to 9 + box 12 minus (box 5 + box 10 + box 11) is positive)

£ · 0 0

17 Total loss to carry forward

£ · 0 0

18 Put an X in the box if this business is in the EEA – *see page UKPN X of the notes*

19 If you want to make a period of grace election, put 'X' in the box

Property income

Do not include furnished holiday lettings, Real Estate Investment Trust or Property Authorised Investment Funds dividends/distributions here.

20 Total rents and other income from property
£ 8 2 5 0 . 0 0

21 Tax taken off any income in box 20
£ . 0 0

22 Premiums for the grant of a lease – *from box E on the Working Sheet on page UKPN X of the notes.*
£ . 0 0

23 Reverse premiums and inducements
£ . 0 0

Property expenses

24 Rent, rates, insurance, ground rents etc.
£ . 0 0

25 Property repairs, maintenance and renewals
£ . 0 0

26 Loan interest and other financial costs
£ . 0 0

27 Legal, management and other professional fees
£ . 0 0

28 Costs of services provided, including wages
£ . 0 0

29 Other allowable property expenses
£ 3 5 0 0 . 0 0

Calculating your taxable profit or loss

30 Private use adjustment – *read page UKPN X of the notes*
£ . 0 0

31 Balancing charges – *read page UKPN X of the notes*
£ . 0 0

32 Annual Investment Allowance
£ . 0 0

33 Business Premises Renovation Allowance (Assisted Areas only) – *read page UKPN XX of the notes*
£ . 0 0

34 All other capital allowances
£ . 0 0

35 Landlord's Energy Saving Allowance
£ . 0 0

36 10% wear and tear allowance – *for furnished residential accommodation only*
£ 5 2 5 . 0 0

37 Rent a Room exempt amount
£ 3 0 0 0 . 0 0

38 Adjusted profit for the year – *from box O on the Working Sheet on page UKPN XX*
£ 1 2 2 5 . 0 0

39 Loss brought forward used against this year's profits
£ 1 8 4 5 . 0 0

40 Taxable profit for the year (box 38 minus box 39)
£ . 0 0

41 Adjusted loss for the year – *from box O on the Working Sheet on page UKPN XX*
£ . 0 0

42 Loss set off against 2011–12 total income – *this will be unusual – read page UKPN XX of the notes*
£ . 0 0

43 Loss to carry forward to following year, including unused losses brought forward
£ 6 2 0 . 0 0

- Take the disposal proceeds (usually the sale price or market value, see page 226). If you owned the asset on 31 March 1982, you use the market value at that date.
- Deduct allowable costs – this includes the purchase price or market value when acquired, and costs such as sales commission or improvements (see page 226).

The result is your gain or your allowable loss. If you are using the working sheet in the notes, this is the figure in box H of the worksheet. However, for some disposals you may be able to claim some form of relief, such as entre-preneurs' relief if you have sold your business or business assets, or lettings relief if you sell your home and you have let part of it out. To claim, put a cross in box 20, make sure the relief you are claiming is explained either in your calculations or under 'Any other information', and check the HMRC notes in case you also have to complete a claim form.

Example 18.7: Working out your gain or loss

Philip bought some shares for £10,000 in July 1990 and sold them in 2011 for £15,000, after deducting brokers' commission. Philip has made a gain of £15,000 – £10,000 = £5,000. But if Philip's shares had sold for only £9,000, he would have made a loss of £1,000.

Which shares or unit trusts are you selling?

Imagine you bought some shares in British Utility plc when the company was privatised, and you bought more later on. Now you are selling half the holding. For the purposes of working out your gain, the purchase 'price' of the shares is normally the average cost of all your shares of the same class in the same company. But if you buy shares of the same type on the same day as the sale, or in the 30 days following the sale, special 'bed-and-breakfasting' rules kick in (see page 229). See HMRC help sheet 284 *Shares and capital gains tax*. The same rules, with added touches, apply to unit trusts and shares in investment trust companies and Open Ended Investment Companies (OEICs).

> ## Selling to family or business partners?

To stop you making artificial sales to create a paper loss, there are special rules if you give or sell something to a 'connected' person such as a close family member or business partner. Any loss on a transaction with a connected person is a 'clogged loss' that can be set against a future gain made only on a disposal to the same person. Read the notes on page CGN 4 carefully if you have made a 'clogged' loss.

Working out your taxable gains for the year

Having worked out the gain or loss on each asset, you can start to fill in the first page of the Capital gains summary. The rate of tax depends on your income. It is 28 per cent if your taxable capital gains, when added to your taxable income, are above the maximum amount taxed at the basic rate (£35,000 in 2011–12, see page 228). Otherwise, it is 18 per cent.

However, you can use your annual tax-free amount and losses to minimise the tax, by deducting them first from gains that might be taxed at 28 and next against gains taxed at 18 per cent. Gains that qualify for entrepreneurs' relief are taxed last, because these are taxed at a lower rate of 10 per cent. You do not have to do all this yourself – it is worked out as part of the overall tax calculation.

Boxes 3 to 6. Total gains or losses of the year

You can find the figures to enter here from box H of the working sheet on page CGN 21 of the notes. If you disposed of more than one asset, complete one sheet for each asset, then add up all your gains (positive figures in box H) and enter them in box 3 or box 5 as appropriate. Your total losses (negative figures in box H) go in box 6.

Now enter any gains included in box 3 that qualify for entrepreneurs' relief. Entrepreneurs' relief may apply on selling a business, but read HMRC help sheet 275 *Entrepreneurs' Relief* and the notes carefully before you begin, because it may affect the losses you can claim and the calculations are complicated if you have deferred gains from before 23 June 2010 (when different rates of capital gains tax applied). Enter the gains in box 4 or box 15 as appropriate.

Box 7. Losses brought forward and used in the year

Any losses you made in 2011–12 (box 6) are deducted from your gains in box 3. There is nothing to enter in box 7 if the amount of gains left after deducting 2011–12 losses is £10,600 or less, because this is the amount you could have tax-free in 2011–12. But if the result is more than £10,600, you can also deduct any losses brought forward from earlier years. You need to deduct only enough losses to reduce your gains to £10,600.

So, look back at your records for earlier years and enter in box 7 any losses made in earlier years that you want to deduct from this year's gains. However, in order to use a loss, you must have 'claimed' it, by telling your tax office about it (by letter or by entering it in your tax return) within a time limit, currently four years after the end of the tax year in which the gain arose. So, it is not too late to claim a loss that you made in the 2008–09 tax year, providing that you tell HMRC by 31 January 2013.

Making the most of losses

Because losses must first be set against gains made in the same year, there is no point in selling an asset just to realise a loss if your gains in the same year are below the annual tax-free amount. Your losses will simply reduce gains that are not taxable in any case. It is worth realising losses only if your gains come to more than the annual tax-free amount, or if you have made a loss on an unlisted trading company which you can set against income (see 'A failed investment' on page 230). See Example 18.8 opposite.

Box 8. Adjustment to capital gains tax

HMRC's computers should work out your tax in the best way for you in most cases. But they may not if you have:

- a capital gain that qualifies for foreign tax credit relief (see page 178)
- an additional liability for non-UK trusts in box 9 (see opposite)
- remitted gains in 2011–12 for which you claimed remittance basis in an earlier tax year (see page 173)

■ losses from a sale to business partners or family (a 'clogged loss', see page 323).

If so, you will need to make an adjustment in box 8 – professional tax advice will probably be necessary.

Example 18.8: **Is it worth realising your loss?**

Philip (from Example 18.7 on page 322) made a gain of £5,000 from selling some shares in July 2011. This was his only gain for the year, so it is below the £10,600 annual tax-free amount. But he still owns other shares on which his loss to date is £2,816. If he had sold them and realised his loss it would have been deducted from his £5,000. He wouldn't have saved any tax. From a tax point of view he might as well hang on to the shares in case he has a taxable gain later on. But he should base his decision on what he thinks will happen to his shares in future – they may be worth even less.

Box 9. Additional liability

There are various anti-avoidance rules to stop people using trusts to avoid capital gains tax. If you fall foul of these rules, gains made by the trust may be 'attributed' to you and taxed as yours. See the HMRC Capital gains summary notes and HMRC help sheet 301 *Beneficiaries receiving capital payments from non-resident trusts: calculation of the increase in tax charge.*

Keeping track of losses

Box 10. Losses available to be carried forward

This box does not affect your tax this year, it is simply a record of unused losses. The figure to enter is the total of:

■ any box 6 losses, minus any gains in boxes 3 or 4 (or zero if the losses were more than the gains)
■ any losses carried forward from previous years, minus losses used in box 7.

Note that if you have carried forward unused losses made before 6 April 1996, you should keep a note of them, because the losses made on or after 6 April 1996 have to be used up first. You should also keep a separate record of losses made on sales to family and business associates (see 'Selling to family or business partners?' on page 323).

Box 11. Losses used against an earlier year's gains

This applies only if somebody made losses in the year they died. See HMRC help sheet 282 *Death, personal representatives and legatees*.

Example 18.9: **Filling in the Capital gains summary**

In 2011–12 Tony sold three assets (see Figure 18.5 opposite). He sold:

- some shares in July 2011 for a gain of £4,800
- his buy-to-let flat in August 2011 for a gain of £28,000
- his business in December 2011 for a gain of £63,000. This qualifies for entrepreneurs' relief, and a tax rate of 10%.

Tony also made a loss of £6,500 on selling antiques in June 2011, and has unused losses of £9,800 from earlier years. First, his 2011 loss is used to reduce those gains which are not eligible for entrepreneurs' relief. This wipes out the gain on his shares, leaving £6,500 − £4,800 = £1,700 of losses unused. He sets these losses against his next gain, the £28,000 gain on the flat. This leaves £28,000 − £1,700 = £26,300 of gain liable to tax. But he also has £9,800 unused losses from earlier years, leaving £26,300 − £9,800 = £16,500 liable to tax. He also has his £10,600 annual tax-free amount, so only £16,500 − £10,600 = £5,900 of the gain on his flat is taxable. As his taxable income is £2,475 below the threshold for higher-rate tax, £2,475 of the gain is taxed at 18% and the remaining £5,900 − £2,475 = £3,425 at 28%.

Finally, the £63,000 gain Tony made on selling his business is taxed at the reduced rate of 10%.

Figure 18.5: Capital gains summary (see Example 18.9)

HM Revenue & Customs

Capital gains summary
Tax year 6 April 2011 to 5 April 2012

1	Your name	2	Your Unique Taxpayer Reference (UTR)
	TONY CAESAR		**9 8 7 6 5 1 2 3 4 5**

Summary of your enclosed computations

Read the notes on pages CGN 10 to CGN 12 before completing this section.
You must enclose your computations, including details of each gain or loss, as well as filling in the boxes.

3 Total gains *(Boxes 19+25+31+32)*
£ **9 5 8 0 0** · 0 0

4 Gains qualifying for Entrepreneurs' Relief (but excluding gains deferred from before 23 June 2010) - *read the notes on page CGN 11*
£ **6 3 0 0 0** · 0 0

5 Box 5 is not in use

6 Total losses of the year - *enter '0' if there are none*
£ **6 5 0 0** · 0 0

7 Losses brought forward and used in the year
£ **9 8 0 0** · 0 0

8 Adjustment to Capital Gains Tax - *see notes*
£ · 0 0

9 Additional liability in respect of non-resident or dual resident trusts
£ · 0 0

10 Losses available to be carried forward to later years
£ · 0 0

11 Losses used against an earlier year's gain (special circumstances apply - *read the notes on page CGN 12)*
£ · 0 0

12 Losses used against income - *amount claimed against 2011-12 income*
£ · 0 0

13 Losses used against income - *amount claimed against 2010-11 income*
£ · 0 0

14 Income losses of 2011-12 set against gains
£ · 0 0

15 Deferred gains from before 23 June 2010 qualifying for Entrepreneurs' Relief
£ · 0 0

Listed shares and securities

16 Number of disposals - *read the notes on page CGN 14*
1

17 Disposal proceeds
£ **7 1 0 0** · 0 0

18 Allowable costs (including purchase price)
£ **2 3 0 0** · 0 0

19 Gains in the year, before losses
£ **4 8 0 0** · 0 0

20 If you are making any claim or election, put 'X' in the box

21 If your computations include any estimates or valuations, put 'X' in the box

Boxes 12 and 13. Losses used against income

In a very few circumstances, you do not have to set this year's losses against this year's gains. If you have made a loss on shares in an unlisted trading company or an Enterprise Investment Scheme, you can claim to set these against your income. See HMRC help sheets 286 *Negligible value claims* and 297 *Enterprise Investment Scheme and capital gains tax*.

Box 14. Income losses of 2011–12 set against gains

This applies only if you made a business loss in 2011–12 and you have claimed to set this against your capital gains (see page 145). If so, you should have an entry in either box 32 of the short Self-employment pages or box 77 of the full pages (and equivalent boxes of the Partnership pages). A few property losses also qualify, in which case you should have an entry in box 42 of the UK property pages.

Box 15. Deferred gains before 23 June 2010 qualifying for entrepreneurs' relief

If you sold business assets before 23 June 2010 that qualify for entrepreneurs' relief but where the gain was deferred, enter the amount here. See HMRC help sheet 275 *Entrepreneurs' relief*.

If you don't know the market value

Your gain is worked out using the market value if you gave something away or sold it on a non-commercial basis. You can estimate the market value if necessary, as long as you take reasonable care, but it may be a good idea to get an independent valuation if it is a valuable asset. You should tell HMRC (on your tax return) how you reached the estimate and its specialist valuers may check it. You can appeal if HMRC's valuer makes a valuation you disagree with. You can also ask your tax office to check a valuation before sending in your return (ask for form CG34).

Listed shares and securities, unlisted shares and securities, property and other assets and gains

The remaining three sections are simply a record of your disposals in separate categories. For each category, you should enter the total number of disposals, and the total disposal proceeds, allowable costs and gains. If you are claiming any relief or election, or using any estimated figures, put a cross in the relevant box and make sure that there is an explanation either in the computations you send in with your tax return and in the 'Any other information' box on the second page.

19

The short tax return

There is a shorter, four-page version of the tax return for people with simple tax affairs, but you can use it only if you are sent one, and it does not cover every type of income you might get, or deduction you can claim. This chapter tells you how to fill it in and what to watch out for.

Top tips

- Even if you are sent the short return, it's your responsibility to tell HMRC if you have income that it does not cover, and to complete the full return if necessary. Read the notes carefully and if in doubt contact your tax office.
- Don't use the short return if you want to claim the tax relief on maintenance payments that is available if you were born before 6 April 1935, or on contributions to Enterprise Investment Schemes or Venture Capital Trusts, or if you want to claim your spouse's unused blind person's or married couple's allowance. It doesn't cover them.
- Also be careful about using the short return if you are self-employed and make a loss – it doesn't allow you to claim immediate tax relief on the loss by setting it against your non-business income, or by carrying it back to earlier years.
- You cannot use the short return if you want to file online – but if you file online the software should guide you through the full return.
- You must file a short return by 31 October 2012. See page 262 for what happens if you miss this deadline.

Getting started

If you have been sent a short tax return, first read page STRG 1 of the notes sent with it, as you won't be able to use it if you are:

■ A pensioner who got a lump sum for deferring your state pension.

■ In partnership, or self-employed with turnover above £73,000 (over a full 12-month period – see page 303), or if you had more than one business, changed accounting date or want the full range of choices for using a loss, or you have a job as well as your own business and want to defer National Insurance contributions (see page 121).

■ A company director (unless you received no pay or benefits and work for a non-trading, non-profit-making or charitable concern).

■ An employee who received a lump sum (unless it was just a redundancy payment of under £30,000), or any taxable share-related benefits (see page 108).

■ A landlord with furnished holiday lettings or more than £73,000 property income.

■ Reporting a taxable life insurance gain (see page 196).

■ Receiving foreign income (except taxed foreign dividends up to £300).

■ Working abroad or claiming to be non-resident, not 'ordinarily' resident or non-domiciled in the UK (see Chapter 10).

If any of these apply to you – or any of the less common situations listed in the notes – contact your tax office. But you can use the short return if you made a capital gain or loss. Put a cross in box 7.4 on page 3 of the form, or phone the HMRC Orderline on 0845 9000 404 to get a copy of the Capital gains summary pages (you can also download them from the HMRC website). These are the same as those for the full return so you can use the information on page 319 to help you fill them in.

Next, collect the documents you need, such as your accounts, P60 or statements of interest received. The 'Record-keeping' sections at the end of each chapter in Parts 1 and 2 of this book will help. You do not need to send these documents with your return unless HMRC requests them.

Now check that the details HMRC holds about you are correct and put a cross in box 1.2 at the bottom of page 1 if they are not. Give your date of birth so that HMRC can check your personal allowance.

Employment income

Employment income

This section is for PAYE earnings – any self-employment income goes in boxes 3.1 to 3.13

2.1 The number of employments you had in the year	**2.4** Benefits and taxable expenses received – *read the notes* £ _ _ _ _ _ **7 1 2 8** · 0 0
2.2 Pay from all employments before tax was taken off £ _ _ **2 5 0 0 0** · 0 0	**2.5** Allowable expenses £ _ _ _ _ _ **1 1 0 0** · 0 0
2.3 Tax taken off box 2.2 £ _ _ _ **3 9 5 5** · 0 0	**2.6** PAYE tax reference of your main or last employer **B R I** / **J E S M I T H** _ _ _

Example 19.1: **Entering employment income**

Martin's P60 shows that in 2011–12 he earned £25,000 as a sales representative, and paid tax of £3,955. He also gets a company car with a taxable value of £6,028 and expenses payments of £1,100, which are shown in his P11D. The expenses were for accommodation while he was on the road, on which he can claim tax relief as an allowable expense.

If you want to check what counts as taxable employment income, see page 97. You can find your taxable pay (box 2.2) and tax taken off (box 2.3) on the form P60 your employer should provide, or P45 if you left a job during the year (see page 26). If you had more than one job in the year you can add together all the amounts within each category.

Benefits cover things like company cars (see page 102), while expenses are amounts your employer has paid you either as a fixed allowance or to reimburse expenses you paid out for work. The taxable value of both will be shown on the form P11D or P9D your employer should give you by 6 July 2012. If you haven't been given a form, you probably haven't received any taxable amounts (or your employer has a 'dispensation' from the tax office to ignore them), but your employer can confirm if this is the case.

Box 2.5 is for 'allowable' expenses on which you can claim tax relief. We list the most common expenses on pages 112 onwards. You will need to get the information from your own records, including expenses claims paid by your employer – but you cannot claim relief for expenses reimbursed by your employer unless the expenses were also shown on your P11D.

Self-employment income

Self-employment income

3.1	**What work do you do?** *For example, plumber, bookkeeper*	

`C H I L D M I N D E R`

3.2	**If you began working for yourself after 5 April 2009, enter the date you began** *DD MM YYYY*

`1 6   0 8   2 0 1 1`

3.3	**If you stopped working for yourself before 6 April 2012, enter the date you stopped**

3.4	**Date you made your books up to** – *please read the notes in the guide*

`0 5   0 4   2 0 1 2`

3.5	**Class 4 National Insurance contributions. Put 'X' in the box if they are excepted** – *read the notes in the guide*

3.6	**Business Start Up Allowance** – *do not include box 3.7*

£ [   ] · 0 0

3.7	**Turnover** (include balancing charges) – *you cannot use this form if your annual turnover was £73,000 or more*

£ **7 5 0 0** · 0 0

3.8	**Expenses allowable for tax** (excluding any capital allowances – *they go in box 3.9*)

£ **3 7 5** · 0 0

3.9	**Capital allowances**

£ **5 0 0** · 0 0

3.10	**Profit** (box 3.7 minus (boxes 3.8 + 3.9))

£ **6 6 2 5** · 0 0

3.11	**Loss** (boxes 3.8 + 3.9 minus box 3.7)

£ [   ] · 0 0

3.12	**Business losses brought forward from earlier years**

£ [   ] · 0 0

3.13	**Deductions on payment and deduction statements from contractors** – *construction industry subcontractors only*

£ [   ] · 0 0

▶ Example 19.2: **Entering income from self-employment**

Joanne started to work as a childminder on 16 August 2011, earning £7,500 up until 5 April 2012 (her year end). Her expenses of £375 included items such as registration fees, insurance and car running costs. She had to buy a bigger car, but she can only claim part of the cost this year, as a capital allowance of £500 (she cannot claim the whole cost because it does not qualify for annual investment allowance and because she uses it privately as well).

In boxes 3.2 to 3.4 enter the date your business started up or ceased (if this was between 5 April 2009 and 6 April 2012) and the date of your year end. These dates will give your tax office the information it needs to check your basis period (the period for which you are paying tax, see page 139). After you have been in business for a couple of years, your basis period will be your accounting period ending in the tax year, but if you are just starting up it may be different and you may not be able to use the short return – see the notes sent with the return.

If you are over state retirement age, you are 'excepted' from paying Class 4 National Insurance and should put a cross in box 3.5 – otherwise leave it empty.

The figures for boxes 3.7 and 3.8 should be in your business records. For a list of what counts as 'turnover' see page 129, and for a list of common expenses that businesses can claim see page 132. If you have bought plant or machinery for your business, it is not an 'expense' but 'capital expenditure', and you can claim either annual investment allowance or capital allowances – see page 136 for how to work them out and enter the total in box 3.9.

You can now deduct your expenses and capital allowances from your business turnover. If you have made a profit, enter it in box 3.10; if you have made a loss, enter it in box 3.11. If you made a loss in previous years (which should be on last year's return), make sure you enter the amount in box 3.12 as HMRC will set it against your profits for this year. Box 3.13 applies only if you are a subcontractor in the building industry. You do *not* need to send in your CIS vouchers.

Did you make a loss?

Unless you say otherwise, any loss you make this year will be taken off future years' profits. But you don't have to do this – you may be able to claim tax relief for your loss now, by setting it against non-business income received in this or earlier years, or against non-business gains made this year (see page 145). You can't use the short tax return if you want to do this, so either ask your tax office for the full return, download it from the HMRC website, or file online.

UK pensions and state benefits received

UK pensions and State benefits received

This section is for the pensions and benefits you get - pensions you are paying into go in boxes 9.1 and 9.2

4.1	State Pension - *enter the amount for the year (not the weekly, or 4-weekly, amount)*	4.4	Tax taken off boxes 4.2 and 4.3
	£ **6 7 6 0** · 0 0		£ **1 1 6 0** · 0 0

4.2	Total of other pensions etc. - *before tax was taken off*	4.5	Jobseeker's Allowance
	£ **8 5 5 0** · 0 0		£ · 0 0

4.3	Taxable Incapacity Benefit and contribution-based Employment & Support Allowance - *read the notes*	4.6	Total of other taxable State benefits
	£ · 0 0		£ · 0 0

Example 19.3: **Entering pensions and benefits**

Benjamin receives a state pension of £6,760 in 2011–12, and an employer's pension of £8,550. Although the state pension is taxable, it is paid out before tax – all his tax (£1,160) is deducted from his employer's pension.

State retirement pension is taxable, but not pension credit and some other state pensions – see the lists on page 72. You should enter in box 4.1 the taxable amount. Contact the Pension Service on 0845 301 3011 if you are not sure. Remember that you cannot use the short return if you received a lump sum from deferring your state pension.

If you receive a private pension (from an ex-employer or personal pension, say), it will usually be paid with tax deducted. Enter the amount before tax in box 4.2, and the tax in box 4.4. You should get an annual statement with this information from the person who pays the pension.

Taxable state benefits are listed on pages 56 and 73. Enter the taxable amount in box 4.3, 4.5 or 4.6, depending on the type of benefit. With some benefits you will get a P60 (or P45 if you stopped claiming before 5 April 2012), showing the taxable amount, but if in doubt ask your benefits office or Jobcentre Plus. Benefits are paid without tax deducted, except for taxable

Incapacity Benefit - if you got this, include in box 4.4 the tax shown on your P60 or P45. If you received a tax refund, enter it in box 4.4 as a minus figure.

UK interest, dividends and other investment income

UK interest, dividends and other investment income

Please read the notes in the guide before filling in boxes 5.1 to 5.3

5.1	Taxed UK interest etc. - *the net amount after tax has been taken off*
£	7 8 · 0 0

5.2	Untaxed UK interest etc. - *total amounts which have not been taxed*
£	4 3 5 · 0 0

5.3	Company dividends (but do not include the tax credits)
£	3 6 · 0 0

Example 19.4: Entering interest and dividends

Emma had a building society account that paid out interest of £78 in 2011–12. This was paid after tax, so she enters the amount she actually received in box 5.1. She also received £435 from National Savings & Investments income bonds – this was paid out before tax so it goes in box 5.2. But she doesn't have to enter the £45 she got from her cash ISA as this is tax-free. Finally, she enters in box 5.3 the £36 she received in share dividends.

You can ignore tax-free income when filling in this section, such as income from an ISA.

Most UK bank and building society accounts pay interest after tax has been taken off – enter the amount actually received in box 5.1. Only enter in box 5.2 interest you have received before tax (such as interest from some National Savings & Investments schemes). Other types of savings income you might have to enter in boxes 5.1 or 5.2 are interest payouts from British Government stock and the taxable portion of a purchased life annuity (an annuity you buy with your own money, not one from a pension plan). But you cannot use the short tax return if you received interest from an offshore account, or have enough British Government stock to bring you within the accrued income scheme (see page 190).

Box 5.3 is for dividends and distributions from shares, investment trusts, unit trusts and Open Ended Investment Companies (OEICs). You can include taxed share dividends from foreign companies, as long as the amount is less than £300. Some unit trusts pay interest ('interest distributions'), not share dividends – enter these in box 5.1 or 5.2, not box 5.3.

UK property

UK property
You cannot use this form if your UK property income was £73,000 or more - if it was, please contact us.

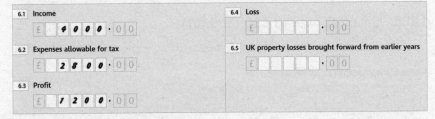

6.1 Income	6.4 Loss
£ 4 0 0 0 · 0 0	£ · 0 0
6.2 Expenses allowable for tax	**6.5 UK property losses brought forward from earlier years**
£ 2 8 0 0 · 0 0	£ · 0 0
6.3 Profit	
£ 1 2 0 0 · 0 0	

Example 19.5: **Entering income from property**

Fred and Ginger received £8,000 from renting out their holiday cottage, against which they can claim expenses of £5,600 (part of their mortgage interest, council tax, letting agents' fees and insurance, and an amount for wear and tear). However, because their property is owned jointly they each enter half of the total amount in their own returns.

You cannot use the short return if your property counts as a 'furnished holiday letting' (as defined on page 158), or if your property income comes to more than £73,000. And you do not need to declare income of up £4,250 from letting a room in your own home under the 'Rent-a-room' scheme (see page 156). All other property income goes in box 6.1. However, you can usually claim some expenses in box 6.2 (see page 160).

Deduct your expenses from your rental income and enter the result in box 6.3 (if you made a profit) or box 6.4 (if you made a loss). If you made a loss in previous years (which should be on last year's return), enter the amount in box 6.5 as HMRC will set it against your profits for this year.

Jointly owned property

Remember that if you have a joint account, or own a property jointly, you only need to enter your share of the income (usually half – see page 314).

Other UK income and capital gains

Other UK income and capital gains
This section is **not** to be used for the types of income listed in the guide.

7.1 Other income	7.3 Where does box 7.1 income come from? *For example, commission, tips, locum fees*
£ 2 2 2 6 · 0 0	J O U R N A L I S M
7.2 Any tax taken off income in box 7.1	7.4 Capital gains - *read the notes to see if you need to fill in the Capital gains summary pages. If so, put 'X' in the box*
£ · 0 0	

Example 19.6: **Entering other UK income**

Angie received £2,300 from some freelance journalism. She can deduct the £74 she spent in travel and telephone costs to do the work, so she enters £2,226 in box 7.1.

Include in this section any taxable income that doesn't belong anywhere else in the return, such as casual earnings. In some cases, you might be able to deduct expenses, but it depends on the type of income; very occasionally, you can deduct a loss from previous years, but if so you will not be able to use the short return. See HMRC help sheet 325 *Other taxable income*. If any tax has been deducted – which is unlikely – enter it in box 7.2.

If you have made a capital gain that you have to declare (listed on page 236), or a loss that you want to claim, put a cross in box 7.4 and you will be sent a separate form to complete.

Gift Aid

Gift Aid

8.1	Gift Aid payments made in the year to 5 April 2012 – *read the notes in the guide*	8.2	Total of any 'one-off' payments included in box 8.1
	£ 2 1 0 · 0 0		£ 1 5 0 · 0 0

Example 19.7: **Claiming Gift Aid**

Roger pays £5 a month to charity under Gift Aid, but he also responded to an emergency charity appeal with a donation of £150. He enters his total donations (£210) in box 8.1 but also enters £150 in box 8.2 so that his tax office can adjust his tax code.

If you gave to charity, enter the amount you handed over under the Gift Aid scheme in box 8.1 (see page 218). Don't give through Gift Aid if you are a non-taxpayer, or HMRC will reclaim from you the tax relief the charity can claim on your gift.

Box 8.2 asks you to say how much of total donations in box 8.1 are 'one-off'. This is because your tax office will adjust your tax code, if you have one, so that less tax is deducted from your pay if you make regular contributions and are a higher-rate taxpayer.

You can opt to have a Gift Aid donation treated as if made in the previous tax year. See page 220. If you asked to do this in last year's return, remember to deduct it from the amount you enter in box 8.1 – but if you want to have a payment made after 5 April 2012 treated as if paid in 2011–12 you cannot use the short tax return. Nor can you use it if you gave property or shares to charity, or gave to a non-UK charity.

Giving through Gift Aid

If you give to charity, always give through Gift Aid unless you are a non-taxpayer. In 2011–12, Gift Aid allowed the charity to claim back £2.50 for every £10 you gave – but if you didn't pay tax HMRC can claim £2.50 back from you. If you are a higher-rate taxpayer you can also claim higher-rate tax relief of £2.50.

Paying into pension schemes

Paying into registered pension schemes or overseas pension schemes

If payments to your pension scheme are deducted from your pay before it is taxed, do not include them here - *read the notes*

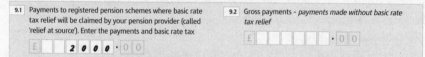

9.1	Payments to registered pension schemes where basic rate tax relief will be claimed by your pension provider (called 'relief at source'). Enter the payments and basic rate tax	9.2	Gross payments - *payments made without basic rate tax relief*
£ **2 0 0 0** · 0 0		£ · 0 0	

Example 19.8: **Entering pension contributions**

Georgina pays £1,600 a year into her personal pension plan. But because the pension company claims back basic-rate tax relief from HMRC which counts as part of her contribution, she enters £1,600 ÷ 0.8 = £2,000 in box 9.1.

Most pension contributions qualify for tax relief, but don't enter here payments to an employer's scheme if you have already had full tax relief on them because the contributions were deducted from your pay before it was taxed (see page 207). Only enter here other payments that qualify for relief, such as a contribution to a personal pension, stakeholder pension, free-standing voluntary contribution (FSAVC) scheme or retirement annuity contract.

Include any payments made between 6 April 2011 and 5 April 2012. The maximum payment that qualifies for tax relief in 2011–12 is the higher of your taxable earnings or payments of up to £3,600 (£2,880 after any tax relief claimed by the company on your behalf). Don't include contributions your employer paid into your plan – you don't get tax relief on these.

Most payments these days are made with basic-rate tax relief given at source and go in box 9.1. Remember, though, that it is the gross amount that you should enter – that is, the amount you handed over, plus the basic-rate tax relief the pension company claims from HMRC. To work this out, divide the amount you paid by 0.8. However, if you pay into a retirement annuity contract and the pension company does not allow you to make payments with tax relief deducted, enter the amount paid in box 9.2.

Blind person's allowance

Blind person's allowance

10.1	If you are registered blind on a local authority or other register, put 'X' in the box	10.2	Enter the name of the local authority or other register
X			E S S E X

Example 19.9: **Claiming blind person's allowance**

Jasper is registered blind, so he puts a cross in box 10.1 and the name of his local authority in box 10.2.

You can claim blind person's allowance of £1,980 for 2011–12 if registered blind or if your eyesight was so bad that you could not do any work for which eyesight is essential (see page 50). Put a cross in box 10.1 and enter the name of the authority with which you are registered as blind in box 10.2, or 'Scotland' or 'Northern Ireland' (where there may be no registers) as appropriate.

Saving tax as a couple

You can transfer blind person's allowance and married couple's allowance to your spouse or civil partner if your income is too low to use it all, but there is nowhere on the short tax return that covers this. Contact your tax office.

Married couple's allowance

Married Couple's Allowance

You can **only** claim Married Couple's Allowance if you, or your spouse (or civil partner) were **born before 6 April 1935**. It is made up of two amounts – a minimum amount (worth up to £280), plus an age-related amount. *Read the notes in the guide.*

11.1	To claim the full allowance, enter your spouse or civil partner's first name
	S H I R L E Y

11.2	If, as a couple, you have already asked us to give all of the minimum amount to you, or your spouse or civil partner, put 'X' in the box

11.3	Your spouse or civil partner's date of birth *DD MM YYYY* – if older than you and you filled in boxes 11.1 or 11.2
	2 5 0 5 1 9 2 6

11.4	Date of marriage or formation of civil partnership – if between 6 April 2011 and 5 April 2012

Example 19.10: Claiming married couple's allowance

Sean is married to Shirley, and as they were already married on 5 December 2005 he gets the whole of the allowance. Because she is older than him, he enters her date of birth in box 11.3.

You can claim married couple's allowance if you or your spouse or civil partner were born before 6 April 1935 (see Table 6.2 on page 82 for the amounts you can claim). However, only the partner who is claiming the allowance needs to fill in this section. Usually, this is the husband, if you married before 5 December 2005, or the higher-income partner if you married on or after that date, but you may have claimed to split the allowance between you.

If you need to fill in this section, enter your date of birth in box 1 on the front page of the tax return and your partner's name in box 11.1, and if he or she is older than you, also enter their date of birth in box 11.3. Box 11.2 applies only if you made a formal allocation to split the allowance before 6 April 2011 (6 April 2012 if you married during the year).

If you married or registered as a civil partner between 6 April 2011 and 5 April 2012, enter the date of marriage or registration in box 11.4 so that your tax office can work out how much of the full allowance to give you (one-twelfth for each month of marriage, see page 83).

Finishing your tax return

If you have paid too much tax

Use boxes 12.1 to 12.6 to say whether you want a repayment to be credited to your bank or building society account, or a payment to be sent to your nominee (such as a tax adviser). HMRC does not send repayments of less than £10, unless requested. And if you have a payment coming up soon, it will usually set the repayment against that bill instead.

Box 12.7 applies only if you received a tax refund part way through the tax year, for example if you are a non-taxpayer and reclaimed tax deducted from a savings account, or if you became unemployed. However, only include tax which has been refunded directly by HMRC or by your Jobcentre Plus – tax refunds from other sources (such as your employer) will be taken into account in your P60 or other end-of-year statement.

If you have not paid enough tax

Boxes 12.8 and 12.9 apply only if you have a job or pension taxed under PAYE. Otherwise, you will have to pay your tax in a lump sum and will get a statement from HMRC saying how much you owe.

Box 12.8. If you owe tax for 2011–12

If you owe less than £3,000, HMRC will usually collect it by adjusting your tax code for 2013–14, if you have a job or pension taxed under PAYE, and providing you get your tax return in by 31 October 2012. Put a cross in this box only if you would prefer HMRC not to collect the tax this way. But if you do, you will have to pay the tax in a lump sum by 31 January 2013, rather than having it spread over your pay or pension during 2013–14.

Box 12.9. If you are likely to owe tax for 2012–13

If your return includes income that was paid out without tax deducted (such as untaxed interest, rental income, or casual earnings), HMRC will assume that it will continue in 2012–13 and adjust your 2012–13 tax code to collect the tax due on it. But if you don't want HMRC to do this, and would prefer to pay tax in a lump sum instead, put a cross in box 12.09. Note that HMRC will not include untaxed income of more than £10,000 in your code, unless you have agreed to this.

Beware, if you ask to pay tax in a lump sum

If you ask to pay tax in a lump sum you may also have to make twice-yearly 'payments on account' in future (see page 30).

What next?

Your tax return must reach HMRC by 31 October 2012 – remember to keep a copy, and get proof of posting. You'll get a statement from your tax office telling you how much tax you owe, but don't take it on trust – the form is machine-processed and entries can occasionally be mis-read, or you might have made a mistake. There is a simple tax calculator in the notes to the tax return that will help you get a rough idea of your tax. And if you are still not sure how HMRC arrived at your tax, phone the number on the statement for an explanation.

20

Filling in a tax repayment form (R40)

The Claim for repayment of tax deducted form (R40) is a simple four-page form that collects the information necessary to assess whether you are entitled to a refund of tax deducted from savings and investments. You won't need one if you are sent a tax return, but you may get one if you contact your tax office about a tax refund, or you might be sent one automatically each year if you normally need to claim tax back.

Top tips

- You do not need to wait until the end of the tax year to make your claim. You can send it in as soon as you have received all your income for the year, or you can send in an interim claim.
- Do not delay claiming a tax refund – the deadline is four years after the end of the relevant tax year. This means you can reclaim tax overpaid going back to 2008–09, provided you claim by 31 January 2013 (see page 37).
- You should not send your dividend vouchers, interest certificates or other documents with the form.
- You should hear from HMRC within 28 days of sending in a repayment claim. If HMRC is being slow, see Chapter 3.
- The form is machine-read, so write clearly in the boxes using black ink.

Claiming a tax repayment

Common reasons why you might need to claim a tax repayment are:

- Tax has been deducted from your savings income but you are liable to pay little or no tax.
- Tax has been deducted from your pay or pension but your circumstances have changed – for example, you have retired or lost your job – and too much tax has been deducted.
- You have started a new job and too much tax was deducted under the 'emergency' code (see page 27), or your employer was using the wrong code.
- You have not claimed an allowance or deduction that might reduce your tax bill.

How you claim a tax repayment depends on the system through which your tax is collected. If you have income that is taxed under PAYE or through a tax return, your repayment will be handled through those systems, so contact your tax office in the first instance. If you do not have a tax office, contact HMRC's Repayment Claim Office in Leicester on 0845 366 7850. The HMRC website has lots of useful information at www.hmrc.gov.uk/incometax/refund-reclaim.htm. There is also a special helpline on 0845 980 0645 if you want to check whether you are entitled to get bank or building society interest paid without tax deducted.

The general time limit for claiming relief is four years after the end of the tax year in question. There may also be specific deadlines for particular claims (e.g. a claim for business loss relief, see page 147).

If you get a tax return

Your repayment will be worked out automatically as part of the tax return process. It will be set against any other tax you owe, but you can ask to have it paid out to you, either by completing page TR5 of the full return or page 4 of the short return or by contacting your tax office (see opposite).

If you think you are due a repayment because you have forgotten to claim a deduction in your return, you can 'amend' your return by contacting your tax office provided that you do so within 12 months of the latest date for filing your return (so, by 31 January 2014 for 2011–12 returns). Claims for earlier years are covered by the general time limit above and you should contact your tax office.

If you are taxed under PAYE and do not get a tax return

■ Contact your tax office if you think you might be due a repayment. You might be sent a form P87 if you are claiming a work-related expense, a form R40 (see below) or a Tax Review form P810 (see page 25). If you have paid too much tax, your tax office may tell your employer to give you a repayment through your pay by adjusting your tax code, or it may send you a cheque.

■ Note that if you have left your job and are now claiming Jobseeker's Allowance, Incapacity Benefit or Employment and Support Allowance, the repayment might be paid through your Jobcentre Plus. Otherwise you might be sent a form P50 *Claiming tax back when you have stopped working* which asks how much pension or earnings you are receiving.

Reclaiming tax through a form R40

Although the R40 looks like a tax return, it is not covered by the rules that apply to returns, and you can use it at any point within the deadline for claiming tax back, as shown on page 37. If you do not get a tax return, you can go back to the 2008–09 tax year provided you send an R40 in by 31 January 2013. Just write the relevant tax year on the front page. You do not need to wait until the end of the tax year to claim – you can claim during the year, or make an interim claim, although HMRC does not pay out claims during the year unless you are owed at least £50.

You can get the R40 from HMRC's Repayment Claim Office in Leicester or download one online. Or you may be sent one automatically if your tax office thinks you can claim. To avoid overpaying tax in future, you may be able to register to have your interest paid before tax (on form R85, see page 189). If you are owed tax, the Repayment Claim Office will send you a cheque (though only on request if you are owed less than £10). Note that you cannot use the R40 if you have capital gains to notify HMRC about. Instead you must register for self-assessment (see page 28).

Claiming on behalf of someone else

Repayment claims may be signed on behalf of a child or an adult who is incapable of doing so. However, you must have legal authority to do this, as the parent or guardian of a child, a Department for Work and Pensions appointee, the person authorised by the courts to look after the affairs of a mentally incapacitated adult, or the executor or administrator of the estate of someone who has died.

Filling in the R40

Personal details

Check the details HMRC holds about you are correct and put a cross in box 1.3 if they are not. Give your date of birth in box 1.1 so that HMRC can give you the right amount of personal allowance once you are 65.

You do not need to wait till the end of the tax year to send in the form, but if you are making an interim claim, put a cross in box 1.5 and enclose an estimate of how much income of each type you expect to receive over the whole year. You may be asked for the actual figures after the end of the tax year.

UK employment income, pensions and state benefits

If you want to check what counts as taxable employment income, see page 97. You can find your taxable pay (box 2.1) and tax taken off (box 2.2) on the form P60 your employer should provide, or P45 if you left a job during the year (see page 26). If you had more than one job in the year, you can add together the amounts for all your jobs.

State retirement pension is taxable, but not pension credit and some other state pensions – see page 72. Enter the taxable amount in box 2.3 – contact the Pension Service on 0845 301 3011 if you are not sure.

If you receive a private pension (from an ex-employer or personal pension, say), it will normally be paid with tax deducted if you are a tax-payer. Enter the amount before tax in box 2.7 and the tax in box 2.8. If you have more than one private pension, tick box 2.9 and attach a note giving the name of the pension scheme and your reference number.

Taxable state benefits are listed on pages 56 and 73. Enter the taxable amount in box 2.5, but if in doubt check with your benefits office or Jobcentre Plus. Benefits are paid without tax deducted – the exception is taxable Incapacity Benefit, but if you get this the Jobcentre Plus should give you a P60 showing the tax deducted to go in box 2.6.

UK interest and dividends

You can ignore tax-free income when filling in this section, such as income from an ISA. And if you have more than one account of a particular kind, you just have to enter the totals in each category. But if you have a joint account, you need only enter your share of the income (see page 52).

Most bank and building society accounts pay interest after tax has been taken off – you may need to check your statements to find the before-tax (gross) amount to go in box 3.3, the after-tax (net) amount for box 3.1, and the tax for box 3.2. See page 357 for how to find these figures. Interest that is paid with no tax deducted (such as interest from some National Savings & Investments schemes) goes in box 3.4.

Other types of saving income you might have to enter in boxes 3.1 to 3.4 are interest payouts from British Government stock and the taxable portion of a purchased life annuity (see page 193). Share dividends and unit trust distributions go in boxes 3.5 and 3.6 – enter the amount actually received. However, if you get an 'interest distribution' from a unit trust it is taxed like savings interest and goes in boxes 3.1 to 3.4 as appropriate. And 'stock dividends' are ones where you get the payout in the form of extra shares (see page 193).

Trust, settlement and estate income

If you have received any income from a trust or the estate of someone who has died, the trustees or the executors (or their solicitors) should give you a form R185 showing how much was taxable, and at what rate. Carry the figures across to boxes 4.1 to 4.11. If you are a non-taxpayer, you may be able to claim back some or all of the tax deducted (see page 189).

UK land and property

You are unlikely to be sent an R40 if you have substantial amounts of income from property. But however small your property income, it is taxed as described in Chapter 9. If you have income from letting a room in your home, this may be tax-free under the Rent-a-room scheme (see page 156). If so, you do not need to enter it on the R40. Remember that if you own a property jointly, you pay tax only on your share of the income.

Foreign income

Foreign income is taxable in the UK, if you are resident here – see Chapter 10. However, you can claim relief for any foreign tax you have already paid. The items you might have to enter here include income from an offshore bank account, foreign dividends or a foreign pension. Note that only 90 per cent of a foreign pension is taxable, so enter only 90 per cent of the amount you received.

Any other income and benefits

This section is for taxable income that doesn't belong anywhere else in the form, such as casual earnings. 'Chargeable event gains' means taxable payouts from a life insurance policy (see page 196) – but this will apply only if you are a higher-rate taxpayer, which is unlikely to be the case if you get a form R40.

Gift Aid

If you gave to charity, enter in box 8.1 the actual amount you handed over under the Gift Aid scheme (see page 218). Don't give through Gift Aid if you are a non-taxpayer, as HMRC can reclaim from you the tax relief the charity can claim on your gift.

Box 8.3 asks you to say how much of the total donations in box 8.1 are 'one-off'. This is because your tax office will adjust your tax code, if you have one, so that less tax is deducted from your pay if you make regular donations and are a higher-rate taxpayer.

You can opt to have a Gift Aid donation treated as if made in the previous tax year (see page 220). If you asked to do this last year, enter the amount in box 8.2, and if you want to have a payment made after 5 April 2012 treated as if paid in 2011–12, enter the amount in box 8.4.

Items not covered by the form

The R40 does not cover every deduction you can claim, such as pension contributions or maintenance payments if you are supporting an ex-spouse and either of you was born before 6 April 1935 (see page 84). Contact your tax office if these apply.

Blind person's allowance

You can claim blind person's allowance of £1,980 for 2011–12 if you were registered blind or if your eyesight was sufficiently bad for you not to be able to do any work for which eyesight is essential (see page 50). Put a cross in box 9.1 and enter the name of the authority with which you are registered as blind in box 9.2 or 'Scotland' or 'Northern Ireland' (where there may not be a register) as appropriate.

Married couple's allowance

You can claim married couple's allowance if you or your spouse or civil partner were born before 6 April 1935 (see Table 6.2 on page 82 for the amounts you can claim). However, only the partner who is claiming the allowance needs to fill in this section. Usually, this is the husband if you married before 5 December 2005, or the higher-income partner if you married on or after that date, but you may have claimed to split the allowance between you.

If you need to fill in this section, make sure you have entered your date of birth on page 1 of the form, your partner's name in box 10.1 and, if they are older than you, their date of birth in box 10.4. Boxes 10.2 and 10.3 apply only if you made a formal allocation to split the allowance before 6 April 2011 (6 April 2012 if you married during the year, see page 83). If you married or registered as a civil partner during the year, enter the date of marriage in box 10.5 so that your tax office knows how much allowance to give you (one-twelfth for each month of marriage, see page 83).

Income too low to use your allowances?

If your income was too low to use your married couple's allowance or blind person's allowance in full, you can transfer the unused amount to your spouse or civil partner by ticking box 10.6 (and see page 80 for other steps to consider).

Finishing the R40

Lastly, fill in the repayment instructions to tell the Repayment Claim Office where you want any repayment to be sent, and sign and date the form before returning it. You should hear back from the Repayment Claim Office within four weeks.

Also check whether you are entitled to fill in form R85 to have your savings income paid out with no tax deducted in future (see page 189).

Example 20.1: **Claiming back tax**

Arnold is 72. He has pensions worth £10,160 a year. However, he also has savings interest of £1,000, which takes his total income for 2011–12 to £11,160. This exceeds his personal allowance of £9,940 by £1,220, but all his taxable interest falls in the 10% band.

Because Arnold is liable to pay some tax, he cannot register to have his interest paid gross. However, the tax on his savings income is deducted at 20% (£200), although he is liable to pay tax at only 10% (£100). He gets a form R40 to claim back the £200 − £100 = £100 tax he has overpaid on his interest. See Figure 20.1 opposite for how he fills it in.

Figure 20.1: R40 Tax Repayment form (see Example 20.1)

HM Revenue & Customs

Claim for repayment of tax deducted from savings and investments

If the address in this box is wrong, please change it. If no address is shown please enter your correct details

Your reference 12345 67890
Tax reference 30 April 2012

MR A RIDLEY
FIRST COTTAGE
2 SECOND STREET
ANYTOWN
X12 2SZ

UK employment income, pensions and state benefits

2.1 Total pay from all employments, before tax taken off (from P60/P45)

£ ⬚⬚⬚⬚⬚⬚ . ⬚⬚

2.2 Tax taken off box 2.1 income

£ ⬚⬚⬚⬚⬚⬚ . ⬚⬚

2.3 State Pension – enter the amount for the year (not the weekly, or 4 weekly, amount). *Do not include Attendance Allowance, Disability Living Allowance or Pension Credits*

£ ⬚⬚ 9 2 5 0 . 0 0

2.4 If you **do not** receive State Pension, put 'X' in the box

⬚

2.5 Total of other taxable state benefits

£ ⬚⬚⬚⬚⬚⬚ . ⬚⬚

2.6 Tax taken off any taxable Incapacity Benefit included in box 2.5

£ ⬚⬚⬚⬚⬚⬚ . ⬚⬚

2.7 Total of other pensions and retirement annuities, before tax was taken off

£ ⬚⬚⬚ 9 1 0 . ⬚⬚

2.8 Tax taken off box 2.7

£ ⬚⬚⬚⬚ 4 4 . ⬚⬚

2.9 Additional information ⬚

UK interest and dividends

With joint accounts, only enter **your share** of the interest received.

3.1 Net interest paid by banks, building societies etc and purchased life annuities – after tax taken off

£ ⬚⬚⬚ 8 0 0 . 0 0

3.2 Tax taken off

£ ⬚⬚⬚ 2 0 0 . 0 0

3.3 Gross amount – the amount before tax taken off

£ ⬚⬚ 1 0 0 0 . 0 0

3.4 If y... interest that has not been taxed at all, put the ...ot in box 3.3

3.5 UK company dividends (but do not add on the tax credit)

£ ⬚⬚⬚⬚⬚ . ⬚⬚

3.6 Dividends from UK authorised unit trusts, open-ended investment companies and investment trusts (but do not add on the tax credit)

£ ⬚⬚⬚⬚⬚ . ⬚⬚

3.7 Stock dividends – enter the appropriate amount in cash/ cash equivalent of the share capital - without any tax

£ ⬚⬚⬚⬚⬚ . ⬚⬚

Fact file

National insurance rates

For rates of income tax, capital gains tax and inheritance tax see the inside front cover. For tax credits, see pages 60 and 61.

National Insurance contributions	2011–12	2012–13
Class 1 contributions		
For employees	12% (10.4%*) on earnings between £139 and £817 p.w. 2% on earnings above £817 p.w.	12% (10.6%*) on earnings between £146 and £817 p.w. 2% on earnings above £817 p.w.
Rate for married women who opted for reduced rate before 6 April 1977	5.85%	5.85%
Lower earnings limit (earnings below this give no right to some state benefits)	£102 p.w.	£107 p.w.
For employers	13.8%* on earnings above £136 p.w.	13.8%* on earnings above £144 p.w.
Class 2 contributions for self-employed	£2.50 p.w. if you earn more than £5,315 p.a.	£2.65 p.w. if you earn more than £5,595 p.a.
Class 3 voluntary contributions to improve benefits	£12.60 p.w.	£13.25 p.w.
Class 4 contributions for self-employed	9% on profits between £7,225 and £42,475, 2% above £42,475	9% on profits between £7,605 and £42,475, 2% above £42,475

* If employer has contracted out of the State Second Pension, lower rates of contribution apply on earnings up to £770 a week in both 2011–12 and 2012–13.

Inheritance tax tax-free bands

Special rules for husbands, wives and civil partners mean that if the first partner to die does not use all their tax-free band, the unused proportion can be transferred to the surviving partner (see page 239). The table below will help you work out how much can be transferred. It starts in 1986 because this is when inheritance tax was introduced – it is possible to transfer unused tax-free bands from before that date, but more complex. HMRC's probate and inheritance tax helpline can give you more information (see page 358).

From	To	Tax-free band
18.03.1986	16.03.1987	£71,000
17.03.1987	14.03.1988	£90,000
15.03.1988	05.04.1989	£110,000
06.04.1989	05.04.1990	£118,000
06.04.1990	05.04.1991	£128,000
06.04.1991	09.03.1992	£140,000
10.03.1992	05.04.1995	£150,000
06.04.1995	05.04.1996	£154,000
06.04.1996	05.04.1997	£200,000
06.04.1997	05.04.1998	£215,000
06.04.1998	05.04.1999	£223,000
06.04.1999	05.04.2000	£231,000
06.04.2000	05.04.2001	£234,000
06.04.2001	05.04.2002	£242,000
06.04.2002	05.04.2003	£250,000
06.04.2003	05.04.2004	£255,000
06.04.2004	05.04.2005	£263,000
06.04.2005	05.04.2006	£275,000
06.04.2006	05.04.2007	£285,000
06.04.2007	05.04.2008	£300,000
06.04.2008	05.04.2009	£312,000
06.04.2009	05.04.2010	£325,000

The tax-free band has been frozen at £325,000 until 2014–15

'Gross' and 'net' figures

When filling in your tax return, you often need to know the gross (before tax) figure of income you receive net (after tax). This is called 'grossing-up'.

For example, the statements from your savings account may show only the net amount of interest received, but the tax return asks for the gross amount and the tax deducted as well. The same applies if you contribute to a personal pension – the amount you hand over is the net amount but the tax return asks for the gross figures.

This is how you can work it out:

- Find the relevant rate of tax or tax relief – 20%, say.
- To find the amount of tax on income at that rate, multiply the income by that percentage – so income of £200 taxed at 20% is £200 × 0.20 = £40. This leaves you with net income of £200 − (1 − 0.20) = £200 × 0.8 = £160.
- If you already know the after-tax amount but want to find the before-tax amount, you simply do the same in reverse. So the gross equivalent of £160, before tax at 20%, is £160 ÷ 0.8 = £200.
- The foolproof way to find the amount of tax, if you know the after-tax amount, is to work out the gross equivalent and deduct the after-tax amount: £200 − £160 = £40.
- For share dividends, you can simply divide the dividend you receive by 9 to find the tax credit.

HMRC helplines

For telephone enquiries about your own tax affairs, ring the phone number on any correspondence from your tax office, or for general income tax and capital gains tax enquiries ring the Taxes helpline on 0845 300 0627. HMRC also has specialist helplines, listed below and in the 'Contact us' section of its website.

Anti-avoidance group   020 7438 6733

Business Payment Support Line	0845 302 1435
Campaigns Voluntary Disclosure helpline	0845 601 5041
Charities and community amateur sports clubs	0845 302 0203
Child Benefit	0845 302 1444
Child Trust Fund	0845 302 1470
Claiming tax back helpline	0845 366 7850
Construction Industry Scheme (CIS)	0845 366 7899
Deceased estates	0845 604 6455
Employers (guidance on PAYE, National Insurance and basic VAT registration)	
New employers	0845 607 0143
Established employers	0845 714 3143
Individual Savings Accounts (general queries about the tax rules for ISAs)	0845 604 1701
IR35 (if you are supplying services through a limited company or partnership, see page 98)	0845 303 3535
National Insurance	
Enquiries for individuals	0845 302 1479
National Insurance for those abroad	0845 915 4811
Registering for a National Insurance number	0845 915 7006
Self-employed helpline	0845 915 4655
National Minimum Wage	0800 917 2368
Newly self-employed	0845 915 4515
Online services technical helpline	0845 605 5999
Orderline for form/leaflet requests	0845 900 0404
Pay and work rights helpline	0800 917 2368
Paying HMRC	0845 366 7816
Probate and inheritance tax	0845 302 0900
Register to receive interest without tax taken off	0845 980 0645
Self-assessment	0845 900 0444
Self-assessment payment difficulties	0845 366 1204
Shares and assets valuation	0845 601 5693
Stamp duty	0845 603 0135
Tax credits	0345 300 3900
Tax evasion hotline	0800 788 887
Trusts	0845 604 6455

| VAT enquiries | 0845 010 9000 |
| Welsh language helpline | 0300 200 1900 |

HMRC websites

The website at www.hmrc.gov.uk includes all leaflets and a wealth of other information, although a lot of information has now been moved to www.direct.gov.uk and www.businesslink.gov.uk. HMRC's own internal guidance manuals are at www.hmrc.gov.uk/manuals and there are many forms you can print off or complete online at www.hmrc.gov.uk/allforms.shtml. There are also toolkits designed to help you avoid common errors – these are aimed mostly at tax advisers but may be helpful if you run your own business or rent out property. They are accessible at www.hmrc.gov.uk/agents/prereturn-support-agents.htm. Below is a selection of other useful pages.

Accessibility – services for people with disabilities and other needs	www.hmrc.gov.uk/contactus/particular-needs.htm
Average exchange rates	www.hmrc.gov.uk/exrate
Business Advice teams	www.hmrc.gov.uk/startingup/bus_sup.htm
Business Income Manual	www.hmrc.gov.uk/manuals/bimmanual
Capital Gains Manual	www.hmrc.gov.uk/manuals/cgmanual
Charities	www.hmrc.gov.uk/charities-donors
Charter (rights and obligations)	www.hmrc.gov.uk/charter
Childcare	www.hmrc.gov.uk/childcare
Child Trust Fund	www.childtrustfund.gov.uk
Claiming a refund	www.hmrc.gov.uk/incometax/refund-reclaim.htm
Company cars	www.hmrc.gov.uk/cars
Complaints and appeals	www.hmrc.gov.uk/complaints-appeals
Construction Industry Scheme	www.hmrc.gov.uk/cis/index.htm
Employment status	www.hmrc.gov.uk/employment-status
Enhanced capital allowances for environmentally beneficial equipment	www.eca.gov.uk
Enterprise Investment Scheme	www.hmrc.gov.uk/eis
HMRC Residency	www.hmrc.gov.uk/cnr

How to pay a tax bill	www.hmrc.gov.uk/payinghmrc
Inheritance Tax	www.hmrc.gov.uk/inheritancetax
Interest rates	www.hmrc.gov.uk/rates/interest.htm
IR35 (if you are supplying services through a limited company or partnership, see page 98)	www.hmrc.gov.uk/ir35
Married women paying reduced National Insurance contributions	www.hmrc.gov.uk/ni/reducedrate/givingupright.htm
National Minimum Wage	www.hmrc.gov.uk/paye/payroll/day-to-day/nmw.htm
Non-resident landlords scheme	www.hmrc.gov.uk/international/nr-landlords.htm
Pre-owned assets	www.hmrc.gov.uk/poa
Property income manual	www.hmrc.gov.uk/manuals/pimmanual
Registered pension schemes manual	www.hmrc.gov.uk/manuals/rpsmmanual
Residence Manual	www.hmrc.gov.uk/manuals/rdrmmanual/index.htm
Self-assessment	www.hmrc.gov.uk/sa
Share schemes	www.hmrc.gov.uk/shareschemes
Selling goods online or at boot sales	www.hmrc.gov.uk/guidance/selling
Students' area	www.hmrc.gov.uk/students
Tax credits	www.hmrc.gov.uk/taxcredits
Trusts	www.hmrc.gov.uk/trusts
Venture Capital Trusts	www.hmrc.gov.uk/guidance/vct.htm

HMRC leaflets

HMRC has been reducing its printed guidance and only a few printed leaflets and factsheets are now available. The most useful are listed below. However, if you don't have access to the internet, or need material in a different format or language, ask a tax office or HMRC Enquiry Centre what help they can give. HMRC is committed to helping people with particular requirements. Leaflets are available from tax offices, from the HMRC Orderline (Tel: 0845 9000 404) or on the HMRC website. HMRC also publishes a number of help sheets, listed on pages 362–5.

480 *Expenses and benefits. A tax guide*
490 *Employee Travel. A tax and NICs guide for employers*

A01 *The Adjudicator's Office for complaints about HM Revenue & Customs and the Valuation Office Agency*

C/FS *Complaints*

CA37 *Simplified Deduction Scheme for employers*

CA44 *National Insurance for Company Directors*

CA5603 *Application to pay voluntary National Insurance contributions*

CIS 340 *Construction Industry Scheme*

CC/FS1 *Compliance checks – General information*

CC/FS2 *Compliance checks – Requests for information and documents*

CC/FS6 *Compliance checks – What happens when we find something wrong*

CC/FS7 *Compliance checks – Penalties for errors in returns or documents*

CC/FS8T *Compliance checks – Help and advice*

CC/FS9 *Compliance checks – Human Rights Act Factsheet*

CC/FS10 *Compliance checks – Suspending penalties for careless errors in returns or documents*

CC/FS11 *Compliance checks – Penalties for failure to notify*

CAP1 *How non-business customers get information about HMRC's interpretation of recent tax legislation*

COP26 *What happens if we've paid you too much tax credit?*

ES/FS1 *Employed or self-employed for tax and National Insurance contributions*

ES/FS2 *Are your workers employed or self-employed for tax and National Insurance contributions?*

HMRC1 *HMRC decisions – what to do if you disagree*

HMRC6 *Residence, domicile and the remittance basis*

How HMRC handle tax credit overpayments

IR115 *Paying for childcare – Getting help from your employer*

IR177 *Share Incentive Plans and Your Entitlement to Benefits*

IR121 *Approaching retirement – A guide to tax and National Insurance contributions*

Making an appeal (Tribunals Service leaflet, see page 370 for address)

NI38 *Social Security abroad – National Insurance contributions, Social Security benefits, Health care in certain overseas countries*

Pride 1 *Taxes and benefits – Information for our lesbian, gay, bisexual and transgender customers*

RK/BK1 *A general guide to keeping records for your tax return*

SE1 *Are you thinking of working for yourself?*

TH/FS1 *Keeping records for business – what you need to know*
TH/FS2 *Self assessment – what you need to know about the three line account*
TH/FS3 *Employing someone for the first time – what you need to know*
TH/FS5 *Working for yourself – what you need to know*
TH/FS6 *Problems paying your tax – what you need to know*
TH/FS7 *Paying your tax – what you need to know*
TH/FS9 *Expenses and allowances for the self-employed*
TH/FS10 *If you stop trading – what you need to know*
TH/FS14 *Paying tax if you buy and sell things from home*
VAT/FS1 *What you need to know about VAT*
WTC1 *Child Tax Credit and Working Tax Credit. An introduction*
WTC2 *Guide to Child Tax Credit and Working Tax Credit*
WTC5 *Working Tax Credit – Help with the costs of childcare*
WTC6 *Child Tax Credit and Working Tax Credit. Other types of help you could get*
WTC7 *Tax Credits penalties*
WTC8 *Child Tax Credit and Working Tax Credit. Why do overpayments happen?*
WTC/AP *Child Tax Credit and Working Tax Credit. What to do if you think your Child Tax Credit/Working Tax Credit is wrong*
WTC/FS1 *Tax credits enquiry*
WTC/FS2 *Tax credits examinations*
WTC/FS3 *Tax credits: formal request for information*
WTC/FS6 *Tax credits – leaving the United Kingdom*
WTC/FS9 *Tax credits – suspension of payments*
Your Charter

HMRC help sheets

HMRC help sheets are designed to help you fill in your tax return, but many contain useful general information and working sheets to help you with particular calculations. Help sheets are available from the HMRC Orderline on 0845 9000 404 or you can download them from www.hmrc.gov.uk.

Employment

Self-employment

Pensions

Other income

Tax reliefs

UK property

Overseas matters

Capital Gains Tax

Useful addresses

Advice Services Alliance
www.advicenow.org.uk

Adjudicator's Office
8th floor, Euston Tower
286 Euston Road
London NW1 3US
Tel: 0300 057 1111
www.adjudicatorsoffice.gov.uk

Age UK
Tavis House
1–6 Tavistock Square
London WC1H 9NA
Information Line: 0800 169 6565
www.ageuk.org.uk

Age Scotland
160 Causewayside
Edinburgh EH9 1PR
Helpline: 0845 125 9732
www.agescotland.org.uk

Age NI
3 Lower Crescent
Belfast BT7 1NR
Helpline: 0808 100 4545
www.ageni.org

Age Cymru
Ty John Pathy
13–14 Neptune Court
Vanguard Way
Cardiff CF24 5PJ
Tel: 029 2043 1555
www.agecymru.org.uk

Association of Chartered Certified Accountants
2 Central Quay
89 Hydepark Street
Glasgow G3 8BW
Tel: 0141 582 2000
www.accaglobal.com

Association of International Accountants
Staithes 3, The Watermark
Metro Riverside
Newcastle upon Tyne NE11 9SN
Tel: 0191 493 0277
www.aiaworldwide.com

The Association of Taxation Technicians
Artillery House, 11–19 Artillery Row
London SW1P 1RT
Tel: 0844 579 6700
www.att.org.uk

Business Debtline
Tel: 0800 197 6026
www.bdl.org.uk

Business Link
Tel: 0845 600 9006
www.businesslink.gov.uk

The Chartered Institute of Taxation
Artillery House, 11–19 Artillery Row
London SW1P 1RT
Tel: 0844 579 6700
www.tax.org.uk

Citizens Advice
Tel (England): 0844 411 1444
Tel (Wales): 0844 477 2020
www.adviceguide.org.uk

Citizens Advice Scotland
www.cas.org.uk

Directgov
UK government's online
   information service
www.direct.gov.uk

Financial Services Authority
25 The North Colonnade
Canary Wharf
London EI4 5HS
Tel: 0845 606 1234
www.fsa.gov.uk

Gilts Registrar
Computershare Investor Services
PO Box 2411
The Pavilions
Bristol BS99 6WX
Tel: 0870 703 0143
www-uk.computershare.com

**HMRC Leicester & Northants
   (Claims)**
Saxon House
I Causeway Lane
Leicester
LEI 4AA
Tel: 0845 366 7850

**HMRC National Insurance
   Contributions and Employer
   Office**
Benton Park View
Newcastle upon Tyne
NE98 IZZ
Tel: 0845 302 1479
www.hmrc.gov.uk/nic

**The Institute of Chartered
   Accountants in England &
   Wales**
Chartered Accountants' Hall
One Moorgate Place
London EC2R 6EA
Tel: 020 7920 8100
www.icaew.com

**Institute of Chartered
   Accountants of Scotland**
CA House
21 Haymarket Yards
Edinburgh EHI2 5BH
Tel: 0131 347 0100
www.icas.org.uk

**Low Incomes Tax Reform
   Group**
Artillery House, II–I9 Artillery Row
London SWIP IRT
Tel: 0844 579 6700
www.litrg.org.uk

Money Advice Service
Holborn Centre
120 Holborn
London ECIN 2TD
Tel: 0300 500 5000
www.moneyadviceservice.org.uk

The Parliamentary and Health Service Ombudsman
Millbank Tower
Millbank
London SW1P 4QP
Tel: 0345 015 4033
www.ombudsman.org.uk

The Pensions Advisory Service
11 Belgrave Road
London SW1V 1RB
Tel: 0845 601 2923
www.pensionsadvisoryservice.org.uk

The Pension Service
Tyneview Park
    Whitley Road, Benton
    Newcastle Upon Tyne NE98 1BA
www.direct.gov.uk
Future Pension Centre (for state
    pension forecasts): 0845 300 0168
National helpline: 0845 606 0265
Pension Tracing Service:
    0845 600 2537

Student Loans Company
100 Bothwell Street
Glasgow G2 7JD
Tel: 0845 0738 891
www.slc.co.uk

TaxAid
304 Linton House
164–180 Union Street
London SE1 0LH
Tel: 0345 120 3779
www.taxaid.org.uk

TOP (TaxHelp for Older People)
Pineapple Business Park
Salway Ash
Bridport
Dorset DT6 5DB
Tel: 0845 601 3321
www.taxvol.org.uk

Tribunals Service, Tax
HM Courts & Tribunals Service
3rd Floor, Temple Court
35 Bull Street
Birmingham B4 6EQ
Tel: 0845 223 8080
www.tribunals.gov.uk/tax

Index